TAX CREDITS FOR THE WORKING POOR

The United States introduced the earned income tax credit (EITC) in 1975, and it remains the most significant earnings-based refundable credit in the Internal Revenue Code. While the United States was the first country to use its domestic revenue system to deliver and administer social welfare benefits to lower-income individuals or families, a number of other countries, including New Zealand and Canada, have experimented with or incorporated similar credits into their tax systems. In this work, Michelle Lyon Drumbl, drawing on her extensive advocacy experience representing low-income taxpayers in EITC audits, analyzes the effectiveness of the EITC in the United States and offers suggestions for how it can be improved. This timely book should be read by anyone interested in how the EITC can be reimagined to better serve the working poor and, more generally, whether the tax system can promote social justice.

Michelle Lyon Drumbl is Clinical Professor of Law at Washington and Lee University and was previously an attorney in the IRS Office of Chief Counsel. Her scholarship focuses on low-income taxpayers and fiscal policy. Her article examining earned income tax credit noncompliance, "Beyond Polemics: Poverty, Taxes, and Noncompliance," was awarded the Cedric Sandford Medal for best paper at the twelfth International Conference on Tax Administration in Sydney.

Lucas,
welcome to W&L Law!
Michelle L Drumbl

Tax Credits for the Working Poor

A CALL FOR REFORM

MICHELLE LYON DRUMBL
Washington and Lee University School of Law

CAMBRIDGE
UNIVERSITY PRESS

CAMBRIDGE
UNIVERSITY PRESS

University Printing House, Cambridge CB2 8BS, United Kingdom

One Liberty Plaza, 20th Floor, New York, NY 10006, USA

477 Williamstown Road, Port Melbourne, VIC 3207, Australia

314–321, 3rd Floor, Plot 3, Splendor Forum, Jasola District Centre, New Delhi – 110025, India

79 Anson Road, #06–04/06, Singapore 079906

Cambridge University Press is part of the University of Cambridge.

It furthers the University's mission by disseminating knowledge in the pursuit of education, learning, and research at the highest international levels of excellence.

www.cambridge.org
Information on this title: www.cambridge.org/9781108415057
DOI: 10.1017/9781108227407

First published 2019

Printed in the United Kingdom by TJ International Ltd. Padstow Cornwall

A catalogue record for this publication is available from the British Library.

Library of Congress Cataloging-in-Publication Data
NAMES: Drumbl, Michelle L., author.
TITLE: Tax credits for the working poor : a call for reform / Michelle Lyon Drumbl, Washington and Lee University School of Law.
DESCRIPTION: 1 Edition. | New York : Cambridge University Press, 2019. |
Includes bibliographical references and index.
IDENTIFIERS: LCCN 2019007313 | ISBN 9781108415057 (hardback) |
ISBN 9781108400206 (paperback)
SUBJECTS: LCSH: Earned income tax credit–United States. | Taxation–Law and legislation–United States. | BISAC: LAW / Taxation.
CLASSIFICATION: LCC HJ4653.C73 D78 2019 | DDC 336.24/216–dc23
LC record available at https://lccn.loc.gov/2019007313

ISBN 978-1-108-41505-7 Hardback
ISBN 978-1-108-40020-6 Paperback

Dedicated to my clients

Contents

Preface and Acknowledgments

This book emerged from my observations of, and reactions to, more than ten years of representing low-income clients before the Internal Revenue Service (IRS). During that time, my students and I have represented dozens of individuals who had problems after claiming the earned income tax credit (EITC) on the return. I was inspired to look outside the United States through conversations with Dutch tax administrators during a sabbatical in the Netherlands. Months later, while presenting at a conference on tax administration in Sydney, a conference participant from New Zealand asked me why the United States was still delivering benefits in a lump sum. I hope this book both answers her question and underscores why she asked it.

I wish to thank many people whose fingerprints are on this book in ways they will never know. More than 100 law students have enrolled in the Tax Clinic at Washington and Lee University School of Law since the clinic's inception in 2008. These students – who have represented the clinic's clients with great passion, zeal, and introspection – have informed my views on the delivery of social benefits through the Internal Revenue Code. Similarly, I have gained invaluable insights from working with our clients, each one of whom had a unique set of circumstances underlying a dispute with the IRS. Our clients teach me the virtues of patience and humility, and I look forward to continuing this work in the years ahead.

For feedback on drafts, conversations, comments, and meaningful insights along the way, I wish to thank: Miranda Fleischer, Shuyi Oei, Keith Fogg, Les Book, Ben Leff, Ariel Stevenson, Lilian Faulhaber, Susan Morse, Nina Olson, Francine Lipman, Diane Ring, Leandra Lederman, Michael Hatfield, Susannah Camic Tahk, Larry Zelenak, Alice Abreu, Katie Pratt, Brian Galle, Damon Jones, Michelle Layser, Kristin Hickman, Heather Field, Bret Wells, Bobby Dexter, Kathleen DeLaney Thomas, Shawna Cheney, David Duff, Wei Cui, Graham Reynolds, Robin Wilson, Blaine Saito, and Patricia McCoy.

This book was greatly enriched through comments received at workshops and presentations at a variety of universities and conferences, including: Boston College Law School, University of British Columbia Allard School of Law, University of Washington School of Law, the 2017 Tax Administration Research Centre workshop at the University of Exeter Business School, the Twelfth International Conference on Tax Administration at the University of New South Wales School of Taxation and Business Law, the 2018 Washington and Lee Journal of Civil Rights and Social Justice Symposium, and the 2018 meeting of the Association for Mid-Career Tax Law Professors.

I am further grateful to Matt Gallaway and the Cambridge University Press editorial staff and also the four anonymous reviewers who reviewed the proposal; their reactions at the earliest stage positively influenced the book's outline and content.

I also wish to thank a number of people at my home institution, Washington and Lee University. Brant Hellwig, Johanna Bond, Chris Seaman, Russ Miller, Kish Parella, Josh Fairfield, Joan Shaughnessy, Mary Natkin, David Eggert, and Margaret Hu in particular have been supportive throughout my writing, as colleagues and as sounding boards. Christopher Bruner, now at University of Georgia, offered advice and insight at the earliest stage. Brianne Kleinert provided key administrative support and helped keep me organized in the clinic while juggling this project. Franklin Runge cheerfully provided research support on short notice as I worked to pull the project together. I am very grateful for the support of the Frances Lewis Law Center, which funded research assistance from several students, most of whom are now lawyers: Abby Mulugeta, Chris Hurley, Kendall Manning, Jay Ha, Thomas Griffin, Michael Brown, William Jenkins, and Kelsey Sherman.

For editorial assistance, I wish to thank Sara Versluis, who helped shape and structure my ideas and research into a better final product. All errors and omissions remain my own.

On a personal note, I am deeply grateful to my family. My parents, Nell and Sherman, both predeceased this project but instilled in me things that made it possible, and my in-laws, Irma and Hubert, are enthusiastic fonts of emotional support for our family's endeavors, including this one. My sons Paul and Luke provide a daily dose of perspective, and I appreciate the light and levity they bring to our house. Finally, heartfelt thanks go to my husband Mark, who for me is the linchpin of all things personal and professional. He joyfully engaged me on refundable credits and social policy over many dinner date nights, kept my spirits high when my energy flagged, and with his wit and intellect helped me connect the dots between things mundane and poetic.

Abbreviations

ACTC	Additional Child Tax Credit
AEITC	Advance Earned Income Tax Credit
AOTC	American Opportunity Tax Credit
APR	annual percentage rate
CBO	Congressional Budget Office
CCB	Canada Child Benefit (Canada)
C-CPI-U	Chained Consumer Price Index for All Urban Consumers
CCTB	Canada Child Tax Benefit (Canada)
CEP	Center for Economic Progress
CFPB	Consumer Financial Protection Bureau
CHIP	Children's Health Insurance Program
CPAG	Child Poverty Action Group (New Zealand)
CPI	Consumer Price Index
CRA	Canada Revenue Agency
CTC	Child Tax Credit
DCIA	Debt Collection Improvement Act of 1996
EITC	Earned Income Tax Credit
FICA	Federal Insurance Contributions Act
FPLP	Federal Payment Levy Program
FWFF	Fix Working for Families (New Zealand)
GAO	US Government Accountability Office
IRS	Internal Revenue Service
NCLC	National Consumer Law Center
NRP	National Research Program
OASDI	Old-Age, Survivors, and Disability Insurance
OBR	offset bypass refund

OECD	Organisation for Economic Co-Operation and Development
PATH	Protecting Americans from Tax Hikes Act of 2015
PAYE	pay-as-you-earn
PPI	Progressive Policy Institute
PTIN	preparer tax identification number
RAC	refund anticipation check
RAL	refund anticipation loan
SECA	Self-Employment Contributions Act
SSA	Social Security Administration
SSDI	Social Security Disability Insurance
SSI	Supplemental Security Income
SNAP	Supplemental Nutrition Assistance Program
TANF	Temporary Assistance for Needy Families
TCE	Tax Counseling for the Elderly
TCJA	Tax Cuts and Jobs Act of 2017
TIGTA	Treasury Inspector General for Tax Administration
VITA	Volunteer Income Tax Assistance
WfFTC	Working for Families Tax Credits (New Zealand)
WIC	Women, Infants, and Children
WITB	Working Income Tax Benefit (Canada)

Introduction

Rethinking the Earned Income Tax Credit

I just wanted to check in and see if you had heard anything . . . I am honestly getting a bit anxious because my transmission just went out in my only vehicle.[1]

Imagine your federal income tax return shows a refund due of several thousand dollars, even though your annual income last year was below the poverty line for a household of your size. This happens to you every filing season; you receive a lump-sum financial windfall that constitutes a significant percentage of your household income each year. This year, however, instead of receiving the lump sum you receive a letter asking you to prove that your child lived in your household last year. Seems easy enough; you gather school records, a letter from a neighbor, a divorce decree and custody order, and you send these to the Internal Revenue Service (IRS), hoping the refund will be released to you soon, because you really need it right now. But it doesn't come. You wait, you inquire, but you cannot reach an IRS representative on the telephone during the limited time you have free in which to call.

I routinely encounter clients in this situation. I direct a low-income taxpayer clinic and provide pro bono legal representation to individuals who have a controversy or dispute with the IRS. Some people are surprised there is even a need for such clinics. In fact, there is a great need, because the Internal Revenue Code is the statutory home of the Earned Income Tax Credit (EITC), a domestic social benefit program for the working poor. Of all the individual income tax returns selected for audit each year, roughly one-third are selected on the basis of an EITC claim.[2] Many of the clients I work with

[1] Email from a former client (writing to inquire when she would receive her EITC refund after we sent substantiating documents to the IRS) (on file with author).

[2] In fiscal year 2017, a total of 933,785 individual income tax returns were selected for examination (representing 0.62 percent of all individual income tax returns filed in calendar year 2016). Of the total individual returns selected for examination, 327,805 (35 percent) were

eventually prevail and receive their refund – but the process can take months, and sometimes more than a year. Others never receive their refund, and face penalties for filing an improper claim. In any of these cases, a delayed or denied refund can be devastating for families with few resources.

The United States introduced the EITC in 1975. It was conceived as an incentive for individuals to work rather than rely on welfare benefits, and a way to mitigate the payroll taxes that apply to the first dollar of wages earned. With time, however, the US EITC policy has shifted thanks to political compromise, stagnant wages, and extensive amendments and expansions. It has expanded from a relatively modest work incentive to one that now also operates as a robust antipoverty program administered by the IRS. Today, more than twenty-five million tax filers claim it each year.

The EITC is the most significant earnings-based refundable credit available in the Internal Revenue Code. It is a refundable tax credit for low-income individuals and couples, particularly those with children. Numerous studies show its positive effect on low-income families. These same individuals may also be eligible for the Child Tax Credit (CTC), another refundable tax credit available to working families. Together, these two credits represent a significant part of the social safety net for low-income individuals and families.

The United States is the oldest example of a country using its domestic tax system to deliver and administer social welfare benefits to lower-income individuals or families. This approach is no longer unique to the United States. Other countries – including the United Kingdom, the Netherlands, New Zealand, France, Canada, Australia, and Sweden – have experimented with or incorporated analogous credits into their tax systems. An EITC-like credit has become "mainstream" in certain other countries that imported the concept from the United States. Forty-plus years after the introduction of the EITC, might the United States now be able to improve upon it by importing experiences and lessons learned in other countries?

The EITC has long enjoyed bipartisan support in the United States because it is thought to incentivize work while lifting millions of families out of

selected for examination on the basis of an EITC claim (representing an audit rate of 1.18 percent on the 27,858,140 returns claiming EITC that year). I.R.S., Pub. 55B, Data Book, 2017 23–26 (2018), https://www.irs.gov/pub/irs-soi/17databk.pdf. These numbers are not anomalous to fiscal year 2017. *See* Kathleen Pender, *IRS Income Tax Audit Chances are Slim, Except for These People*, SAN FRANCISCO CHRONICLE (Apr. 15, 2015), https://www.sfchronicle.com/business/networth/article/IRS-income-tax-audit-chances-are-slim-except-for-6202608.php; David Cay Johnston, *I.R.S. More Likely to Audit the Poor and Not the Rich*, N.Y. TIMES (Apr. 16, 2000), https://www.nytimes.com/2000/04/16/business/irs-more-likely-to-audit-the-poor-and-not-the-rich.html.

poverty. At the same time, the EITC suffers much criticism because of its consistently high error rate, its failure to reach all eligible families, and its limited impact in reducing poverty among childless workers. Other challenges degrade the integrity of the credit, such as return preparer fraud and tax-related identity theft.

Even with the higher audit selection rate for EITC returns (relative to non-EITC returns) and myriad approaches aimed at improving accuracy and educating taxpayers, the IRS nonetheless has been unsuccessful at reducing the rate of EITC overclaims. Since 2003, the estimated rate of improper payments on EITC claims has exceeded 20 percent. Annual improper EITC payments have ranged between an estimated minimum of $8.6 billion (in 2004) to an estimated maximum of $18.4 billion (in 2010). To provide context for these figures, federal spending on the National School Lunch Program was nearly $12.6 billion in 2014. In other words, in some years more federal money flows to improper EITC claims than to subsidizing lunches for schoolchildren.

The EITC is an undeniably important program. Despite its error rate and other shortcomings, it effectively helps many low-income families. But from my perspective as an advocate for low-income taxpayers, its implementation is far from ideal. This book tells the story of the EITC, examines the shortcomings of its administration, and imagines ways in which this social benefit might be delivered more effectively. This book is a call to reimagine how a largely successful social program – by certain metrics – can be improved upon as part of a broader effort to address poverty in the United States.

I first trace the evolution of the US EITC from a work bonus incentive into an antipoverty program. The first chapters identify the modern challenges that the IRS faces with administering the EITC. I then examine how other countries have chosen to administer similar social benefits through their respective tax systems. One striking difference is that some countries, even those that administer the credit through their tax agencies, choose to deliver the benefit in regular increments throughout the year instead of in one annual lump sum as a tax refund. In particular, Canada and New Zealand provide useful case studies for assessing year-round delivery of tax-based family credits to a significant percentage of their population. By examining their systems in depth, it is possible to consider the advantages and feasibility of importing such a model to the United States.

I conclude that Congress should restructure the EITC, importing ideas from how Canada and New Zealand have implemented work and family tax credits. In short, I argue that the EITC should be returned to its original function as a credit to incentivize work and ease the regressive nature of payroll taxes. At the same time, the antipoverty income support element that currently results from claiming one or more qualifying children should be reconfigured as a family-support credit. In repackaging it, I argue that Congress should split off this portion of the credit from the tax refund, such that it can be delivered quarterly rather than annually. Further, I recommend that at least a portion of the family-support element be made exempt from offset or application toward other debt.

The potential benefits of such a restructuring are fourfold. First, it would convey a more coherent tax policy to the public – both those who receive the credit and those who do not. Second, it presents an opportunity to simplify the current structure of the EITC and related family benefits. Third, if structured properly it would reduce the rate of improper payments, as well as reduce opportunities for tax return preparer fraud and tax-related identity theft. Finally, restructuring would allow the EITC to function better as a true antipoverty program because funds would be made available regularly instead of as an annual lump sum subject to offset.

This book does not question the importance of the EITC program to those who rely upon it. Rather, it questions whether the program is living up to its potential from an administrative perspective. It considers why and how the EITC should be restructured. It provides an in-depth look at the problems and challenges of how it is currently delivered. It balances these flaws against the benefits and the stated purpose of the program. It contemplates administrative methods that might work more effectively and be more beneficial to low-income individuals. It examines ways in which other countries have developed their EITC analogs, and considers how the United States might borrow ideas from these foreign systems to improve its own.

The reimagination I propose in this book is largely inspired by my work with low-income taxpayers. As I have found with so many of my clients, poor administration and design can wreak havoc on the lives of EITC recipients. There are also undesirable consequences for the government and all taxpayers. It is time to rethink the EITC.

1

A History of the EITC

How It Began and What It Has Become

The origins of the earned income tax credit can be traced back to ideas that emerged from the broader political conversation about welfare reform during the 1960s and 1970s.[1] In the early 1960s, economist Milton Friedman advanced the concept of a "negative income tax" to deliver welfare benefits to the poorest individuals in the United States.[2] This was a pragmatic proposal – Friedman sought to replace the costly assortment of welfare measures then available. In general terms, a negative income tax represents payments from the government to those whose incomes are below a certain threshold. A negative income tax, argued Friedman, would work to alleviate poverty by establishing "a floor under the standard of life of every person."[3]

Friedman's proposal sparked a conversation about distributing basic income through the income tax system. President Richard Nixon, intrigued by

[1] Bryan Camp has written an interesting historical piece on an earlier "earned income credit" that was enacted in 1924 and eliminated in 1943. Bryan T. Camp, *Franklin Roosevelt and the Forgotten History of the EITC*, 20 Green Bag 2d 337 (2017). Camp describes the earlier EITC as a "subsidy for the rich" because it provided relief to income earned from labor as a way of mitigating the unfairness of using wages earned to pay taxes (rendering those individuals less able to accumulate capital) while those who earned income from capital had investments to rely on in their old age. While the earlier EITC served a different function and was not an antipoverty program, Camp notes that "both subsidies rest on a normative concept of progressivity, grounded in the concept of ability to pay tax." *Id.* at 349.

[2] Milton Friedman, Capitalism and Freedom (University of Chicago Press 1962, 40th anniversary edition, 2002). Friedman was not the first to propose a basic income; for example, his work builds upon that of Lady Juliet Rhys-Williams, who advocated a similar idea in the United Kingdom. *See* Lily L. Batchelder, Fred T. Goldberg, Jr., & Peter R. Orszag, *Efficiency and Tax Incentives: The Case for Refundable Tax Credits*, 59 Stan. L. Rev. 23, 32 (2006). For an in-depth discussion of Friedman's theory and an analysis of its impact on subsequent welfare reform, *see* Robert A. Moffitt, *The Negative Income Tax and the Evolution of U.S. Welfare Policy*, 17 J. Econ. Persp. 119 (2003).

[3] Friedman, Capitalism and Freedom, *supra* note 2, at 191.

Friedman's concept, introduced his own idea for welfare reform – the Family Assistance Plan – in 1969. The plan called for guaranteed income supplements to all poor families with children. It proved to be politically unpopular in both parties: liberals found it "insufficiently generous," while conservatives criticized its cost and felt it had "insufficiently stringent work requirements."[4] Congress ultimately did not adopt it.

Work remains an enduring question in the conversation about welfare reform: Does welfare disincentivize work? Conversely, can welfare be used to encourage work? What happens when employment income is insufficient, and what about those unwilling or unable to work? As Nixon wrote in 1972, a few years after the introduction of his Family Assistance Plan,

> To those who deride the "work ethic," Americans must respond that any job for an able-bodied man is preferable to life on the public dole. No task, no labor, no work, is without dignity or meaning that enables an individual to feed and clothe and shelter himself, and provide for his family. We are a nation that pays tribute to the working man and rightly scorns the freeloader who voluntarily opts to be a ward of the state.[5]

Senator Russell Long, a conservative Democrat, opposed Nixon's Family Assistance Plan due to its guaranteed income supplements.[6] Long wanted to aid the working poor and prevent the poor from relying on welfare; thus, he developed an alternative plan to reward work.[7] In 1972, in his capacity as chair of the Senate Finance Committee, Long recommended a comprehensive "workfare" program that would "increase the economic value" of work.[8] Consistent with Nixon's notion that the United States is a nation that celebrates work over "freeloading," Long and the committee sought to replace a House proposal for guaranteed welfare income with an alternative proposal for guaranteed employment opportunity. In announcing the committee's recommendation, Long quoted Nixon's words about the American work ethic and

[4] V. Joseph Hotz & John Karl Scholz, *The Earned Income Tax Credit, in* MEANS-TESTED TRANSFER PROGRAMS IN THE UNITED STATES at 144 (Robert A. Moffitt ed. 2003).

[5] Richard Nixon: "Statement on Signing a Bill Amending the Social Security Act," Dec. 28, 1971, Online by Gerhard Peters and John T. Woolley, The American Presidency Project. www.presidency.ucsb.edu/ws/?pid=3282.

[6] Hotz & Scholz, *supra* note 4, at 144.

[7] *See* 118 CONG. REC. S33011 (Sept. 30, 1972) (statement of Sen. Long).

[8] 92ND CONG., WELFARE REFORM: GUARANTEED JOB OPPORTUNITY – EXPLANATION OF COMM. DECISIONS BEFORE THE S. COMM. ON FIN. 3 (Comm. Print 1972).

stated that the proposal was intended to "break the cycle of dependency characterizing today's welfare system."[9]

Long's proposal described the existing welfare system as having "work disincentives." It explained how a mother eligible for welfare would find her payment reduced if she returned to the work force.[10] The thrust of the proposal was to move those who were fit to work off welfare rolls and onto employment rolls. Similar language was used years later to describe the function of the earned income tax credit (EITC).[11]

Under the Senate committee proposal, those family heads who were physically able to work (including families headed by mothers once the youngest child was at least six years old) would be ineligible for welfare, but would be guaranteed employment opportunities through a federal program. The proposal was designed to include a supplement to wages paid by the private employer if the job paid less than minimum wage, with wage subsidies that would be paid by the government.[12]

Another key component of the committee's workfare proposal was the "work bonus" for low-income workers who were the head of a family. Low-income workers would receive a monetary benefit as a reward for participation in the work force. The proposed work bonus was to be equal to 10 percent of wages taxed under social security, up to $4,000 of a married couple's total wage income. Once wages exceeded $4,000, the bonus would be subject to a phase out, and would phase out completely once total wages reached $5,600.

The work bonus concept was fixed – the benefit would not vary "by family size, but only by income, providing no economic incentive for having additional children."[13] The committee noted that this feature "preserves the principle of equal pay for equal work."[14] The EITC as first enacted retained this structure. Over time, however, the EITC has departed from this model,

9 *Id.* at 2.
10 *Id.* at 5.
11 *See, e.g.*, 124 CONG. REC. S18030 (Oct. 10, 1978) (statement of Sen. Bellmon).
12 92ND CONG., WELFARE REFORM: GUARANTEED JOB OPPORTUNITY, *supra* note 8, at 3. The subsidized wage proposal applied to jobs not covered under the minimum wage law at the time, which included certain jobs in small retail stores, small service establishments, domestic service, and agricultural labor. *Id.* at 7.
13 *Id.* at 6. When asked why the benefit did not vary by family size, Long emphasized that the work bonus credit was a refund of social security taxes paid: "He gets the money back whether he has one child or five children. The social security tax is levied on that man, and if he has five children he pays the same amount of social security tax as if he has one." 118 CONG. REC. S33013 (Sept. 30, 1972) (statement of Sen. Long).
14 *Id.* at 3.

varying significantly in dollar amount according to whether the claimant has one, two, or three or more children (or no children at all).

The Joint Committee on Taxation later described Senator Long's work bonus plan as having a twofold purpose: it was "a way of decreasing work disincentives in the case of persons on welfare who were provided an opportunity to work" and "a way of removing much of the regressivity of the social security taxes."[15] The social security tax and the separate Medicare tax, which apply to all wages, salaries, and self-employment income (and are referred to collectively as Federal Insurance Contributions Act [FICA] taxes), are described as regressive because the same tax rate applies to all earners, while the maximum wage cap on the social security tax means individuals with earnings above the cap pay an overall lower rate relative to their income. In addition, FICA taxes apply even at the lowest earning levels, whereas a worker can earn many thousands of dollars before becoming subject to federal income tax.[16] It is likely the latter factor that the Joint Committee on Taxation had in mind when they described the social security taxes as regressive.

THE ORIGINAL EITC (1975)

Senator Long's workfare program ultimately did not pass the House, but several elements of the work bonus plan were incorporated into the EITC when it was enacted in 1975. The original EITC was a temporary measure to be made available only for that tax year. It was born in an economic climate of inflation and recession, during a time in which President Gerald Ford's administration and Congress sought to craft a tax reduction that would stimulate the economy without increasing inflation.[17] In contrast to today, the original EITC was available only to individuals with a dependent child in the household; the legislation identified these households as "those who are most in need of relief."[18]

[15] Joint Comm. on Internal Revenue Taxation, 94th Cong., Analysis of the House Version of the Tax Reduction Act of 1975 (H.R. 2166) and Possible Alts. 33 (Comm. Print 1975).

[16] As of 2018, the standard deduction for a single filer is $12,000. Thus, the first $12,000 of that individual's income is not subject to federal income tax, but it is subject to the 7.65 percent payroll tax.

[17] Joint Comm. on Internal Revenue Taxation, 94th Cong., *supra* note 15, at 6–7.

[18] S. Rep. No. 94-36, at 11 (1975).

A 1975 Senate Finance Committee report describes the EITC as consistent with Senator Long's work bonus concept.[19] This legislative history describes the EITC as an inducement for low-income individuals to work, and references social security taxes:

> This new refundable credit will provide relief to families who currently pay little or no income tax. These people have been hurt the most by rising food and energy costs. Also, in almost all cases, they are subject to the social security payroll tax on their earnings. Because it will increase their after-tax earnings, the new credit, in effect, provides an added bonus or incentive for low-income people to work, and therefore, should be of importance in inducing individuals with families receiving Federal assistance to support themselves. Moreover, the refundable credit is expected to be effective in stimulating the economy because the low-income people are expected to spend a large fraction of their increased disposable incomes.[20]

Indeed, the 1975 EITC looked a lot like the work bonus plan that Long's committee had proposed in 1972. Like the work bonus proposal, the EITC was calculated based on the tax filer's earned income, without regard to the size or number of children in the household. The maximum available credit was $400,[21] the same dollar amount that Long's committee had proposed. The EITC began to phase out if the filer had adjusted gross income greater than $4,000, the same figure that Long's committee had chosen for the work bonus. The EITC phase-out curve was less steep: while the work bonus plan would have fully phased out once wages reached $5,600, the EITC did not fully phase out until total earnings exceeded $8,000.

The EITC has always been a refundable credit. This means that the credit first offsets any tax liability, and then to the extent it exceeds the return filer's liability, the filer receives the remaining amount as a tax refund. The EITC was not the first refundable tax credit enacted by Congress – the first was a refundable gasoline tax credit, enacted ten years earlier in the Excise Tax

[19] *Id.* at 33. For a comprehensive summary of the legislative history of the EITC, tracing the "idea that became the EITC" back to Nixon's proposal, *see* Christine Scott & Margot L. Crandall-Hollick, Cong. Research Serv., RL31768, The Earned Income Credit (EITC): An Overview 21–28 (2014).

[20] S. Rep. No. 94-36, at 11.

[21] Tax Reduction Act of 1975, Pub. L. No. 94-12, § 204(a), 89 Stat. 25, 30. Adjusted for inflation, $400 in 1975 is worth approximately $1,936 in 2019. *See* www.saving.org/inflation/inflation.php?amount=400&year=1975.

Reduction Act of 1965.[22] But the EITC was the first refundable credit designed to widely deliver a social benefit to low-income individuals.

In the time since the EITC was introduced, Congress has created several other refundable credits for the Internal Revenue Service (IRS) to administer, some of which have been temporary and some of which are permanent. The EITC and the child tax credit are earnings-based refundable credits, meaning the amount of the credit is tied to the return filer's earnings. Most refundable credits are expenditure-based: the amount is tied to an expense the individual has incurred. Expenditure-based credits often serve as a method to encourage or support certain behaviors or decisions. Most recently, Congress created the premium tax credit to help offset the cost of obtaining health insurance in connection with the Affordable Care Act.

Throughout the decades, the EITC has been hailed as a bipartisan success, but there have been skeptics and critics of the credit since its enactment. Though President Ford signed the bill into law that enacted the EITC, it was not his idea, and his administration is on record as criticizing the provision. The Ford administration had made a different proposal, which was not adopted by Congress. In connection with its energy tax package, the administration had proposed an annual payment of up to $160 to married filers and up to $80 to single filers. The proposed annual payment would have a dollar phase out as filers' income exceeded $4,500 and $2,750, respectively. The scope of the Ford proposal was not limited to families with children, because the purpose of the payment was "to offset the effect of higher energy prices resulting from the administration's energy proposals."[23]

An unsigned White House memorandum summarizing the Tax Reduction Act of 1975 for Ford labeled the EITC as one of several "especially undesirable" items in the bill. The memo framed the EITC within the debate on the regressive nature of the payroll tax:

> This is a new and undesirable welfare type program, which tends to undercut the insurance concept of social security. Since both the House and Senate bills contained an earned income provision (with differences of detail), we are unlikely to get rid of it unless something worse is put in its place. A redeeming aspect of the earned income credit is that it makes other, worse approaches somewhat less likely.

[22] While the gasoline tax credit had previously been available to farmers on a separate form, the legislative history explains that Congress incorporated the credit into the individual income tax form to "simplify tax administration for both farmers and the Government." S. Rep. No. 89-324, at 54–55 (1965).

[23] Joint Comm. on Internal Revenue Taxation, 94th Cong., *supra* note 15, at 32.

> Payroll taxes are virtually certain to become a major political issue in the next two years. There has been much debate on whether they are too high and too regressive, and the debate is part of the larger issue of whether we can really afford the kind of social security system we have. Something along the lines of the earned income credit may be the best defense to a much more radical change, such as the other proposed funding of a part of social security from the general revenues. It reduces the impact of the payroll taxes, but confines the reduction to a relatively small amount and a relatively small group of persons. At the same time, it operates indirectly through the income tax system, and permits us to keep intact the principle that social security is an insurance scheme under which people get what they pay for.[24]

The memo suggests that there was political disagreement over using payroll taxes to fund the social security program, as well as whether the structure of the program would remain viable. While the memo writer clearly disliked the EITC, worse was the idea of restructuring how social security was funded. While we do not know Ford's personal views on the matter, the memo and other records demonstrate that some of his advisors counseled him to oppose the EITC.[25]

While acknowledging that the EITC was technically to be enacted as a temporary provision, the White House memo disapprovingly noted that the EITC (and certain other provisions in the Tax Reduction Act of 1975) were "very likely" to be made permanent. Indeed, the memo's author proved to be correct. The EITC was extended in one-year increments for tax years 1976, 1977, and 1978[26] before it was made permanent by the Revenue Act of 1978.[27]

THE FIRST EXPANSION OF THE EITC (1978)

In addition to making the EITC permanent, the Revenue Act of 1978 increased both the maximum earned income credit amount and the eligibility limit. Effective in 1979, the new maximum credit was $500. A 12.5 percent phase out applied to earnings over $6,000, and the credit fully phased out once earnings or adjusted gross income reached $10,000. As before, an individual had to have a dependent child (or a disabled dependent child of

[24] Memorandum from the White House to the US President, 2 (Mar. 29, 1975), https://www.fordlibrarymuseum.gov/library/document/0204/1511983.pdf.

[25] *See, e.g.*, Philip Shabecoff, *Ford Approves Tax Cuts, Saying He Has No Choice; Bars a New Spending Rise*, N.Y. TIMES (Mar. 30, 1975), https://www.nytimes.com/1975/03/30/archives/ford-approves-tax-cuts-saying-he-has-no-choice-bars-a-new-spending.html.

[26] Scott & Crandall-Hollick, *supra* note 19, at 21.

[27] Revenue Act of 1978, Pub. L. No. 95-600, § 103, 92 Stat. 2763.

any age) in order to qualify. The Joint Committee on Taxation's general explanation of the Act explains that Congress felt it necessary to increase the credit because the cost of living had increased since the original enactment.[28] The explanation also restates the view that the EITC is dual purpose in providing both work incentives and relief from the regressive nature of social security taxes. The Senate Finance Committee report projected that the expanded EITC, coupled with other expanded credits, "should greatly increase the employment of people who are now on welfare."[29]

Senator Harry Byrd Jr. of Virginia, a Democrat turned independent who served as chairman of the Subcommittee on Taxation and Debt Management, was an outspoken opponent of expanding the EITC. He commented that the Senate Finance Committee version of the bill (only slightly different from the version that passed) contained a "dramatic expansion of the earned income credit," and that this was "disturbing."[30] Byrd was concerned by the increase in cost to the government, but also expressed broader concerns about the EITC. In a lengthy statement, Byrd described his concern that the Finance Committee had not sufficiently considered the EITC's role in relation to other welfare programs. He further criticized the fact that it only went to filers with children:

> This dramatic expansion of the earned income credit, as a tax reduction measure, is not appropriate. It is a supplemental welfare program. It should be viewed in this broader context. While introducing the negative income tax concept into the tax law, the committee has structured the benefits to go narrowly to one group of taxpayers, those who have children. It is of no benefit for those taxpayers who are married without children or who are single ... Disparities in the effect of the earned income credit highlight the basic difficulties which arise when a supplemental welfare program is inserted into a tax reduction measure without full consideration of its total ramifications ... I certainly do not mean to suggest that the proposed earned income credit should be expanded beyond the committee's recommendation in order to eliminate inequities among workers or to remove possible disincentives to hard work. On the contrary, I am pointing out that the full consequences of this provision have not been adequately considered, and that it should be studied in conjunction with possible revisions in the welfare system.[31]

28 *Id.*; Joint Comm. on Internal Revenue Taxation, Gen. Explanation of Revenue Act of 1978 (66 CCH Fed. Tax. Reps.) 51 (Mar. 12, 1979).

29 S. Rep. No. 95-1263, at 5 (1978).

30 *Id.* at 267–68.

31 *Id.* at 268–69.

Other senators, including Republican Henry Bellmon of Oklahoma, took a different view. Bellmon urged a still more generous expansion, lauding the credit as an important tax innovation that helps low-income families make ends meet and "avoid falling into welfare dependency."[32]

The 1978 Act also introduced the option of an "advance earned income credit." This provision allowed an employee to elect to receive a portion of the EITC in each paycheck, which required coordination with the employer. This concept was sometimes referred to as "reverse withholding," reflecting the method of distribution. For reasons explored in the next chapter, this method of distribution never caught on among claimants.

FURTHER EITC EXPANSIONS IN THE REAGAN YEARS

In his 1985 State of the Union address, President Ronald Reagan reiterated his commitment to protecting the working poor:

> Low-income families face steep tax barriers that make hard lives even harder ... To encourage opportunity and jobs rather than dependency and welfare, we will propose that individuals living at or near the poverty line be totally exempt from Federal income tax.[33]

Reagan was one of many politicians at the time who spoke in favor of dropping the poorest taxpayers from the tax rolls.[34] This could be accomplished by increasing the so-called zero bracket amount (those taxpayers with no taxable income) through increases to the standard deduction and personal and dependent exemptions, as well as by offsetting the payroll tax burden through use of the EITC.

During his presidency, Reagan made proposals to expand the EITC in significant ways. Thanks to his support of the EITC, Reagan is perhaps the most prominently cited Republican advocate of the credit.[35] The Deficit Reduction Act of 1984 increased the EITC to 11 percent of the first $5,000

[32] 124 CONG. REC. S18029-30 (Oct. 10, 1978) (statement of Sen. Bellmon).

[33] President Ronald Reagan, *Address before a Joint Session of Congress on the State of the Union* (Feb. 6, 1985), Online by Gerhard Peters & John T. Woolley, The American Presidency Project, https://www.presidency.ucsb.edu/node/258923.

[34] GOV'T PRINTING OFFICE, THE PRESIDENT'S TAX PROPOSALS TO THE CONGRESS FOR FAIRNESS, GROWTH, AND SIMPLICITY 5 (1985).

[35] Reagan is sometimes misquoted as having called the credit "the best anti-poverty, the best pro-family, the best job creation measure to come out of Congress." The full context of the quote reveals that Reagan was speaking of the Tax Reform Act of 1986 as a whole, not the EITC in particular.

of earned income, meaning a maximum available credit of $550. However, Reagan pushed for further expansion of the credit. He advocated for a higher credit percentage and a phase out at a higher income level. Recognizing that these dollar-amount increases were not keeping up with inflation, thereby eroding the value of the credit, Reagan proposed that both the maximum amount of the credit and the earned income limit should be indexed for inflation according to the Consumer Price Index for All-Urban Consumers (CPI-U).

The Tax Reform Act of 1986 increased the maximum credit again, to 14 percent of the first $5,714 of earnings, with a maximum available credit of $800. This legislation also reduced the phase-out rate from 12.22 percent to 10 percent, which meant more people would receive the credit. Perhaps most significantly, the Tax Reform Act adopted Reagan's proposal that both the credit amount and the income limit be indexed annually for inflation going forward.[36]

The legislative debate preceding this expansion of the EITC characterized it as "a powerful work incentive," and one which "eases the transition from tax-exempt welfare benefits to taxable earned income."[37] It also emphasized the EITC's function in offsetting the burden of payroll taxes for families in poverty. For the time being, the EITC remained available only to taxpayers with children, and the benefit did not fluctuate according to family size.

TRANSFORMATION TO AN ANTIPOVERTY PROGRAM AND CONTINUED EXPANSION (1989–2015)

In 1989, House Ways and Means Chairman Dan Rostenkowski, a Democrat, introduced a proposal to expand the EITC.[38] As others had proposed in the mid-1980s,[39] Rostenkowski sought to increase the amount of the maximum credit according to family size: a taxpayer with two children would receive a

36 Tax Reform Act of 1986, Pub. L. No. 99-514, § 111, 100 Stat. 2107.

37 *Tax Burdens of Low-Income Wage Earners: Hearing before the Subcomm. on Select Revenue Measures*, 99th Cong. 6–7 (1985).

38 Joint Comm. on Taxation, Description of Proposal by Chairman Rostenkowski Relating to Child Care and the Earned Income Credit, Expiring Tax Provisions, Medicare Catastrophic Ins. Provisions, and Certain Other Revenue Provisions (JCX-31-89) (July 18, 1989).

39 *See, e.g.*, *Tax Burdens of Low-Income Wage Earners: Hearing before the Subcomm. on Select Revenue Measures*, 99th Cong. 110–14 (1985) (discussing the Kemp-Kasten Fair and Simple Tax Act).

larger EITC, and a taxpayer with three or more children would receive an even larger credit.

This proposed change was a significant departure from the EITC as it existed then. In its first fifteen years, the EITC retained its work bonus roots. Recall that the original school of thought was that the credit should not provide "an economic incentive for additional children." Senator Long had argued for a fixed amount regardless of family size to preserve "the principle of equal pay for equal work."

Rostenkowski's idea to vary the credit by family size was adopted, though in a slightly more modest fashion than what he had proposed: the Omnibus Budget Reconciliation Act of 1990, signed into law by President George H. W. Bush, increased the EITC for families with two or more children.[40] Increasing the credit by family size was arguably the pivotal moment when the EITC was transformed from functioning primarily as a labor incentive to an antipoverty program. While the credit serves in part as a labor incentive even today, a credit that varies by family size is directly tied to the notion that a bigger household needs more financial support than a smaller one.

By 1991, there was talk on Capitol Hill of further expanding the EITC or using additional refundable credits to provide greater support to low-income families with children.[41] Senator Bill Bradley proposed a refundable tax credit for each child under the age of eighteen. Representative Tom Downey and Senator Al Gore Jr. proposed a refundable tax credit for low-income families in lieu of a personal exemption deduction for dependent children. Though the child tax credit (CTC) was not adopted until 1997, these bills were an early version of that concept. Congress debated several different plans, and some took the view that the EITC should be not just an income supplement but rather an income floor for poor families.

Early in his presidency, Bill Clinton supported the idea of creating an income floor for the full-time working poor, stating that this type of EITC expansion "will reward work and family and responsibility and make a major down payment on welfare reform."[42] In this discussion of his economic plan, Clinton explicitly framed the EITC as a work incentive, but also as an antipoverty program:

[40] Omnibus Budget Reconciliation Act of 1990, Pub. L. No. 101-508, § 1111, 104 Stat. 143.

[41] *See* James R. Storey, Cong. Research Serv., Issue Brief, Refundable Tax Credits for Fams. with Child. 12–13 (1991) (listing the various proposals).

[42] William J. Clinton, *Remarks on the Earned-Income Tax Credit and an Exchange with Reporters* (July 29, 1993), Online by Gerhard Peters & John T. Woolley, The American Presidency Project, www.presidency.ucsb.edu/node/220334.

> But the most important thing of all to reward work is that this will be the first time in the history of our country when we'll be able to say that if you work 40 hours a week and you have children in your home, you will be lifted out of poverty.[43]

With only minor changes, Clinton's proposal passed as part of the Omnibus Budget Reconciliation Act of 1993.[44] The Act increased the credit rates quite significantly: from 23 percent to 34 percent for a taxpayer with one child, and from 25 percent to 40 percent for a taxpayer with two or more children. This was the largest expansion of the EITC to date, and data from the late 1990s shows it achieved its goal. In a short number of years, millions of families were lifted out of poverty, the adult and child poverty rates dropped significantly, and the percentage of single mothers working (and receiving no welfare) rose by 14 percentage points.[45]

The 1993 Act included another type of expansion: for the first time, workers without children at home (sometimes referred to as "childless workers") became eligible for the EITC. Childless workers between age twenty-five and sixty-four were eligible for a credit of 7.65 percent on their first $4,000 of earnings; the credit was fully phased out by $9,000. These figures were indexed annually for inflation, but the credit for childless workers was (and still is today) far more modest than that received by working parents.

The most recent EITC expansions were in 2001,[46] when the income level phase out for married couples was increased, and in 2009,[47] when the credit was made larger for families with three or more children.

As the program grew over the years, so did the complexity of claiming the credit and determining eligibility. For tax year 1990, the instructions for Form 1040 devoted two pages to the EITC (including a worksheet) and a two-page earned income credit table. For tax year 1994, the IRS created a separate thirty-eight-page publication explaining the EITC.

43 *Id.*

44 P. Law No.103-66, § 13131, 107 Stat. 312 (1993).

45 Press Release, White House, President Clinton Proposes to Expand the Earned Income Tax Credit in Order to Increase the Reward for Work and Family (Jan. 12, 2000), https://clintonwhitehouse4.archives.gov/WH/New/html/20000112_2.html.

46 Economic Growth and Tax Relief Reconciliation Act of 2001, Pub. L. No. 107-16, § 303, 115 Stat. 38. This change was temporary, but later made permanent by the Protecting Americans from Tax Hikes Act, Division Q of the Consolidated Appropriations Act of 2016, Pub. L. No. 114-113 (2015).

47 American Recovery and Reinvestment Act of 2009, Pub. L. No. 111-5, § 1002, 123 Stat. 115. Like the increase in phase out for married couples, this was a temporary expansion later made permanent by the Protecting Americans from Tax Hikes Act, Division Q of the Consolidated Appropriations Act of 2016, Pub. L. No. 114-113 (2015).

As the EITC expanded, Congress more sharply defined its contours. It added new limitations to exclude those taxpayers who were not intended to benefit from the credit. For example, the Personal Responsibility and Work Opportunity Reconciliation Act of 1996 added a requirement that filers claiming the EITC must be authorized to work in the United States, and stipulated that individuals claiming the EITC must list a valid social security number and, if married, that of their spouse.[48] The same legislation provided that if a return lacked a valid social security number or numbers, the EITC could be summarily denied without full taxpayer due process, such as examination procedures and the opportunity to petition the Tax Court. The legislative history explains that this change was made to streamline the procedures for denying the EITC to undocumented workers.[49] The same act also broadened the definition of "earned income" for purposes of calculating the phase out; it specified certain investment losses, passive losses, and business losses that would be disregarded in determining the taxpayer's income in this calculation.

Concerns about EITC abuse and fraud also grew as the credit expanded. The Taxpayer Relief Act of 1997 included two significant new "improved enforcement" provisions that remain in the Code today. One of these new provisions was section 32(k), which authorizes the IRS to impose a ban: a disallowance period of two years for reckless (but not fraudulent) EITC claims and ten years for fraudulent claims. Section 32(k) further requires taxpayers who are denied the credit to recertify eligibility on a special form the next time they claim the credit.

The other new enforcement provision introduced in 1997 was section 6695(g), a due-diligence requirement for return preparers. Congress authorized the Treasury Department to promulgate regulations to impose these requirements, and preparers who failed to meet the requirements would face a $100 penalty per failure (the penalty has since been increased to $500). Sections 32(k) and 6695(g), and their impact, are discussed in greater detail in Chapter 3.

The Taxpayer Relief Act of 1997 brought yet another income-based (and partially refundable) family credit onto the scene: the child tax credit. Because low-income taxpayers are eligible for the refundable portion once they have

48 Personal Responsibility and Work Opportunity Reconciliation Act of 1996, Pub. L. No. 104-193, § 451, 110 Stat. 2277.

49 Joint Comm. on Taxation, Gen. Explanation of Tax Legis. Enacted in the 104th Cong. (JCS-12-96) 394 (Dec. 18, 1996).

met a certain earning threshold, the CTC is another vital component of the Code's antipoverty benefits.

THE CHILD TAX CREDIT AND ITS RELATIONSHIP TO THE EITC

The idea of a child tax credit arose in the early 1990s as a way to further ease the tax burden on families with children. Variants of the idea were proposed by a bipartisan commission, the Republican Party, and President Clinton.[50] The Code had long provided a deduction for personal exemptions for each taxpayer and their dependents in order to reflect the economic variations between differently sized households. In other words, there was an understanding that the tax burden on a household of two people should not be the same as that on a household of five people. By the 1990s, however, there was a recognition that the personal and dependent exemption amounts had declined in value over time, and a sense that families needed greater relief.[51] Those who favored a CTC argued that simply increasing the exemption amount per dependent would not help those who owed no federal income tax, and would disproportionately favor those in higher marginal tax brackets.

In 1987, President Reagan signed into law a bill passed by a Democratic-controlled Congress, establishing the bipartisan National Commission on Children. The commission's work culminated in a report that recommended a range of proposals to promote income security, improve children's health, promote better educational achievement, and strengthen families.[52] The commission was chaired by Democratic Senator John D. (Jay) Rockefeller IV of West Virginia, who framed the report as "not . . . about poor families and poor children," but "about all children and all families."[53] The unanimously adopted report proposed the creation of a $1,000 refundable CTC for all

[50] For a comprehensive summary of the legislative history of the CTC, *see* Margot L. Crandall-Hollick, CONG. RESEARCH SERV., R45124, THE CHILD TAX CREDIT: CURRENT LAW AND LEGIS. HIST. (2018).

[51] *See, e.g.*, JOINT COMM. ON TAXATION, GEN. EXPLANATION OF TAX LEGIS. ENACTED IN 1997, (JCS-23-97) 6–7 (Dec. 17, 1997) ("over the last 50 years the value of the dependent personal exemption has declined in real terms by over one-third"); NAT'L COMMISSION ON CHILDREN, BEYOND RHETORIC: A NEW AM. AGENDA FOR CHILD. & FAMS.: FINAL REP. OF THE NAT'L COMMISSION ON CHILD. 85–86 (1991) ("The personal exemption is designed to recognize differences in household size . . .. The value of the personal exemption has eroded substantially since its establishment in 1948, however, even though the Tax Act of 1986 greatly increased the exemption and linked its growth to the CPI.")

[52] NAT'L COMMISSION ON CHILDREN, *supra* note 51.

[53] Marlene Cimons, *Panel Urges $1,000 Tax Credit for Each Child*, L.A. TIMES (June 25, 1991), http://articles.latimes.com/1991-06-25/news/mn-1260_1_child-tax-credit.

children through the age of eighteen. Significantly, it did not link the credit to earned income – it envisioned a universally available credit, noting that "[t]he United States is the only Western industrialized nation that does not have a child allowance policy or some other universal, public benefit for families raising children."[54] The recommendation was for the full $1,000 credit to be available even to unemployed parents. To partially offset the cost, it proposed the elimination of the personal exemption for dependent children. The proposal intended for the CTC to be in addition to, not a replacement of or a change to, the EITC as it then existed.[55] The commission recommended that the credit be paid to the adults primarily responsible for the child's care, whether that be a parent or parents, members of the extended family, or foster parents. Moreover, the commission recommended the new CTC be indexed for inflation, as the EITC is.[56] The report described its proposed CTC as follows:

> Because it would assist all families with children, the refundable child tax credit would not be a relief payment, nor would it categorize children according to their "welfare" or "nonwelfare" status. In addition, because it would not be lost when parents enter the work force, as welfare benefits are, the refundable child tax credit could provide a bridge for families striving to enter the economic mainstream. It would substantially benefit hard-pressed single and married parents raising children. It could also help middle-income, employed parents struggling to afford high-quality child care. Moreover, because it is neutral toward family structure and mothers' employment, it would not discourage the formation of two-parent families or of single-earner families in which one parent chooses to stay at home and care for the children.[57]

The idea of a CTC caught on in Congress, though not in the ambitious and universal manner envisioned by the bipartisan commission. The House Republicans included a nonrefundable earnings-based CTC of $500 per child as a legislative proposal in their 1994 "Contract with America." President Bill Clinton made a similar proposal, but the 104th Congress did not come to an agreement on the specifics.

The next Congress did find common ground, and enacted the CTC as part of the Taxpayer Relief Act of 1997. Although the EITC already provided some

54 Nat'l Commission on Children, *supra* note 51, at 94.

55 The report praised the EITC and recommended adjusting it for family size up to three qualifying children. *Id.* at 97.

56 *Id.* at 95.

57 *Id.*

relief to families with children, the CTC was created as an additional form of relief that reached a broader income base. The Joint Committee on Taxation noted that an increase in family size reduced a family's ability to pay taxes because of the cost of raising children. The committee further indicated that the value of the dependent exemption had declined by over one-third in real terms in fifty years' time.[58] Interestingly, their report framed this new credit as a matter of "family values": "The Congress believed that a tax credit for families with dependent children will reduce the individual income tax burden of those families, will better recognize the financial responsibilities of raising dependent children, and will promote family values."[59]

Initially, the CTC was $500 per qualifying child under age seventeen, and included the possibility of a refundable portion only if a taxpayer had three or more qualifying children.[60] Legislative modifications in 2001 provided a gradual dollar-amount increase in the maximum credit over a period of ten years, reaching $1,000 by 2010.[61] The 2001 amendments also provided a calculation for a refundable portion that applied to all families, regardless of the number of qualifying children, but only to the extent the taxpayer had earned income above $10,000.[62] Subsequent legislation enacted in 2003, 2004, and 2008 accelerated the timetable for the increase of the credit's maximum dollar amount, increased the rate of refundability, and reduced the income threshold used to calculate refundability.[63] In 2009, Congress lowered the refundability threshold to a minimum income of $3,000, which benefited taxpayers at lower income levels.[64]

The IRS refers to the refundable portion of the CTC as the "additional child tax credit," though it is not called that in the Internal Revenue Code. In this book, when I write about the CTC, I refer to the overall credit, including the refundable portion, unless stated otherwise.

58 Joint Comm. on Taxation, Gen. Explanation of Tax Legis. Enacted in 1997, (JCS-23-97) 6–7 (Dec. 17, 1997).

59 *Id.* at 7.

60 Taxpayer Relief Act of 1997, Pub. L. No. 105-34, § 101, 111 Stat. 787.

61 Economic Growth and Tax Relief Reconciliation Act of 2001, Pub. L. No. 107-16, § 201(a), 115 Stat. 38. The EGTRRA had a sunset provision, meaning all of these changes would expire on December 31, 2010 and revert back to the prior law. Congress extended the changes several times and eventually made them permanent.

62 *Id.* at § 201.

63 This legislative history is described in more detail by Crandall-Hollick, *supra* note 50.

64 American Recovery and Reinvestment Act of 2009, Pub. L. No. 111-5, § 1003, 123 Stat. 115. As enacted, this reduction was only for tax years 2009 and 2010, but subsequent legislation extended it, and it was made permanent with the passage of Protecting Americans from Tax Hikes Act, Division Q of the Consolidated Appropriations Act of 2016, Pub. L. No. 114-113, § 101 (2015).

From 2010 until 2017, the refundable portion of the CTC was calculated as 15 percent of earnings that exceed \$3,000, up to a maximum of \$1,000 per child. This meant that a low-income taxpayer with one child must earn more than \$3,000 to receive any portion of the credit and must have at least \$9,664 in earnings to receive the full \$1,000 credit.[65] For some taxpayers, the credit is entirely refundable because they owe no income tax but meet the minimum earning threshold. Other taxpayers receive only a portion of the CTC because they earn more than \$3,000, but not enough to maximize the \$1,000 per child credit once the formula for determining the refundable portion is applied.

The Tax Cut and Jobs Act of 2017 provided for a temporary doubling of the credit amount, from \$1,000 to \$2,000; as enacted, this increase is effective only for tax years 2018 through 2025.[66] The increased credit is not fully refundable for any taxpayer: the maximum refundable amount for those years is capped at \$1,400 per qualifying child; however, the earned income threshold for refundability was lowered further, from \$3,000 to \$2,500. The Tax Cut and Jobs Act of 2017 also added a new \$500 nonrefundable credit (again, available for tax years 2018–25) for qualifying dependents other than qualifying children.

Today, the CTC bears certain similarities to the EITC: it is refundable, it increases with the number of children, and it benefits taxpayers beginning at a very low income level. Both the EITC and CTC are earnings-based and thus are wholly unavailable to the unemployed.

However, the CTC differs from the EITC in several significant ways. The income phase out is set at a far higher level, with the result that the CTC benefits both low-income and middle-income families. In 1997, the income phase-out threshold starting point was fixed at \$75,000 for single taxpayers and \$110,000 for married taxpayers filing jointly. The CTC is also available to married taxpayers filing separate returns; phase out for that status begins at \$55,000. The Tax Cuts and Jobs Act of 2017 greatly increased these phase-out thresholds, making more taxpayers eligible for the credit: the phase out for married couples filing jointly begins at \$400,000, and the credit begins to

[65] A special rule applied for filers with three or more children: they received the greater of the refundable portion as calculated by the 15 percent rule or the excess of social security taxes over the amount of the EITC for the year. I.R.C. § 24(d)(1)(B). This provided relief from regressivity to those parents who had several children but did not earn enough to benefit from full refundability, ensuring that at a minimum these individuals would receive a full refund of the social security taxes they paid.

[66] An Act to Provide for Reconciliation Pursuant to Titles II and V of the Concurrent Resolution on the Budget for Fiscal Year 2018, Pub. L. No. 115-97, § 11022, 131 Stat. 2054 (2017) (known unofficially as "The Tax Cuts and Jobs Act").

phase out at $200,000 for all other taxpayers (including married taxpayers filing separately); this increased phase out is only in effect for tax years 2018–25.

In contrast, in 2017, the EITC began to gradually phase out starting at $8,350 for a single taxpayer with no children, at $13,950 for married taxpayers filing jointly with no children, at $18,350 for single taxpayers with children, and at $23,950 for married taxpayers filing jointly with children. Unlike the CTC, the EITC is not available to married taxpayers filing a separate return at any income level.[67]

A taxpayer's EITC increases if the taxpayer has one, two, or three qualifying children, but there is no further increase for a taxpayer with four or more children. In contrast, taxpayers receive the same maximum CTC for each qualifying child, no matter how many children they have. Thus, a taxpayer with eight children under age seventeen is entitled to up to $8,000 in CTC (or double that amount in the years 2018–25), which – subject to the refundability calculation and the phase-out rules – would be refundable to the extent the credit exceeds the tax owed.

The EITC and the CTC vary in their definitions of "qualifying child." For the CTC, the qualifying child must be under age seventeen at the end of the tax year. For the EITC, the qualifying child must be under age nineteen, or under age twenty-four if a full-time student. Moreover, the EITC age requirement is waived for dependents who are permanently and totally disabled; for example, a taxpayer whose 30-year-old disabled child resides with her can claim him as a qualifying child for the EITC. There is no similar waiver for the CTC; the same taxpayer cannot claim this child for the CTC, because he is older than seventeen.

Another difference is that the EITC does not include a requirement that the claimant must support the child financially. So long as the qualifying child meets the age, relationship, and residency requirements, it is not relevant whether the taxpayer claiming the EITC provided support to the child. In contrast, the CTC requires that the qualifying child must not have provided one-half or more of his or her own support during the tax year.

Divorced or separated parents encounter yet another difference in the credits: Code section 152(e)(2) allows a noncustodial parent to claim the children for the purposes of the dependent exemption if the custodial parent

[67] As I discuss in more detail in Chapter 5, there is no explanation in the legislative history for why married taxpayers filing separately are excluded from the credit. I have argued elsewhere that Congress should liberalize this rule. *See* Michelle Lyon Drumbl, *Joint Winners, Separate Losers: Proposals to Ease the Sting for Married Taxpayers Filing Separately*, 19 FLA. TAX REV. 399 (2016).

provides written consent on IRS Form 8332. If the noncustodial parent claims the child as a dependent, that parent can also claim the child for purposes of the CTC. This special rule is effectively a waiver of the residency requirement. However, the noncustodial parent may not claim the child for the EITC. Despite waiving the dependent exemption and the CTC, the custodial parent is still entitled to claim the child for the EITC, and can still use the head-of-household filing status. This is the only circumstance in which more than one taxpayer can claim the same child for different purposes. This rule remains in effect for the CTC and EITC after the Tax Cuts and Jobs Act of 2017, which suspended the personal and dependent exemptions for tax years 2018–25.

Though Congress had reasons for establishing different eligibility requirements and different exceptions for the two different credits, this adds complexity to the Code and confusion for taxpayers who prepare their own returns. As I discuss in Chapter 3, this complexity contributes to EITC errors and makes administration of the credit more difficult.

THE IMPORTANCE OF THE PRESENT-DAY EITC

The modern-day EITC is very different from the one enacted in 1975. In 1975, 6.2 million families claimed the EITC. The average amount received (in 1975 dollars) was $201, and the total cost to the government (including both tax offsets and the refundable portion) was $1.25 billion.[68] This amount is approximately $5.8 billion in 2018 dollars. In contrast, in 2016, over twenty-seven million families and individuals received $67.9 billion in EITC benefits.[69] The average EITC was more than $2,400. Many of these families who received the EITC also benefited from the CTC; over nineteen million families received $25.7 billion of refundable CTC in 2016.[70]

Coupled together, these two refundable credits can and do lift millions of working families out of poverty. Research shows that the EITC expansion

[68] Scott & Crandall-Hollick, *supra* note 19, at 8; INTERNAL REVENUE SERV., GOV'T PRINTING OFFICE, STATISTICS OF INCOME–1975, INDIVIDUAL INCOME TAX RETURNS tbl. 3B (1978).

[69] Internal Revenue Serv., Statistics of Income-Individual Income Tax Returns, Preliminary Data 2016 tbl. 1 (Spring 2018), www.irs.gov/pub/irs-soi/soi-a-inpd-id1802.pdf. Of this total, $58.1 billion was the refundable portion of the EITC.

[70] *Id.* at 2. More than 22.3 million families or individuals claimed a total CTC in 2016 of $52.8 billion, which represents both the portion of the credit used to offset income taxes ($27.1 billion) and the refundable portion ($25.7 billion). Like the EITC, some of the refundable portion may be used to offset other taxes, such as self-employment taxes, and thus may not be received as a refund but is still beneficial to the taxpayer.

achieved its intended effect of incentivizing work, particularly among single mothers earning low wages.[71] One study of single women found that "EITC recipients who were induced to take jobs experience subsequent earnings growth," in part because these women obtain new skills.[72] To the extent the EITC boosts employment and earnings, it also ultimately boosts the worker's social security benefits.

Importantly, studies also show the EITC has several positive life-long outcomes for children. Remarkably, these benefits to children seem to start at birth: A 2014 study of EITC expansions concluded that "the EITC reduces the incidence of low birth weight and increases mean birth weight."[73] Multiple studies have linked the EITC to improved academic performance in school, including higher test scores, higher high school graduation rates, an increased likelihood of attending college, and improved employment outcomes.[74]

What began as a modest work bonus for low-income families has expanded and evolved into a critical antipoverty program that seeks to incentivize work. Both the EITC and CTC have long enjoyed bipartisan success in part because of their work requirements. Clearly, these two refundable credits play an important social role in the United States. This importance underscores why it is so important to improve upon, and reimagine, the administration of these benefits.

[71] For a summary of research studies on the EITC, *see* Chuck Marr, Chye-Ching Huang, Arloc Sherman, & Brandon DeBot, *EITC and Child Tax Credit Promote Work, Reduce Poverty, and Support Child.'s Dev., Res. Finds*, CTR. ON BUDGET AND POLICY PRIORITIES (2015).

[72] Molly Dahl, Thomas DeLeire, & Jonathan A. Schwabish, *Stepping Stone or Dead End? The Effect of the EITC on Earnings Growth*, INST. FOR THE STUDY OF LAB., IZA Discussion Paper No. 4146 19 (2009), http://ftp.iza.org/dp4146.pdf.

[73] Hilary Hoynes, Doug Miller, & David Simon, *Income, the Earned Income Tax Credit, and Infant Health*, 7 AM. ECON. J. 172, 174 (2015).

[74] Raj Chetty, John N. Friedman, & Jonah Rockoff, *New Evidence on the Long-Term Impacts of Tax Credits*, STAT. OF INCOME PAPER SERIES (Nov. 2011), www.irs.gov/pub/irs-soi/11rpchettyfriedmanrockoff.pdf; Jacob Bastian & Katherine Michelmore, *The Long-Term Impact of the Earned Income Tax Credit on Child.'s Educ. & Emp. Outcomes*, 36 J. OF LAB. ECONS. 1127 (2018).

2

Why the United States Uses Lump-Sum Delivery

The Earned Income Tax Credit (EITC) is a sizable social benefit program, and an important one. When combined with the Child Tax Credit (CTC), these two tax credits are the largest means-tested cash assistance program administered by the federal government. In 2012, the refundable portion of these credits paid to taxpayers totaled $81 billion.[1] By comparison, in the same year the government paid $50 billion in Supplemental Security Income (SSI) and $17 billion in Temporary Assistance for Needy Families (TANF) benefits. The government also spent $80 billion that year on Supplemental Nutrition Assistance Program (SNAP) benefits and $18 billion on child nutrition programs. The federal cost of Medicaid in 2012, meanwhile, was $251 billion.[2]

The administrative characteristics of the EITC are unique in a variety of ways. It is a social benefit administered by the federal revenue agency. Taxpayers self-declare eligibility on an annual income tax form rather than via an application at a government office. Applications for social benefits through other agencies generally require the applicant to establish eligibility to the agency before receiving any benefits. For example, to apply for SNAP benefits, one generally fills out an application that is processed through a local office. While the EITC is centralized through a common federal tax return,

[1] William Carrington, Molly Dahl, & Justin Falk, *Growth in Means-Tested Programs and Tax Credits for Low-Income Households*, Cong. Budget Office 27 (Feb. 2013), www.cbo.gov/sites/default/files/113th-congress-2013-2014/reports/43934-means-testedprogramso.pdf. This figure includes only the portion of the EITC and CTC that exceed tax liabilities, because these are treated as outlays in the federal budget. The Congressional Budget Office (CBO) treats the portion of these refundable credits used to reduce the amount of taxes owed as a reduction in revenues.

[2] *Id.* All figures represent only federal spending and do not include any state dollars spent. Federal spending on administrative costs is included in the data for Medicaid, TANF, SNAP, and child nutrition programs.

the SNAP application form and process are different from state to state because the program is primarily administered through the states. In Virginia, for instance, an applicant completes a two-page application form with only two pages of instructions. In conjunction with an in-person interview at a local social services office, this Virginia common application form is used to determine eligibility for a variety of social security programs, including (but not limited to) SNAP, TANF, Medicaid, and Energy Assistance. Virginians can request food stamps using an expedited short form (in conjunction with an interview). Maryland also has a common application form for TANF, SNAP, and medical assistance; it is seven pages long, with seven pages of instructions.

Unlike other social benefits, for EITC claimants a commercial third party is often involved – the tax return preparer. In tax year 2013, 55 percent of EITC claimants used a paid preparer.[3] This places the claimants in the unusual position of paying money to receive an antipoverty cash benefit. It also interjects a dynamic that is ripe for miscommunication, misunderstanding, and abuse. I address these concerns in detail in Chapter 3. Meanwhile, among self-filers (that is, those who do not use a return preparer), most use commercial tax preparation software.[4] While many of the software programs are available at no charge through an Internal Revenue Service (IRS) initiative known as the "Free File Alliance," use of the free online software is quite low,[5] meaning a cost is often attached even for those who do not use a commercial third-party preparer. In addition, taxpayers who choose to self-prepare their taxes are at risk of misinterpreting the EITC's complex statutory requirements.

Another distinct aspect of the delivery is that claimants receive the EITC benefit as a "tax refund." Because of this delivery format, many taxpayers are perhaps incognizant of the degree to which it is a social benefit, because a refund can also represent overwithholding of wages earned. Even the name "earned income" tax credit can be confusing. While it refers to a social benefit calculated based on the amount of income that is earned, it could be

[3] *Written Statement of Nina E. Olson, National Taxpayer Advocate, Hearing on the Nat'l Taxpayer Advocate's 2014 Annual Report to Congress before the Subcomm. on Gov't Operations, Comm. on Oversight and Gov't Reform, H.R.*, 114th Cong. 28 (Apr. 15, 2015). The percentage of EITC claimants using a paid preparer has declined in recent years: An IRS National Research Program study based upon tax years 2006–08 found that approximately 68 percent of EITC claimants in those years used a paid preparer.

[4] Jay Soled & Kathleen DeLaney Thomas, *Regulating Tax Return Preparation*, 58 B.C. L. Rev. 152, 192–93 (2017).

[5] *Id.* at 165–66.

construed (correctly) as a benefit that one "earns" rather than one that is given for free.

The delivery structure of the EITC is distinct from other social benefits, the result of its genesis and evolution over the past decades. As described in Chapter 1, the credit developed out of conversations about welfare reform. In the 1960s, economist Milton Friedman advocated for a negative income tax as an appropriate way to provide guaranteed income through the tax system. Generally speaking, a negative income tax refers to the idea that people earning below a certain amount should receive money from, rather than pay income tax to, the government.[6] Friedman envisioned a negative income tax as a universal antipoverty program that would substitute for what he called the "ragbag" of various welfare measures then available.[7] He argued that welfare recipients should be guaranteed some level of income even if not working, but favored a benefit formula that would provide incentives for work, with those entering the work force eventually receiving a larger income in correlation with increased work hours.[8] Friedman believed that having the IRS administer a negative income tax would save administrative costs because it would replace multiple welfare programs. He further argued it would reduce stigma between the poor and the nonpoor.[9]

The EITC as we know it is different from Friedman's negative income tax proposal. Friedman favored work incentives but would not have imposed work requirements, because he envisioned the negative income tax as replacing the welfare programs.[10] Friedman's idea never gained political traction in its purest form. But today's EITC bears similarities in that it is run through the

[6] *See, e.g.*, Sheldon S. Cohen, *Administrative Aspects of a Negative Income Tax*, 117 U. PA. L. REV. 678, 678 (1969) (writing that the term *negative income tax* "was developed from the notion that an individual whose income is too low to allow him to use all his income tax exemptions and deductions should receive from the federal government a payment determined by application of a negative tax rate to the unused value of those exemptions and deductions.").

[7] MILTON FRIEDMAN, MILTON FRIEDMAN ON FREEDOM: SELECTIONS FROM THE COLLECTED WORKS OF MILTON FRIEDMAN 99 (Robert Leeson & Charles G. Palm eds., Hoover Institution Press 2017); Robert A. Moffitt, *The Negative Income Tax and the Evolution of U.S. Welfare Policy*, 17 J. OF ECON. PERSP. 119, 121 (2003).

[8] Moffitt, *supra* note 7, at 120.

[9] *Id.* at 121–22. In addition to the advantages listed here, Moffitt writes that Friedman saw an advantage to providing support to poor families on the basis of income rather than another characteristic (such as age) purported to correlate with need. Moffitt writes that Friedman favored distributing a cash benefit, which the negative income tax would do. Finally, Moffitt states that Friedman felt a negative income tax would not distort market prices in the way that a minimum wage, farm supports, or tariffs do.

[10] *Id.*

Code, incentivizes work, and operates as a refundable tax credit. As later parts of this chapter describe, it arguably accomplishes some of Friedman's stated goals about administrative costs and stigma.

Friedman favored a negative income tax as a substitute for welfare. However, the EITC became (and remains) politically popular precisely because it was *not* traditional welfare. Traditional welfare, as I use the term, is means-tested cash assistance available to the poorest Americans, such as the Aid to Families with Dependent Children program created by the Social Security Act of 1935 (the predecessor to today's TANF program). The EITC, meanwhile, requires that recipients have a minimum amount of earned income. This distinction was reinforced when the EITC was expanded in the 1990s as part of a broader political movement to shift from welfare to "workfare." Not long after the Clinton-era expansion of the EITC, tax scholar Anne Alstott wrote that the EITC had found a "secure niche in welfare policy" because it responded to "a bipartisan consensus on work-based welfare reform and widespread dissatisfaction with traditional welfare administration."[11]

Tax scholar Lawrence Zelenak has described the EITC as "a welfare program that happens to be administered through the tax system."[12] Steve Holt characterizes it as "a government transfer payment administered through the tax system that provides cash assistance to low-income workers."[13] These descriptions highlight the unique place that the EITC and CTC have come to occupy in the Code – as social benefits administered at the federal level by the agency charged with collecting revenue.

ADMINISTRATIVE BENEFITS OF A LUMP-SUM APPROACH

The EITC and CTC are also unique in that they are delivered as an annual lump sum rather than smaller amounts dispersed periodically. This delivery is unusual both compared to how other social benefits are delivered in the United States and compared to how similar refundable tax credits are delivered in other countries.

Allowing taxpayers to self-declare eligibility and receive social benefits as a lump-sum tax refund provides a number of advantages to the government. These include reduced administrative costs, increased participation rates, and

11 Anne L. Alstott, *The Earned Income Tax Credit and the Limitations of Tax-Based Welfare Reform*, 108 Harv. L. Rev. 533, 537 (1995).

12 Lawrence Zelenak, *Tax or Welfare? The Administration of the Earned Income Tax Credit*, 52 UCLA L. Rev. 1867, 1869 (2005).

13 Steve Holt, *The Role of the IRS as a Social Benefit Administrator*, Am. Enter. Ins. iii (July 2016), www.aei.org/wp-content/uploads/2016/07/The-Role-of-the-IRS.pdf.

positive public perception. Appreciating these advantages helps explain why the United States has chosen lump-sum delivery. My reimagination of the EITC proposes that EITC payments be delivered throughout the year; to fully understand how and why such a reimagination is advantageous, it is crucial to understand why they have been structured as they have.

The total overhead costs of the EITC are approximately $600 million. In fiscal year 2014, the government paid out $60.3 billion in total benefits, meaning the overhead costs were only 1 percent of the cost of the program. Both as a dollar figure and as a percentage, National Taxpayer Advocate Nina Olson notes that this is the least expensive overhead cost of nine means-tested federal payment programs aimed at families.[14] Among the other eight programs, administrative costs range from 4.7 percent (Medicaid, with overhead costs of $11.7 billion) to 41.8 percent (Women, Infants, and Children [WIC], with overhead costs of $1.9 billion) of total program costs (as measured by total benefits paid out).[15]

As the next chapter will detail, one trade-off of the low direct costs of administering a social benefit program through the Code is a high improper payment rate. An improper payment is a payment made in an incorrect amount (either an underpayment or an overpayment), or one that is made to an ineligible recipient. Since 2003, the estimated rate of improper payments on EITC claims has exceeded 20 percent and ranged as high as 30 percent.[16] The estimated annual dollar amounts for improper EITC payments range between $8.6 billion (the minimum estimate in 2004) to $18.4 billion (the maximum estimate in 2010). These figures long have drawn the attention of the Treasury Inspector General for Tax Administration (TIGTA) and the Government Accountability Office (GAO).[17] The overpayment dollar amounts are significant enough that the Office of Management and Budget

[14] *See* Taxpayer Advocate Service, 2016 Annual Report to Congress (Vol. 1) 341. The other eight federal payment programs are: SNAP, WIC, SSI, TANF, HUD, CHIP, Medicaid, and the School Lunch Program.

[15] *Id.*

[16] Treasury Inspector Gen. for Tax Admin., Ref. No. 2014-40-027, *The Internal Revenue Service Fiscal Year 2013 Improper Payment Reporting Continues to Not Comply with the Improper Payments Elimination and Recovery Act*, Treasury Dept. 5 (Mar. 31, 2014), www.treasury.gov/tigta/auditreports/2014reports/201440027fr.pdf.

[17] *See, e.g.*, Treasury Inspector Gen. for Tax Admin., Ref. No. 2014-40-093, *Existing Compliance Processes Will Not Reduce the Billions of Dollars in Improper Earned Income Tax Credit and Additional Child Tax Credit Payments*, Treasury Dept. (Sept. 29, 2014), www.treasury.gov/tigta/auditreports/2014reports/201440093fr.pdf; US Gov't Accountability Off., GAO-16-92T, Fiscal Outlook: Addressing Improper Payments and the Tax Gap Would Improve the Government's Fiscal Position 13–15 (2015).

has designated the EITC as a "high-risk program"; it is the only Code-based program designated as such.[18] Politicians generally praise the social function of the EITC, but the high improper payment rate is major point of criticism.

However, Olson points out that when both overhead costs and improper payments are calculated as a percentage of total benefits paid, the overall cost ratio of the EITC (relative to benefits paid) is very similar to TANF and the School Lunch program, and significantly lower than WIC or the Children's Health Insurance Program (CHIP), which have a cost percentage of 42.8 percent and 44.5 percent, respectively.[19] At the same time, the EITC has a participation rate among its eligible population of nearly 80 percent, which is among the highest rate of the federal payment programs. SNAP has a similar participation rate (79 percent), but the rates for programs such as TANF and SSI are significantly lower (32 percent and 58 percent, respectively).[20] Olson attributes the relatively high EITC participation rate to the ease of claiming it on a tax return; she cites the rate as evidence that the EITC is "a highly effective method of delivery."[21]

Delivery through the Code is easier for the government while also less stigmatizing for recipients. Delivery through the Code also arguably makes the program more popular politically, because it casts the benefit as part of the tax system rather than a welfare entitlement. Alstott writes that "the EITC's redistributive function is cloaked in anti-welfare rhetoric to attract maximum political support."[22] Zelenak writes that an advantage of structuring social benefits as a refundable credit might be that the public finds this structure more palatable, hypothesizing that "a dollar of welfare overpayment is considered more objectionable than a dollar of excessive tax reduction from the overclaiming of a tax benefit, and that a dollar of EITC overpayment is viewed

[18] Treasury Inspector Gen. for Tax Admin., *supra* note 16, at 3. I use the term overpayment throughout the book to refer to an amount of money received by a taxpayer in excess of the correct amount due. The term is also used in the Code to refer to a taxpayer's refund shown due on the return. *See* I.R.C. §§ 6401, 6402.

[19] *See* Taxpayer Advocate Service, *supra* note 14. Figure 2.1.5, Costs and Benefits of Federal Payment Programs shows overhead costs and improper payments as a percentage of total benefits paid for EITC were 25 percent in FY 2014, compared to 24.7 percent for TANF in FY 2011 and 26 percent for School Lunch in FY 2013. Meanwhile, the comparable percentage for WIC in FY 2010 was 42.8 percent and for CHIP in FY 2012 was 44.5 percent.

[20] *Id.*

[21] *Written Statement of Nina E. Olson, National Taxpayer Advocate, Hearing on Internal Revenue Service Oversight, before the Subcomm. on Fin. Serv. and Gen. Gov't, Comm. on Appropriations, H.R.*, 113th Cong. 32 (Feb. 26, 2014), www.irs.gov/pub/tas/nta_testimony_houseppprops_oversight_022614.pdf.

[22] Alstott, *supra* note 11, at 537.

as an intermediate case (although probably closer to the tax pole than to the welfare pole)."[23]

Public opinion surveys generally confirm Zelenak's hunch about the public's view of delivering social benefits as tax expenditures. In reviewing a number of studies, Susannah Camic Tahk discusses the significance of public opinion favoring a "tax war on poverty." Tahk finds that "public opinion views tax-embedded programs more favorably than their nontax counterparts" and that "individuals are more likely to favor the exact same hypothetical program designed as a tax provision than designed as a nontax spending program."[24] Importantly, Tahk notes these surveys "reveal significantly more support for refundable credits than for otherwise identical direct-spending programs."[25]

Alstott, Zelenak, and Tahk identify a psychological component to housing the EITC in the Internal Revenue Code, and its administration within the IRS. I agree that the EITC finds its political viability in this home. My perspective is that the administration is flawed and in need of a reimagination; one of my primary proposals is to remove a portion of the EITC from the annual return filing process and discontinue delivering it as a tax refund. However, for the reasons evoked by Alstott, Zelenak, Tahk, and others, I believe the EITC's statutory authority should remain in the Code, and the IRS should remain the EITC's administrating agency.

TAXPAYER PREFERENCES AND BEHAVIOR ASSOCIATED WITH LUMP-SUM DELIVERY

Economists, sociologists, and policy analysts have studied many aspects of the EITC. Two types of studies shed light on the appropriateness and effectiveness of lump-sum delivery. First, qualitative empirical studies offer interesting and important insights into how the EITC recipients themselves view the program and, specifically, how they view the delivery of benefits in an annual lump sum.[26] Second, researchers have used both quantitative and qualitative

[23] Zelenak, *supra* note 12, at 1888.

[24] Susannah Camic Tahk, *The Tax War on Poverty*, 56 Ariz. L. Rev. 791, 822–23 (2014).

[25] *Id.* at 838.

[26] *See* Jennifer Sykes, Katrin Križ, Kathryn Edin, & Sarah Halpern-Meekin, *Dignity and Dreams: What the Earned Income Tax Credit (EITC) Means to Low-Income Families*, 80 Am. Sociological Rev. 243 (2015); Sarah Halpern-Meekin, Kathryn Edin, Laura Tach, & Jennifer Sykes, It's Not Like I'm Poor (University of California Press 2015); Sara Sternberg Greene, *The Broken Safety Net: A Study of Earned Income Tax Credit Recipients and a Proposal for Repair*, 88 N.Y.U. L. Rev. 515 (2013); Ruby Mendenhall, Kathryn Edin, Susan Crowley, Jennifer Sykes, Laura Tach, Katrin Križ, & Jeffrey R. Kling, *The Role of Earned Income Tax Credit in the Budgets of Low-Income Households*, 86 Soc. Serv. Rev. 367 (2012).

methods to shed light on how EITC recipients use their lump-sum refunds.[27] Both types of studies suggest that delivery through the tax filing system offers many benefits to recipients as compared to other means-tested programs, and that the lump-sum nature is desirable to the recipients.

Sociologists Jennifer Sykes, Katrin Križ, Kathryn Edin, and Sarah Halpern-Meekin collaborated to analyze qualitative interviews of 115 parents who received the EITC in 2006. The authors examined their findings within the framework of behavioral economists and cultural sociologists who previously had found that people perceive and spend money differently depending on whether it is a gift, windfall, compensation, or an entitlement.[28]

Sykes and her collaborators concluded from the interviews that EITC recipients derive a feeling of social inclusion from the credit and view EITC dollars differently than they do wages or welfare dollars.[29] The researchers tie this feeling to three elements of the EITC delivery: the annual lump-sum nature, the universal nature of tax filing, and the connection between work and the benefit.[30]

Sykes and her coauthors also found that EITC recipients distinguish between traditional welfare and refundable tax credits, regarding the former as a "handout" for the "lazy" and the latter as a "reward for hard work."[31] There is a perceived stigma attached to a trip to the welfare office.[32] EITC recipients value the privacy afforded by the "invisible" delivery of the EITC: "When refund checks come, there is no 'scarlet letter' on checks distinguishing individuals who overpaid from those who are receiving a government 'handout.'"[33]

In a subsequent project analyzing the qualitative interviews, Sarah Halpern-Meekin, Kathryn Edin, Laura Tach, and Jennifer Sykes noted that the EITC recipients took pride in their trip to the commercial tax preparation chain

27 *See* Andrew Goodman-Bacon & Leslie McGranahan, *How Do EITC Recipients Spend Their Refunds?*, 32 Econ. Persp. 2Q, (2008), at 17, www.chicagofed.org/publications/economic-perspectives/2008/2qtr2008-part2-goodman-etal; Jennifer L. Romich & Thomas Weisner, *How Families View and Use the EITC: Advance Payment versus Lump-Sum Delivery*, 53 Nat'l Tax J. 1245 (2000).

28 *See* Sykes *et al.*, *supra* note 26, at 246–47 (citing Hersh M. Shefrin, Richard H. Thaler, Nicholas Epley, Ayelet Gneezy, Viviana Zelizer, and others). I discuss the work of Gneezy, Epley, and Zelizer more extensively in Chapter 5.

29 *Id.* at 244.

30 *Id.* at 246.

31 *Id.* at 257–59.

32 Greene, *supra* note 26, at 541–42.

33 Sykes *et al.*, *supra* note 26, at 257.

H&R Block. Halpern-Meekin and her coauthors frame this as a stark contrast to the dread associated with a trip to see the welfare caseworker, and the authors observe: "At H&R Block, one is a client, a taxpayer."[34]

The irony of this perception of oneself as a taxpayer is that in a given year many EITC recipients pay no federal income tax at all.[35] In 2017 a married couple with two children with an adjusted gross income of up to $28,900 would have had no tax due on a joint income tax return after the subtractions for the standard deduction ($12,700 for married filing jointly), two personal exemption deductions ($4,050 each), and two dependent deductions for the children ($4,050 each). Assuming the statutory criteria are met, a couple with that exact adjusted gross income would receive an EITC of $4,554 and a refundable CTC of $2,000. The refund of $6,554 is equal to more than 22 percent of their total wages for 2017.[36] This refund is indeed a reward for hard work, but it is also in its entirety a social benefit; it is an antipoverty supplement for working families. Notably, the very word *taxpayer* is so intertwined with the delivery of refundable credits that it appears as a noun twenty times in the Code section authorizing the EITC, even though individuals who are not subject to any tax at all are eligible to receive the credit.[37]

Because many working parent wage-earners will owe no federal income tax, these taxpayers can use IRS Form W-4 to reduce the withholding their employer subtracts from each paycheck, resulting in a slightly bigger paycheck from week to week. While this sounds like a rational choice that most informed employees would make, empirical research suggests that many people do the opposite. In fact, in interviews, some claimants speak about "claiming zero," meaning they claim no exemptions on the form in order to maximize overwithholding.[38] The interviewees spoke about how claiming

[34] Halpern-Meekin *et al.*, *supra* note 26, at 69.

[35] The federal budget calculates the portion of refundable credits used to reduce the amount of taxes owed as a reduction in revenue, whereas the "refundable" portion exceeding the liability is treated as a budgetary outlay. Historically, the portion of the EITC that is an outlay far exceeds that portion that is a reduction in revenue. The same is not true for the CTC because it is available to both low- and middle-income earning taxpayers.

[36] The refund would be even higher if either spouse had any federal income tax withheld from his or her paycheck, because any withholding would be refunded because no tax is due.

[37] Similarly, I have chosen to use the terms *EITC claimant* and *taxpayer* interchangeably throughout the text of this book, even to refer to claimants with no federal or social security tax liability. I.R.C. § 7701(a)(14) defines taxpayer to mean "any person subject to any internal revenue tax."

[38] Halpern-Meekin *et al.*, *supra* note 26, at 86.

zero is a sacrifice, but it ensures no money is owed to the IRS and it functions as a "savings account."[39]

Economist Damon Jones has studied the EITC within the specific context of individual overwithholding and income tax refunds.[40] Jones notes that low-income taxpayers are "particularly prone to overwithholding," despite having limited to no tax liability.[41] Jones theorizes that this may be explained in part by inertia, though he also notes that "a complete understanding of the connection between the EITC and tax liability ... may yet be elusive for recipients."[42]

That the EITC is one sizable annual payment is another characteristic that sets it apart from more traditional social benefit programs. For example, TANF benefits arrive in monthly installments. TANF benefits vary from state to state and by family size. In July 2016, the median state TANF benefit was $432 per month.[43] The average EITC received in 2016 was $2,455,[44] which equates to a monthly benefit of just over $204. There is ample evidence that working parents like the lump-sum nature of the refund, in particular because it is a large figure received all at once. Some taxpayers describe this as like "hitting the lottery" or "found money."[45] Psychologically, this money feels special to them, and feels different and more meaningful than a slightly larger paycheck would feel.

So how do taxpayers spend this much-awaited sum? Sykes and her coauthors found that 90 percent of those interviewed had some form of debt, including credit card debt and overdue utilities, rent, or both. They note that the windfall of a lump-sum EITC allowed these recipients to make progress in paying down these outstanding debts in part or in full: "It would have been nearly impossible for these parents to pay down debts and back bills without

39 *Id.* at 87. *See also id.* at 70–71; Laura Tach & Sarah Halpern-Meekin, *Tax Code Knowledge and Behavioral Responses among EITC Recipients: Policy Insights from Qualitative Data*, 33 J. Policy Analysis and Mgmt. 413, 429 (2014).

40 Damon Jones, *Inertia and Overwithholding: Explaining the Prevalence of Income Tax Refunds*, 4(1) Am. Econ. J.: Econ. Policy 158 (2012).

41 *Id.* at 179.

42 *Id.* at 178.

43 Megan Stanley, Ife Floyd, & Misha Hill, *TANF Cash Benefits Have Fallen by More than 20 Percent in Most States and Continue to Erode*, Ctr. on Budget & Policy Priorities (Oct. 17, 2016) (hard copy on file with author).

44 I.R.S., *Statistics for Tax Returns with EITC* (Apr. 17, 2017). At $1,000 per child, the child tax credit increases the total refund substantially, and that is not reflected in this figure.

45 Halpern-Meekin *et al.*, *supra* note 26, at 65.

their refunds; they found making so much progress on their debts all at once quite gratifying."[46]

The Halpern-Meekin study found that the families allocated nearly 90 percent of their EITC to late or past-due debts and bills, household expenses, consumer durables, fees, and savings.[47] In addition to paying down debts, recipients had enough left over from the lump sum to spend money on special purchases for their kids, and doing so "offered powerful validation to parents' identity as providers."[48] The authors found that the remaining 11 percent portion of the interviewees' collective tax refunds went to "treats," a category that includes eating out, gifts, toys, and vacations.[49]

Halpern-Meekin and her coauthors posit that the uncertainty of an anticipated annual tax refund windfall in an unknown sum is what allows households to allocate a substantial portion (nearly half) of the refund to things other than current consumption and debt payoff, such as applying money toward a home, a car, or durable goods and treats.[50] In other words, the uncertainty "seems to dampen the temptation to overconsume" in the months leading up to the refund, and the authors argue that greater certainty "might actually decrease the amount that families were able to set aside" for what the authors term assets and mobility purposes.[51]

These findings are consistent with previous research based not on recipient interviews but on data from the US Bureau of Labor Statistics' Consumer Expenditure Survey; the latter correlated receipt of the EITC with a larger effect on spending on durable goods than nondurable goods. Specifically, those studies found a concentration in vehicle purchases.[52]

These findings also beg the question: If recipients are using the EITC to pay off past-due debt, does that not signal that the taxpayers lack access to the money they need to get by throughout the year? Sociologist and law professor Sara Sternberg Greene writes about the EITC and "financial shock events," which can include medical problems, loss of a job, separation and divorce,

[46] Sykes *et al.*, *supra* note 26, at 251–52.
[47] Halpern-Meekin *et al.*, *supra* note 26, at 64.
[48] Sykes *et al.*, *supra* note 26, at 253.
[49] Halpern-Meekin *et al.*, *supra* note 26, at 64.
[50] *Id.* at 75.
[51] *Id.*
[52] Goodman-Bacon & McGranahan, *supra* note 27, at 30 (finding that "The EITC increases relative average monthly spending on vehicles in February by about 35 percent for EITC families compared with their non-EITC counterparts.").

incarceration, car or home repairs, and loss of housing, among other possibilities.[53] Individuals without adequate savings rely on high-interest financial products such as credit cards, payday loans, and title loans to make it through such events. The much-awaited lump-sum EITC allows taxpayers to pay down these debts, but a percentage of the EITC is then allocated to fees and interest. Many taxpayers are so eager, and some cases desperate, to access their EITC that they pay high fees for refund anticipation loans or other refund-related financial products at tax filing time. As I discuss in more detail in Chapter 3, these products are associated with unscrupulous behavior among some tax return preparers, leaving the low-income taxpayer especially vulnerable if the return is not prepared accurately.

THE ADVANCE EARNED INCOME CREDIT: AN UNDERUTILIZED PERIODIC PAYMENT OPTION

For many years, Congress provided an option for taxpayers to receive their EITC benefit more evenly throughout the year. This advance payment option was available for more than thirty tax years, but it never caught on among taxpayers. The Advance Earned Income Tax Credit (AEITC) was introduced in 1979, four years after the EITC was first enacted. The Senate Finance Committee believed that making the EITC available throughout the year instead of as a lump sum at filing time would increase the incentive for individuals to work, and thus make the program more effective.[54] The AEITC was also intended to help taxpayers make ends meet throughout the year rather than waiting until the year's end for a lump sum.[55]

The amendments, enacted as part of the Revenue Act of 1978, provided the option for a taxpayer to elect to receive advance payment of the EITC through his or her paycheck. The taxpayer's employer provided the delivery mechanism for the advance payment option, and the option was not available to self-employed individuals.

A taxpayer electing to receive the advance payments was required to certify his or her EITC eligibility to the employer on Form W-5. Form W-5 was short, with only four "yes or no" responses required. Taxpayers were asked to affirm that they expected to claim the EITC in that tax year; to indicate whether they

[53] Greene, *supra* note 26 (discussing how, since welfare reform in the mid-1990s, credit card debt has replaced welfare benefits as a safety net during financial shocks).

[54] S. Rep. No. 95-1263, at 52 (1978).

[55] US Gov't Accountability Off., GAO/GGD-92-96, Earned Income Tax Credit: Advance Payment Option is Not Widely Known or Understood by the Public 10 (1992).

expected to have a qualifying child; to state whether they were married; and, if married, to indicate whether their spouse was choosing AEITC payments. The AEITC election expired at the end of each year, such that taxpayers would fill out a new Form W-5 at the start of each tax year.

After a taxpayer completed Form W-5 and submitted it to his or her employer, the employer then added an amount to the employee's paycheck according to an IRS table designed for this purpose. The amount of the advance payment was based on the taxpayer's income as well as whether the taxpayer's spouse was also claiming the advance payment. The advance payment was not treated as a reduction in withholding; it was accounted for separately as an addition and then listed in a separate box on the taxpayer's Form W-2 at the end of the year. An individual claiming the AEITC was then required to file an income tax return to report the AEITC; because the actual amount of the EITC benefit would not be known until the end of the year, the advance payments received had to be reconciled on the return against the full amount of the EITC due. Taxpayers who received too much AEITC or who ultimately were not eligible for the EITC were liable for the excess advance payments received.[56]

Why Wasn't the AEITC More Popular?

Taxpayer take-up of the AEITC was very low. For two reasons, this was perhaps less surprising in the early years. First, the program was new. Second, recall that the early EITC was more a work incentive than an antipoverty program. The maximum EITC available in 1979 was only $500; in 1984 the maximum increased to $550, and in 1986 the maximum increased to $800. When these sums became available as an advance in paychecks, perhaps the sums seemed less significant to taxpayers – even for those eligible for the maximum EITC in the later years of the AEITC program, the advance portion was approximately $30 per week.[57] In 1989, the AEITC participation rate was less than 0.5 percent of eligible workers, and the GAO undertook a

[56] S. Rep. No. 95-1263, at 54 (1978).

[57] US Gov't Accountability Off., GAO-07-1110, Advance Earned Income Tax Credit: Low Use and Small Dollars Paid Impede IRS's Efforts in Reduce High Noncompliance 8 (2007). The same report found that over a period of three years reviewed, most individuals received amounts that were significantly less than the yearly maximum: "about half of all individuals who got AEITC received $100 or less each year and about 75 percent received $500 or less." *Id.* at 10.

study to determine why this rate was so low and what could be done to increase it.[58]

The GAO surveyed a sample of eligible employees and found that fewer than half of those surveyed knew about the EITC at all. Of those who knew about the EITC, fewer than one in four knew about the advance payment option.[59] Among those who were aware of the advance payment option, some said they did not elect advance payments because they feared owing the IRS money at the end of the year. Others stated a preference for receiving a lump sum. The GAO noted that this was consistent with taxpayer behavior generally: "Historically, 75 percent of taxpayers have more income taxes withheld from their paychecks than needed and then get a refund at the end of the year."[60] Interestingly, the GAO discovered that the IRS had not emphasized the advance payments option in its EITC outreach efforts to workers: "IRS officials informed us that they are reluctant to promote the advance payment option because of taxpayer noncompliance."[61] The GAO urged the IRS to increase its outreach both to employees and to employers. The GAO also surveyed employers, finding that many did not understand the advance option or were unclear about their role in delivering it.

The IRS concerns about taxpayer noncompliance arose from the fact that the advance credit was paid before eligibility was confirmed: all a worker had to do was give his or her employer Form W-5. If the worker did not file a tax return, the IRS could not determine whether the worker was eligible or not.[62] The GAO reported an eight-month lag between the close of the tax filing season and the matching of Form W-2s with tax returns.[63] Based on its survey, the GAO estimated that approximately 45 percent of individuals who received advance payment did not file a tax return, which meant the IRS could not determine their eligibility or reconcile the payment amounts.[64] Among those who did file a tax return and had received the advance payment, an estimated 49 percent did not report having received the advanced payment; upon filing,

[58] US Gov't Accountability Off., *supra* note 55, at 14.

[59] *Id.* at 15.

[60] *Id.* at 16.

[61] *Id.* at 17. The report further noted: "Contemporaneous matching of information and tax returns is one of IRS' long-term goals." *Id.* at 28. Twenty-five years later, the IRS is still trying to accomplish this goal.

[62] *Id.* at 24–25.

[63] *Id.* at 27.

[64] *Id.* at 3.

these taxpayers appeared eligible to receive the full lump-sum EITC, resulting in an overpayment.[65]

Involving employers in the advance distribution of the EITC had certain advantages, such as reducing stigma and minimizing administrative costs to the government. At the same time, it shifted part of the onus and burden of administering a social program onto a population that did not directly benefit from it. In the GAO survey, the majority of employers who had employees claiming the AEITC described the program as not burdensome on them.[66] However, there was speculation that employers would not want to inform or encourage their workers to sign up for the AEITC because of the perceived administrative burden, especially for smaller businesses.[67]

Was it appropriate to involve employers? Unlike paid return preparers, employers had no incentive to inflate a credit or facilitate one for a taxpayer who was not eligible. At the same time, they would not want to be responsible, even if indirectly, for creating a situation in which the employee received payments but ultimately was not eligible and had to repay the IRS.

Interestingly, the IRS did not require employers to submit the Form W-5 to the Service, even though the GAO noted that there would have been at least two advantages to having done so.[68] First, it could have prevented noncompliance related to invalid social security numbers. Second, it would have given the IRS a database of AEITC recipients to which it could have sent notices reminding those taxpayers to file. In part because of low participation rates in the AEITC option, the IRS felt such a database would not have a worthwhile return on investment.[69]

Following the first GAO report, Congress required the IRS to notify eligible taxpayers of the advance payment option.[70] But this did not have the desired effect of increasing participation. The GAO studied the AEITC again more than a decade later, using data from tax years 2002 through 2004 in a report released in August 2007. It found that despite the various publicity efforts

65 *Id.*

66 *Id.* at 21.

67 Saul D. Hoffman & Laurence S. Seidman, The Earned Income Tax Credit: Antipoverty Effectiveness and Labor Market Effects 83–85 (W.E. Upjohn Int. for Emp't Res. 1990) (recommending "serious consideration be given to terminating the advance payment system"); *see also Selected Aspects of Welfare Reform: Hearing before the Subcomm. on Select Revenue Measures and Subcomm. on Human Resources of the H. Comm. on Ways and Means*, 103rd Cong. 126 (1993) (statement of Robert Greenstein, Executive Director, Center on Budget and Policy Priorities); S. Rep. No. 95-1263, at 52 (1978).

68 US Gov't Accountability Off., *supra* note 57, at 42.

69 *Id.*

70 Omnibus Budget Reconciliation Act of 1993, Pub. L. No. 103-66, § 13131, 107 Stat. 312, 433–35.

about the program, take-up remained very low: only 3 percent of eligible individuals.[71] At the same time, AEITC noncompliance was quite high. Among AEITC recipients, 79 percent failed to comply with at least one program requirement. Some were noncompliant in multiple respects, in multiple years, or both. The GAO found that more than 100,000 AEITC recipients had an invalid social security number; nearly 200,000 did not file the tax return as required; and among those who filed a tax return, approximately 60 percent misreported the amount of AEITC received.[72]

A study conducted by Damon Jones considered whether taxpayers prefer the "forced savings" of a lump sum to an advance receipt option; his experiment allowed a group of participants the option to channel AEITC payments into a company-matched 401(k) savings plan.[73] He concluded that his experiment results "imply that low participation in the Advance EITC option is not simply due to a lack of information, administrative costs, stigma, procrastination, or long-term forced savings motives."[74] Jones discussed two alternative explanations for the low take-up rate: risk aversion, that is, recipients' fear of learning they would have to pay back the AEITC at year's end if ultimately ineligible; and a short-term forced savings motive.

The End of the AEITC

Whatever the reasons, US taxpayers never embraced the AEITC option. After decades of low take-up, President Obama proposed eliminating the AEITC option as part of a broader budget proposal that passed in 2010. Of course, taxpayers who anticipate an EITC large enough to offset their income tax liability could still adjust their withholding downward to receive a bit more money in their paychecks. The Joint Committee on Taxation noted this in its report describing the proposal, and also wrote in its analysis:

> Eliminating the advance payment option would not affect the timing of the EITC for most EITC recipients because the vast majority of recipients do not elect it. Eliminating the advance payment option resolves noncompliance

[71] US Gov't Accountability Off., *supra* note 57, at 3.

[72] *Id.* at 4.

[73] Damon Jones, *Information, Preferences and Public Benefit Participation: Experimental Evidence from the Advance EITC and 401(k) Savings*, 2(2) Am. Econ. J.: Applied Econ. (2010), 147–49.

[74] *Id.* at 160.

problems associated with it, according to proponents of the repeal, and simplifies the tax law for all EITC taxpayers.[75]

Ultimately, the AEITC may be remembered as a well-intended but failed experiment. As referenced, the possibility of owing the credit back at tax filing time was a significant downside – and risk – of the AEITC program for both the taxpayer and the IRS. Taxpayers had to be diligent about notifying their employers of any change in personal circumstance that would affect eligibility, such as a change in marital status.

Perhaps this is illustrative of one way in which the ease of using the Code to deliver benefits obscures people's cognizance that they are part of a social program. Recipients in other social programs – such as SNAP, Social Security Disability Insurance (SSDI), and TANF – recognize the nature of those programs as social benefits and likely understand the connection between reporting changes and the benefit due. This is not to suggest that recipients in these other programs are always timely about reporting changes, but they are more likely to understand the requirement to do so.

A notable difference with the AEITC was the involvement of the employer as an intermediary between the recipient and the program. First, because taxpayers received the AEITC as part of their paychecks, it did not have the feel of a government benefit, and taxpayers probably gave little thought to the requirement to report changes. Second, taxpayers may have been reluctant to report personal changes to their employer.

The AEITC was also the opposite of what empirical data suggests taxpayers want. Among the small number of taxpayers who opted into the AEITC, 50 percent of them received an advance credit of $100 or less per year, and 75 percent received $500 or less per year.[76] For an employee with a biweekly paycheck, this translates into $4 per check if receiving $100 per year or $19 per check if receiving $500 per year. No taxpayer, no matter what the wage level, will feel the benefit of an extra $5 in his or her biweekly paycheck. Contrast this to the interviews conducted by Sykes, Halpern-Meekin, and others, in which taxpayers expressed a strong preference for lump-sum delivery because the money could be used for a specific purpose.

[75] Joint Comm. on Taxation, JCS-2-09, Description of Revenue Provisions Contained in the President's Fiscal Year 2010 Budget Proposal, Part One: Individual Income Tax and Estate and Gift Tax Provisions 132 (2009).

[76] US Gov't Accountability Off., *supra* note 57, at 10. The yearly maximum of AEITC one could receive in 2002, 2003, and 2004 was $1,503, $1,528, and $1,563, respectively. Only 8 percent of AEITC recipients received an AEITC amount between $1,001 and the maximum in any of the three years in the study. *Id.* at 11.

An anonymous commenter echoed this preference with specific reference to the AEITC in the following reaction to a news story about President Obama's proposal to end the AEITC: "I personaly do not like this AEITC ... 10 dllrs extra dont do nothing for my fam. I feel that we would do a lot more getting the EITC all together. Do we have a choice on this or what?"[77] The AEITC was an effort to put the credit into the taxpayer's hands more than once a year. That specific program ultimately failed, for any number of the reasons described herein. But that does not mean the idea is fatally flawed. What if the benefits were delivered quarterly, as part of a broader reimagination of the EITC program?

EXPERIMENTING WITH PERIODIC PAYMENT

The AEITC was ended in 2010, but conversation about policy alternatives to an annual lump-sum EITC has continued. Many scholars and policy analysts recognize the ways in which EITC recipients could benefit from periodic payment of the benefit. Steve Holt at the Brookings Institution proposed a new design by which EITC recipients would receive a quarterly direct deposit payment administered by the IRS.[78] Holt (and others) argued that the AEITC was ineffective in part because of the "too-small disbursements," and he proposed a quarterly distribution of the EITC.[79] Holt surveyed other recent proposals for periodic distribution, and categorized the proposals into three distinct types: accelerated disbursement, early advance, and deferred savings.[80] As I will discuss in my proposal for year-round delivery of the reimagined family-support benefit, these distribution methods carry different implications for administration and recipient access.

Holt defines *accelerated disbursement* as the distribution of four equal advance payments of the EITC.[81] In other words, taxpayers receive the expected benefit before earning the income, then reconcile any difference at tax time.

[77] Anonymous, Comment to Elaine Maag, *Giving Up on the Advanced Earned Income Tax Credit*, TaxVox: Federal Budget and Economy (Mar. 4, 2009), www.taxpolicycenter.org/taxvox/giving-advanced-earned-income-tax-credit (hard copy on file with author).

[78] Stephen D. Holt, *Periodic Payment of the Earned Income Tax Credit*, The Brookings Inst. (June 5, 2008), https://www.brookings.edu/research/periodic-payment-of-the-earned-income-tax-credit; Steve Holt, *Periodic Payment of the Earned Income Tax Credit Revisited*, The Brookings Inst. (Dec. 17, 2015), https://www.brookings.edu/research/periodic-payment-of-the-earned-income-tax-credit-revisited.

[79] Holt, *Periodic Payment of the Earned Income Tax Credit Revisited*, *supra* note 78, at 5.

[80] *Id.* at 8.

[81] *Id.* at 32.

Early advance proposals envision an option for taxpayers to access benefits on demand once or twice a year.[82] Taxpayers could access the benefit after it accrues in part, but before the end of the tax year. Senator Sherrod Brown proposed such an "early refund" program that would allow taxpayers to take an advance of up to $500, which would be subtracted from their EITC when the return is filed. As Brown noted: "We can use the EITC to provide an alternative to payday loans and make sure that families are no longer forced to take on payday loans and then use their EITC to dig out of the trap of indefinitely rolling over the initial debt."[83]

Deferred savings proposals are designed to incentivize EITC claimants to save or defer part of their EITC benefit, rather than receive the entire lump sum at once. Under these proposals, there is no need to estimate and reconcile income, because it is received at tax filing time rather than in advance.[84] Sara Sternberg Greene proposed an idea she coined the "Savings and Emergency Fund Account" (SAEF), whereby a portion of the EITC would be directed into an interest-bearing account, and recipients additionally would be eligible to receive a bonus based on the amount of the account balance retained.[85] Along with Halpern-Meekin, Greene was also among a group of scholars who proposed a similar bonus match, the "Rainy Day EITC" proposal.[86] In 2016, Senators Cory Booker and Jerry Moran introduced a bipartisan proposal, the Refund to Rainy Day Savings Act, which draws on these scholars' proposals.[87] Both the proposed Refund to Rainy Day Savings Act and Sara Sternberg Greene's SAEF proposal would create matching savings incentives to encourage recipients to set aside money for emergencies.

82 *Id.*

83 Press Release, Sen. Sherrod Brown, Brown Outlines Efforts to Expand Economic Opportunity to All Americans, Make Tax Code Work Better for Families (June 7, 2016), https://www.brown.senate.gov/newsroom/press/release/brown-outlines-efforts-to-expand-economic-opportunity-to-all-americans-make-tax-code-work-better-for-families.

84 Holt, *Periodic Payment of the Earned Income Tax Credit Revisited*, *supra* note 78, at 33.

85 Greene, *supra* note 26.

86 Sarah Halpern-Meekin, Sara Sternberg Greene, Ezra Levin, & Kathryn Edin, *The Rainy Day Earned Income Tax Credit: A Reform to Boost Financial Security by Helping Low-Wage Workers Build Emergency Savings*, 4(2) The Russell Sage Foundation J. of the Social Sciences 161 (2018), http://muse.jhu.edu/article/687580/pdf. The authors note that this would increase the administrative cost of the EITC as well as the overall EITC expenditures, with the amount of the increase varying depending on how the proposal is structured.

87 The Booker–Moran proposal would allow all tax filers (not just EITC filers) to defer their tax refund in an interest-bearing account. *See* Press Release, Sen. Cory Booker, Booker, Moran Introduce Bill Empowering Taxpayers to Defer Refund for Rainy Day Savings (Apr. 13, 2016), www.booker.senate.gov/?p=press_release&id=403.

As part of this conversation, policy makers and scholars have collaborated to survey taxpayer preferences and conduct small-scale experiments with different frequencies of EITC delivery. The most notable experiment since the termination of the AEITC was an EITC periodic payment pilot program in Chicago in 2014–15. The Center for Economic Progress (CEP) administered this extensive pilot program as part of a collaborative effort with the Chicago Department of Family and Support Services, the Office of Chicago Mayor Rahm Emanuel, the Chicago Housing Authority, and the University of Illinois at Urbana-Champaign. The pilot program sought to explore the "administrative feasibility" and "recipient utility" of disbursing the EITC in quarterly advance payments.[88]

The pilot program selected 343 participants using four selection criteria: participants had to both have a qualifying child and have received the EITC benefit in the previous tax year; their estimated EITC had to be at least $600; their EITC could not be subject to offset due to other outstanding federal debt; and they had to be a current recipient of housing assistance.[89] The CEP provided four equal periodic payments to the participants on a fixed schedule throughout 2014, with a maximum of $2,000 paid to the participants. At the same time, the CEP measured the effects of the pilot by using a control group of 164 individuals who did not receive periodic payments. Participants signed a loan agreement as a condition of participation: in exchange for receiving the four payments, they agreed to repay the CEP from their 2014 EITC.[90]

The pilot program was sensitive to research showing that EITC recipients prefer year-end lump-sum payments. The project explained to participants that they would be obligated to repay the quarterly funds upon receiving their 2014 tax refund; six eligible individuals declined to participate after attending an information session about the program.[91]

The pilot program, which is discussed in more detail in Chapter 6, resulted in a number of findings that support the need for a reimagination of both the design and the administration of the EITC in the United States. Ninety

[88] David Marzahl, *Chicago Earned Income Tax Credit Periodic Payment Pilot Interim Report*, Ctr. for Econ. Progress (Dec. 2014) (on file with author).

[89] *Id.*

[90] Participants were expected to have their 2014 income tax return prepared by CEP in order to facilitate the repayment. Approximately one-third of participants did not complete the pilot program, in many cases because they chose not to have their 2014 tax return prepared at CEP. Those who did not complete the program are excluded from the project findings. Dylan Bellisle & David Marzahl, *Restructuring the EITC: A Credit for the Modern Worker*, Ctr. for Econ. Progress 5 (2015), www.economicprogress.org/assets/files/Restructuring-the-EITC-A-Credit-for-the-Modern-Worker.pdf.

[91] Marzahl, *supra* note 88.

percent of those who received quarterly payments reported this as a preference over any other payment method. Of those who completed the pilot program, a majority made income and household predictions that produced "reasonably accurate" estimates of the amount of EITC they would receive, and only 3 of 229 participants (1.3 percent) overestimated their refund such that they had a balance due at tax time. Finally, participating households reported a variety of positive benefits resulting from the periodic payments, including less stress in meeting monthly expenses.[92]

The EITC's current design presents advantages to both the government and the taxpayer. But despite much evidence highlighting taxpayer preference for an annual lump-sum payment, many low-income taxpayers still rely on credit cards and payday loans when financial shock events occur or simply to make ends meet until tax time. Distributing the EITC throughout the year would offer taxpayers a periodic safety net that could help cushion these shocks. The CEP pilot program study shows that taxpayers responded positively to a quarterly distribution of the EITC when given that option.

The next chapter explores several other flaws in the way the United States currently administers the EITC. These shortcomings must be balanced with taxpayer preferences in reimagining the EITC. While it is clear that the AEITC was not an attractive option to taxpayers, the current design does not function optimally for many taxpayers or for the IRS.

[92] Bellisle & Marzahl, *supra* note 90.

3

How Inexpensive Administration Creates Expensive Challenges

The first submission was constantly being worked on but was never completed . . . If K., wearied by all the talk, happened to remark that things were proceeding at a very slow pace . . . he was told that things were not proceeding slowly at all.[1]

The delivery of refundable credits through the Internal Revenue Code allows for inexpensive administration and high participation rates. The rationale for lump-sum delivery is further reinforced by taxpayer preferences and attitudes. Nonetheless, there are several significant ways in which the delivery of refundable credits through the Code is problematic.

Allowing taxpayers to self-declare eligibility for the Earned Income Tax Credit (EITC) and Child Tax Credit (CTC) keeps overhead costs on the government side to a minimum, but creates several problems and challenges. From a budgetary and enforcement perspective, the primary challenge is the persistently high rate of overpayment. The self-declaration design makes the credit difficult to administer and enforce because the Internal Revenue Service (IRS) relies on return-processing filters and an inefficient automated examination process to pursue questionable EITC claims.

Self-declaration also creates problems and challenges for taxpayers. Examination statistics reveal that the IRS is more likely to examine, or audit, an individual return on which EITC is claimed, with approximately one-third of all individual examinations involving an EITC claim.[2] The high examination

[1] Franz Kafka, The Trial 88 (Ritchie Robertson ed., Mike Mitchell trans., Oxford University Press 2009), copyright in the translation Mike Mitchell 2009, copyright in the editorial matter Ritchie Robertson 2009, reproduced with permission of the Licensor through PLSclear.

[2] In recent years, less than 1 percent of individual income tax returns were selected for audit; for example, in calendar year 2014, 0.84 percent of individual returns were subject to audit. While 1.57 percent of returns claiming EITC that year were selected for audit explicitly on the basis of the EITC claim, only 0.66 percent of non-EITC returns were audited on any basis. I.R.S., Pub.

rate of EITC returns is, at least in part, an agency response to the high rate of improper payments of the EITC. However, a significant percentage of EITC claimants selected for examination prove to be eligible for the credit. Claimants selected for examination suffer from the slow and punitive nature of the examination process, which is overwhelmingly conducted by mail correspondence rather than face to face. The confusing and inefficient examination process creates untimely delays in benefit delivery, assuming the taxpayer can even navigate the examination successfully: studies show a significant portion of eligible taxpayers are unable to do so because of systemic barriers.

The filing process in itself is complex and can be overwhelming; many EITC claimants turn to return preparers. At best, these EITC claimants bear a financial cost; a percentage of the benefit intended to relieve poverty is paid to the preparer. Many of these filers owe no federal income tax, but they must file a return to claim their social benefit. Furthermore, because extra forms are required to claim the EITC with qualifying children, return preparers charge more for these returns. In this regard, the administrative costs of benefit delivery are borne by the recipient, not the government. At worst, taxpayers are enticed into predatory lending practices related to their tax refunds or become unknowing victims of return preparer fraud. With a maximum available credit of over $6,000, the EITC, like other sizeable refundable credits, also attracts large-scale tax-related identity theft.

The various empirical works of Jennifer Sykes, Sarah Halpern-Meekin, Sara Sternberg Greene, and others are filled with interviews of happy EITC recipients who received their refund in the expected fashion: promptly and in full. Missing from these interviews are the stories of taxpayers whose refunds were frozen even though they qualified for the EITC. Missing are the tales of those who had to fight the IRS during examinations, appeals, and the Tax Court for more than a year to receive the benefit to which they were entitled, and which they needed to make ends meet. Missing are the tales of ambiguity when

55B, DATA BOOK, 2015 23 (2016), www.irs.gov/pub/irs-soi/15databk.pdf. In some tax years, the audit rate of EITC claimants was twice as high as the audit rate for non-EITC returns. For example, of the nearly 148 million individual income tax returns filed in calendar year 2015, 0.7 percent were subject to audit. Of the 28,060,849 returns claiming the EITC, 380,260 were selected for audit on the basis of the EITC claim (meaning that 1.3 percent of all EITC returns were audited on the basis of the EITC claim); only 606,748 (0.5 percent) of the 119,906,475 non-EITC returns were audited on any basis. I.R.S., PUB. 55B, DATA BOOK, 2016 23 (2017), https://www.irs.gov/pub/irs-soi/16databk.pdf. *See also* TAXPAYER ADVOCATE SERVICE, 2009 ANNUAL REPORT TO CONGRESS (VOL. 2) 86 (citing I.R.S., PUB. 55B, DATA BOOK, 2008 tbl. 9a, which showed an average audit rate of slightly more than 2 percent for taxpayers claiming the EITC as opposed to about 1 percent for taxpayers overall). EITC returns are selected for audit based on third-party database information, a risk score, or at random.

taxpayers actually met the statutory requirements but were denied the refund because they could not document it in the fashion expected by the IRS. Missing are stories of divorced custodial parents who did not receive the money they needed because the noncustodial parent filed first and claimed the credit despite not being entitled to it. Missing are stories of taxpayers taken advantage of by unscrupulous return preparers. Missing are the stories of taxpayers whose return preparers pressured them into purchasing or selecting a financial product that diminished the refund.

This chapter speaks to those stories.[3] It presents an argument that the present administration of social benefits through the Code is not working as well as it should for many recipients, for the IRS, or for the taxpaying public as a whole.

THE STUBBORNLY HIGH IMPROPER PAYMENT RATE

The Improper Payments Information Act of 2002 requires federal agencies to annually review programs to identify those that are "susceptible to significant improper payments."[4] The act defines an "improper payment" as a payment that should not have been made (including one to an ineligible recipient) or that was made in an incorrect amount (including either an overpayment or an underpayment).[5]

The rate of EITC overclaims and overpayments has been, and continues to be, persistently high. Since 2003, the estimated rate of EITC improper payments has exceeded 20 percent and ranged as high as 30 percent. The EITC is the only IRS program classified as a "high-risk" program by the US Office of Management and Budget.[6] Despite many legislative and

[3] This chapter draws in part on my previous work, including Michelle Lyon Drumbl, *Beyond Polemics: Poverty, Taxes, and Noncompliance*, 14 eJournal of Tax Research 253 (2016), and Michelle Lyon Drumbl, *Those Who Know, Those Who Don't, and Those Who Know Better: Balancing Complexity, Sophistication, and Accuracy on Tax Returns*, 11 Pitt. Tax Rev. 113 (2013).

[4] Improper Payments Information Act of 2002, Pub. L. No. 107-300, 116 Stat. 2350 (2002) [hereinafter IPIA]. The IPIA has been expanded by Exec. Order No. 13520, 3 C.F.R. 274 (2010) and two subsequent acts: Improper Payments Elimination and Recovery Act of 2010, Pub. L. No. 111-204, 124 Stat. 2224 [hereinafter IPERA] and the Improper Payments Elimination and Recovery Improvement Act of 2012, Pub. L. No. 112-248, 126 Stat. 2390 [hereinafter IPERIA].

[5] IPIA § 2(d)(2).

[6] Treasury Inspector Gen. for Tax Admin., Ref No. 2017-40-030, *Revised Refundable Credit Risk Assessments Still Do Not Provide an Accurate Measure of the Risk of Improper Payments*, Treasury Dept. 3 (Apr. 28, 2017), www.treasury.gov/tigta/auditreports/2017reports/201740030fr.pdf.

administrative approaches over the years, which this chapter discusses in detail, the IRS has been unable to meaningfully reduce the overpayment rate.

More recently, the Treasury Department has broadened the scope of its annual risk assessment review to include two other refundable credits: the Additional Child Tax Credit (ACTC) and the American Opportunity Tax Credit (AOTC). The ACTC is the term the IRS uses to refer to the refundable portion of the CTC. The AOTC is a refundable credit for qualified higher education expenses. In its first review of these refundable credits, the IRS rated the risk of ACTC and AOTC improper payments as "low." However, the Treasury Inspector General for Tax Administration (TIGTA) drew a different conclusion based on the same compliance data that the IRS used. For fiscal year 2015, TIGTA estimated an ACTC improper payment rate of 24.2 percent (with improper payments estimated to be between \$4.9 and \$6.4 billion) and an AOTC improper payment rate of 30.7 percent (with improper payments estimated to be between \$1.6 and \$2.1 billion).[7]

It is important to note that the improper payment rate does not differentiate between intentional and unintentional overclaims. Many policy makers and observers mistakenly (or deliberately, to serve a political agenda) conflate the EITC improper payment rate with that of taxpayer fraud, which is not measured. As this chapter explains, overpayments and fraud are far from synonymous, and understanding this is crucial to a reimagination of EITC administration.

Treasury Department and IRS officials offer a variety of responses to criticism of the high improper payment rate. These responses include critiques of EITC design, which is in essence blame directed at Congress. For example, in 2017 Ursula Gillis, chief financial officer of the IRS, wrote:

> Our risk assessments continue to show that improper payments from refundable credits are not rooted in internal control weaknesses, financial management deficiencies, or financial reporting failures, but instead, from the inherent difficulty of delivering benefits through the tax system. It is difficult to administer these programs since errors frequently stem from how Congress structured them, and because the IRS lacks available tools for verifying data or correcting issues identified during filing or through our fraud prevention programs ... With the majority of erroneous payments stemming from the statutory design of the refundable tax credit programs, and the IRS's limited ability to correct and audit returns, there is little we can do to reduce payment

7 *Id.* at 4.

errors in refundable tax credits, absent legislative changes or increased funding.[8]

The Treasury Department has identified six specific factors as contributing to EITC noncompliance and presenting difficulties for reducing the rate of EITC overclaims: the complexity of the tax law, the structure of the EITC, confusion among eligible claimants, high turnover of eligible claimants, unscrupulous tax return preparers, and fraud.[9]

It is important to note that these factors contribute to both intentional and unintentional noncompliance. While it is hard to discern how much noncompliance is intentional versus unintentional, many believe the latter may be more common. IRS Commissioner John Koskinen, for one, emphasized the extent of unintentional noncompliance in remarks he gave in 2014: "Our biggest problem isn't that people are stealing the money who have no right to it at all. It is that the program is so complicated that people are inadvertently having difficulty figuring out where they fit and where they don't."[10]

The IRS's National Research Program (NRP) data and compliance studies provide important insights into EITC noncompliance, though the data cannot distinguish between intentional and unintentional noncompliance. The NRP studies are based on audits of a random sample of tax filers, rather than audits selected by the IRS based on risk or other factors. The most recent NRP study of the EITC, published in 2014, was based on EITC claimed in tax years 2006–2008.[11] One important shortcoming of the NRP data is that approximately 15 percent of taxpayers who were selected for an NRP audit in this study did not participate in the audit; in these cases, the EITC was disallowed because the taxpayer did not substantiate the claim. The study authors acknowledge the possibility that some nonresponsive taxpayers may in fact have been eligible for the EITC; they account for this missing group by providing a "higher end" and "lower end" range in the study's estimates.

[8] *Id.* at 28. Gillis does not specify what she means by "erroneous payments stemming from the statutory design," but I interpret this to refer to the complexity of the statute and the challenge faced by the agency in verifying eligibility requirements, such as where a child resides.

[9] *US Dept. of Treasury, Agency Financial Report: Fiscal Year 2013* 214 (Dec. 16, 2013), www.treasury.gov/about/budget-performance/annual-performance-plan/Documents/2013%20Department%20of%20the%20Treasury%20AFR%20Report%20v2.pdf.

[10] William Hoffman, *Koskinen Kicks off Filing Season with Spotlight on EITC*, 142 Tax Notes 617 (2014).

[11] I.R.S., *Pub. No. 5162, Compliance Estimates for the Earned Income Tax Credit Claimed on 2006–2008 Returns* (Aug. 2014), www.irs.gov/pub/irs-soi/EITCComplianceStudyTY2006-2008.pdf.

Unlike the improper payment estimates, the NRP study did not adjust its estimates to account for IRS actions to prevent or recover EITC overclaims. As a result, the study's overclaim estimates are higher than the improper payment rate, and the study does not "reflect the cost of EITC errors to the Federal government."[12] Put differently, the NRP study is an estimate of taxpayer overclaims, not net errors that impact the federal budget. It sheds lights on what taxpayers are getting wrong in their filings, although it does not capture the segment of taxpayers who are entitled to claim EITC yet do not do so.

With that caveat in mind, the NRP study is perhaps most usefully viewed as raw data on taxpayer behavior – both erroneous and intentional. As discussed later in this chapter, the IRS has developed a number of initiatives in response to these findings (and findings from a similar study in 1999) to reduce the rate of overpayments. The data can also be useful in reimagining credit eligibility and delivery more generally.

Significantly, the 2014 NRP study reported that an estimated 79–85 percent of taxpayers who overclaim the EITC are altogether ineligible for the credit, as opposed to overstating the amount to which they are entitled.[13] Through its NRP data, the IRS has isolated the main errors underlying EITC overclaims. There are three significant categories of errors, as well as several other types of errors that are less common, which I do not discuss here.[14]

The two most significant taxpayer errors are "income misreporting errors" and "qualifying child errors." Income misreporting errors are the most common error (appearing in two-thirds of known overclaim returns) and are frequently the only error (an estimated 51 percent of the time).[15] Qualifying child errors are less common, but are more significant from a dollar amount perspective: On an estimated 21 percent of returns, the only error is a qualifying child error, but the average estimated overclaim on these returns is $2,327.[16] In contrast, on returns in which income misreporting is the only error, the average overclaim is $673.[17]

Qualifying child errors present the greatest difficulties for taxpayers and the IRS alike, because the eligibility requirements are factually intensive and not

[12] *Id.* at iv.

[13] *Id.*

[14] The less common errors include tie-breaker errors (occurring when more than one taxpayer meets the criteria to claim the same child), errors resulting from an invalid social security number, errors corrected during processing, errors relating to citizenship or residence status, and others.

[15] I.R.S., *supra* note 11, at 16–17.

[16] *Id.*

[17] *Id.*

easily verifiable. For example, the statute includes both a "relationship test" and a "residency test." The latter requires an EITC claimant to document that the child shared the same "principal place of abode" as the taxpayer for at least one-half of the year. The IRS does not have an easy way to make such a factual determination – it generally does not have access to third-party information about where children are living – and thus relies on the taxpayer to provide documentation. Substantiating documentation is often very difficult for taxpayers to provide, including in cases where custody is shared.

The third most common taxpayer error is an incorrect filing status, representing between 9 and 17 percent of total overclaim dollars.[18] As is the case with qualifying child errors, filing status is a fact-intensive determination that the IRS is not well positioned to verify; the IRS does not have ready access to state marriage records. Errors of filing status often involve a married taxpayer misrepresenting himself or herself as unmarried to receive a higher EITC or to meet the eligibility criteria.

There are two incentives for taxpayers to misrepresent filing status this way. One is the scenario in which two married taxpayers collectively earn an amount above the EITC income phase out. The income phase out for a married couple filing jointly is higher than that for an unmarried taxpayer, but the phase-out amount is not doubled. Thus, at some income levels, if the taxpayers file as unmarried, one or even both may appear income-eligible for the EITC, whereas their collective income would exceed the phase-out level on a joint return. In contrast, a cohabitating but unmarried couple's EITC eligibility is determined individually, even if their collective household income exceeds the phase out that they would be subject to if married and filing jointly.

The second reason a taxpayer may misrepresent filing status is because married taxpayers filing separate returns are ineligible for the EITC, regardless of income level.[19] Joint filing for married couples is an election, and both spouses must consent to file a joint return. Thus, if one spouse refuses to file jointly (or if the claimant spouse is unable to do so), the claimant spouse will not receive the credit even if the income and qualifying child eligibility criteria are met. There is no exception allowing a married filing separate filer to claim the EITC. A special rule does allow a married individual to file as head of household if he or she furnishes more than half the cost of maintaining a household with a child residing there more than half the year, but only if the filer's spouse did not live in the household during the last six months of the

[18] *Id.* at 30.

[19] I.R.C. § 32(d). There is no stated rationale for this rule in the Code or legislative history.

taxable year.[20] This rule does not help everyone. For example, married taxpayers who separate from their spouses during the second half of the year are not eligible to file as head of household, even if a child resided with them during the entire year. This is problematic in cases of a recent estrangement or separation, especially in cases of domestic violence. It may be unsafe to request joint filing, and if individuals shared a household with their spouse after June 30, they cannot claim head of household status. Thus they cannot access the EITC unless they misrepresent their filing status.

The stubbornly high improper payment rate remains so for complex and varied reasons. Understanding the causes of EITC overclaims is pivotal to a reimagination of EITC delivery. The IRS does not have a way to measure the extent to which overclaims are intentional or unintentional, although as noted earlier, the agency estimates that a significant amount of noncompliance is unintentional.[21] To some extent, Congressional and agency responses to noncompliance must address intentional and unintentional noncompliance as two separate phenomena, because the underlying causes are different. The response must also consider differences between taxpayer and return preparer noncompliance.

INTENTIONAL AND UNINTENTIONAL TAXPAYER NONCOMPLIANCE

Fewer than half of taxpayers who claim the EITC prepare their own income tax return. The most recent NRP study (based on tax years 2006–2008) reported that 68 percent of EITC claimants used a paid preparer, also noting that the percentage of taxpayers self-preparing EITC returns had increased since those tax years.[22] In 2014, IRS Commissioner John Koskinen reported that 57 percent of EITC claimants used paid preparers.[23]

20 I.R.C. § 7703(b).

21 *US Dept. of Treasury, Agency Financial Report: Fiscal Year 2016* 231 (Nov. 15, 2016) ("Much of the difficulty administering the EITC derives from the complexity of its statutory eligibility requirements. Whether a taxpayer meets these eligibility rules may be difficult for the taxpayer to understand and cannot be independently confirmed by the IRS using third-party corroborating data"), www.treasury.gov/about/budget-performance/annual-performance-plan/Documents/Treasury%20FY2016%20AFR.pdf; Robert Greenstein, John Wancheck, & Chuck Marr, *Reducing Overpayments in the Earned Income Tax Credit*, CTR. ON BUDGET & POLICY PRIORITIES (Apr. 7, 2014) (hard copy on file with author) (citing two older studies on this point); Leslie Book, *The Poor and Tax Compliance: One Size Does Not Fit All*, 51 U. KAN. L. REV. 1145, 1166 (2003).

22 I.R.S., *supra* note 11, at v n. 4.

23 *Written Testimony of John Koskinen, Commissioner Internal Revenue Service, before the House Ways and Means Comm., Subcomm. on Oversight on the 2014 Filing Season and Improper Payments*, 113th Cong. 13 (May 7, 2014). *See also Written Statement of Nina E. Olson, National*

Taxpayers who choose to self-prepare are likely to use commercial software programs, such as Turbo Tax or Tax Act. Some "do-it-yourself" taxpayers rely on a friend or family member to assist (with or without the use of such software), and still others may navigate the paper forms on their own. Using software is significantly less expensive than using a tax return preparer and may even be available for free. Low-income taxpayers are generally eligible to access free return preparation software through the IRS Free File Alliance program, which allows taxpayers to select from among a dozen commercial providers to prepare and electronically file a federal and state income tax return.

The IRS encourages low-income taxpayers to self-prepare, promoting its Free File Alliance program as a fast, safe, and free option.[24] One the one hand, the IRS should be lauded for making self-preparation accessible for no charge to low-income taxpayers. Ironically, however, this may fuel both intentional and unintentional EITC noncompliance.

Unintentional EITC Noncompliance

The statutory complexity of the EITC poses challenges for taxpayers who choose not to use a preparer. I.R.C. section 32 is over 2,400 words long and includes more than twenty cross-references to other sections or subsections of the Code. The IRS publication explaining the EITC is thirty-seven pages long. The various benefits for families – filing status, dependent exemptions, EITC, and CTC – do not align perfectly, even after Congress adopted a uniform definition of "qualifying child" in 2004. For example, to claim a qualifying child as a dependent, the child must not have provided half of his or her own support for the tax year. The EITC does not have such a support requirement. Yet taxpayers claiming head of household filing status must be able to claim a dependent and also show that they furnished over half of the cost of maintaining the household during the taxable year. A qualifying child must be the taxpayer's child, stepchild, or descendant of such a child (grandchildren) or the sibling, stepsibling, or descendant of such a sibling (nephew or niece).

Taxpayer Advocate, Hearing on the Nat'l Taxpayer Advocate's 2014 Annual Report to Congress Before the Subcomm. on Gov't Operations, Comm. on Oversight and Gov't Reform, H.R., 114th Cong. 28 (Apr. 15, 2015), www.irs.gov/pub/foia/ig/tas/Nina_Olson_Testimony_2015_Annual_Report_to_Congress-4-15-2016.pdf (with data showing that 55 percent of EITC returns in tax year 2013 were paid preparer returns).

[24] I.R.S., *Do Your Federal Taxes for Free* (hard copy on file with author).

If the "qualifying child" test is not met, the taxpayer can claim a "qualifying relative" as a dependent; that definition is much broader: It additionally includes parents, stepparents, grandparents, aunts, uncles, certain in-laws, and any unrelated individual (other than a spouse) who was a member of the taxpayer's household for the entire year. In a twist on the support test for "qualifying child," the taxpayer must have provided more than half of the qualifying relative's total support for the year. There is a subtle but real distinction between having to show that the *dependent* did not provide half or more of his own support (as required to claim a qualifying child) and showing that the *taxpayer* provided more than half the dependent's support (required to claim a qualifying relative). Furthermore, to be a qualifying relative, that person's gross income must be less than the exemption amount for the calendar year.

A qualifying relative can be claimed as a dependent, but cannot be claimed for the EITC or CTC. This distinction is very confusing to many taxpayers, who do not understand why they can claim a person in their household as a dependent but not claim the same person for the EITC or CTC (if that individual otherwise meets the age requirement for the credit). For example, an unmarried taxpayer can potentially claim his girlfriend and her minor children as dependents on his tax return if they reside with him and he supports them financially, but he cannot claim those minor children for the EITC and CTC because they are not his stepchildren.

The tax reform enacted in 2017 introduced yet another confusing wrinkle: It suspended the personal exemption deduction for taxpayers and dependents for tax years 2018–25. At first blush, this would seem to simplify things for low-income taxpayers, especially given that the definition of dependent doesn't fully align with who one can claim for the CTC and EITC. However, the definition of dependent remains in the Code, as it provides a critical cross-reference definition for calculating the premium tax credit, for determining head of household status, and for a newly enacted $500 nonrefundable credit for dependents other than qualifying children.

Additional special rules for divorced or separated parents are not easy to navigate: It is possible for the custodial parent (with whom the child lives for more than half the year) to "release" the dependent exemption to the noncustodial parent. If this is done, the noncustodial parent can claim the child as a dependent and as a qualifying child for the CTC, despite not having met the residency requirement. However, the noncustodial parent cannot claim head of household status solely on this basis and cannot claim the child for the EITC. The custodial parent can claim head of household status and the EITC for the child, despite relinquishing the dependent exemption and the CTC.

Even during 2018–25, the years in which the deduction for personal and dependent exemptions is suspended, the custodial parent can still release the dependent for purposes of allowing the noncustodial parent to claim the CTC.

As if statutory complexity were not enough to contend with, household composition is often complex and does not necessarily conform to the statutory definitions. The proportion of children living in a nuclear family with married parents has declined over time; today, 40 percent of children are born to unmarried parents.[25] The percentage of children living in households with cohabitating unmarried parents is relatively small, but on the rise.[26] Children in low- and moderate-income families are more likely than other children to experience a change in family type from one year to the next, as are children in families with cohabitating unmarried parents.[27] Nearly one-fifth of children in single-parent families live in a multigenerational household.[28]

There are complicated "tie-breaker" rules when more than one taxpayer can claim the same qualifying child for the EITC. These would apply commonly in households with cohabitating unmarried parents and also in multigenerational homes. If the child resides with both unmarried parents who file separate returns, either parent can claim the child; if both were to claim the child, the IRS would award the credit to the parent with the higher adjusted gross income. If the child resides with one or both parents and also a grandparent or other family member, the other relative can claim the qualifying child if the parent chooses not to, but only if that relative's adjusted gross income is higher than either parent's adjusted gross income.[29]

Each of these statutory terms is a precise term of art, sometimes further defined in the Treasury Regulations, but taxpayers understandably conflate the concepts and do not appreciate the technical distinctions. In some cases, they file with imperfect information, believing they are entitled to claim a child based on what they know. The results can be sad, and at least one Tax Court judge has remarked on this in an opinion. In *Smyth v. Commissioner*, a grandmother provided all financial support for her household, which included her adult son, his wife, and their two young children. Smyth's

[25] Elaine Maag, H. Elizabeth Peters, & Sara Edelstein, *Increasing Family Complexity and Volatility: The Difficulty in Determining Child Tax Benefits*, Tax Policy Ctr. 1 (Mar. 3, 2016), www.taxpolicycenter.org/sites/default/files/alfresco/publication-pdfs/2000641-increasing-family-complexity-and-volatility-the-difficulty-in-determining-child-tax-benefits.pdf.

[26] *Id.* at 10.

[27] *Id.* at 13–14.

[28] *Id.* at 18.

[29] I.R.C. § 152(c)(4)(C).

grandchildren were "qualifying children," and she claimed them on her return. Her son told her he was not going to file a return, so the tie-breaker rule did not seem to come into play. After she was audited, her son admitted that he had filed a return and spent the tax refund on himself (though not relevant to the statutory analysis, the court pointed out that it was spent on drugs). Because of the tie-breaker rule, Smyth was denied the dependency exemptions, EITC, and CTC. Judge Holmes wrote in his decision:

> It is difficult for us to explain to a hardworking taxpayer like Smyth why this should be so, except to say that we are bound by the law. And it is impossible for us to convince ourselves that the result we reach today – that the IRS was right to send money meant to help those who care for small children to someone who spent it on drugs instead – is in any way just. Except for the theory of justice that requires a judge to follow the law as it is but explain his decision in writing so that those responsible for changing it might notice.[30]

The *Smyth* case is an excellent example of one taxpayer's unintentional EITC noncompliance. Smyth met all the eligibility requirements to claim her grandchildren and believed, in good faith, that the children's parents had not filed a return. Though her son lived under her roof, it was the IRS who informed her that someone else had claimed the same children, making her ineligible for the EITC and CTC.

Intentional Noncompliance

At least some EITC noncompliance, however, is intentional. What drives intentional EITC noncompliance? The answer, at first blush, appears simple: A relatively large amount of money is at stake, and it can be obtained with "relative ease."[31]

Leslie Book has written several articles examining EITC noncompliance through the lens of social psychology and behavioral economics. Book argues that the design of the EITC includes structural incentives for taxpayers to engage in intentional noncompliance. He further argues that some taxpayers engage in "intentional symbolic noncompliance" in response to perceived injustices in the EITC design.[32] Book cites two examples: taxpayers who have more than the maximum number of qualifying children for the EITC; and

[30] Smyth v. Commissioner, T.C. Memo 2017–29 (Feb. 7, 2017).

[31] Taxpayer Advocate Service, 2009 Annual Report to Congress (Vol. 2) 82.

[32] Leslie Book, *Freakonomics and the Tax Gap: An Applied Perspective*, 56 Am. U. L. Rev. 1163, 1176–77 (2007); *see generally*, Book, *supra* note 21.

noncustodial parents who financially support their children but cannot claim them for EITC because they do not meet the residency requirements.[33] The latter may be especially true in instances in which the custodial parent has no earned income and therefore cannot claim the EITC; collectively, the parents may agree that the noncustodial parent should claim the child as if the child lived with that parent.[34] Other possible perceived injustices may motivate noncompliance, such as the disparity in phase-out levels between married taxpayers and unmarried cohabitating parents. Taxpayers may engage in intentional noncompliance if they hear of other people who are improperly claiming children on their tax return and not getting caught. Citing Dan Kahan's reciprocity theory, Book writes: "if taxpayers believe that others are not complying, then taxpayers will resent complying and be more inclined to cheat."[35]

Jay Soled and Kathleen DeLaney Thomas argue that tax return preparation software may also contribute to noncompliance by encouraging aggressive return positions.[36] They cite the "audit risk meters" that provide users with real-time feedback on the likelihood of an audit, which stands in stark contrast to the ethical rules prohibiting regulated return preparers from factoring the likelihood of audit risk into tax advice.[37] Soled and Thomas further note the tendency of tax return software programs to oversimplify the law. For the EITC, however, the most significant and troubling feature is the software's display of the taxpayer's refund due or balance owed: A taxpayer can change information on the return and immediately see how this impacts the bottom line.[38] In the EITC context, this may encourage income misreporting – taxpayers may inflate self-employment income or inflate Schedule C deductions (self-employment deductions such as mileage, travel expenses, or expenses for a home office) to maximize the credit, and with simple tinkering in the software they can see the results of these adjustments.

Taxpayers who self-prepare using software may fail to understand the underlying EITC requirements as they complete their return. As Soled and Thomas suggest, some of these taxpayers may deliberately flout the requirements, thinking they can get away with it, and not appreciating the consequences if they are caught. Paid preparers are subject to extra due diligence

[33] Book, *supra* note 32, at 1176–77.
[34] Book, *supra* note 32, at 1178.
[35] Book, *supra* note 21, at 1176.
[36] Jay A. Soled & Kathleen DeLaney Thomas, *Regulating Tax Return Preparation*, 58 B.C. L. Rev. 152, 179 (2017).
[37] *Id.* at 180.
[38] *Id.* at 180–81.

requirements when claiming the EITC on a return; they must fill out Form 8867 and submit it with the return. Self-preparing taxpayers are not subject to these same due diligence requirements.

William Cobb, CEO of H&R Block, has raised this discrepancy to Congress and to the IRS and Treasury. In a March 2015 letter to the Senate Finance Committee and the House Committee on Ways and Means, Cobb advocated for the IRS to require all taxpayers to answer the same eligibility questions and submit responses to the IRS, regardless of whether they self-prepare or use a paid preparer. Cobb wrote: "The implementation of inconsistent EITC eligibility standards and documentation requirements has resulted in a movement of [improper payments] out of the assisted tax space and into the self-prepared channel (DIY), contributing to a material change in EITC taxpayer behaviors."[39]

Similar proposals have been made in Congress,[40] but as of the time of writing, none have passed. Cobb argued that the IRS can change Form Schedule EIC without statutory authority, meaning the agency could change the form to require self-preparing taxpayers to answer the same due diligence questions that paid preparers must answer on Form 8867. This form implements Code section 6695(g)'s due diligence requirement. Paid preparers must affirmatively answer questions to demonstrate the level of due diligence performed during return preparation; for example, whether the preparer made reasonable inquiries of the taxpayer, whether they documented those inquiries, and whether they asked if the taxpayer would be able to provide documentation to substantiate the credit should the return be selected for audit. Not everyone agrees with Cobb that requiring a due diligence form for self-preparing taxpayers is a good idea. David Williams, chief tax officer of Intuit and a former director of the EITC office at the IRS, worries that making self-preparation harder will increase rather than reduce EITC errors. Increasing the information required of taxpayers, Williams says, is a "very bad idea because it puts the burden of tax compliance squarely on lower-income working taxpayers."[41]

Some degree of taxpayer noncompliance, both intentional and not, is an inevitable consequence of self-declaring EITC eligibility because there is no

[39] Letter from William Cobb, Pres. & C.E.O., H&R Block, to the S. Comm. on Fin. and H. Comm. on Ways & Means (Mar. 10, 2015) (on file with author).

[40] *See, e.g.*, S. Rep. No. 114-97, at 37 (2015).

[41] Leslie Book, *Intuit Chief Tax Officer Says Reducing EITC Errors Should Not Come on Backs of Poor*, FORBES (Mar. 6, 2015, 7:16 AM), www.forbes.com/sites/procedurallytaxing/2015/03/06/intuit-chief-tax-officer-says-reducing-eitc-error-shouldnt-come-on-backs-of-low-income-taxpayers.

government intermediary to prescreen eligibility. In a sense, such noncompliance may be a "cost" of the current EITC design. But it is far from the only cost.

RETURN PREPARER MISCONDUCT

The universe of paid preparers includes two worlds of return preparers: those who are professionally credentialed and therefore subject to federal regulation under Treasury Department Circular 230, and those who are not. The former category includes attorneys, certified public accountants, and enrolled agents. Those who are not credentialed or subject to regulation are often referred to as "unenrolled and unregulated" preparers. While some studies describe commercial tax return preparers as empowering low-income taxpayers,[42] others reveal a much more pernicious side of commercial tax return preparation and the ways that some return preparers can take advantage of taxpayers, often without their knowledge.

As National Taxpayer Advocate Nina Olson points out, before the "ubiquitous availability" of inexpensive tax return software, knowledge of the tax law was a barrier to entry into the profession.[43] Not so today: Software programs make it relatively easy to prepare returns because most include an interview mode to follow. No math is required, and (assuming one is either an expert or is not concerned with accuracy) a preparer can complete a return without consulting a single IRS publication or instruction booklet. Thus, an unregulated preparer industry has emerged as a market player, and it disproportionately serves the low-income community.

A tax return preparer is defined in Treasury Regulation section 301.7701-15 (a) as "any person who prepares for compensation, or who employs one or more persons to prepare for compensation, all or a substantial portion of any return of tax or any claim for refund of tax under the Internal Revenue Code." A dozen distinct penalties in the Internal Revenue Code apply to the conduct of "tax return preparers"; these penalties are the only common federal regulation of the profession. The penalties impose monetary fines for misdeeds such as failing to sign a return or failing to provide a copy of the return to the taxpayer. Some of these penalties carry a criminal sanction; for example,

[42] *See generally* Sarah Halpern-Meekin, Kathryn Edin, Laura Tach, & Jennifer Sykes, It's Not Like I'm Poor (University of California Press 2015).

[43] Nina E. Olson, *More Than a 'Mere' Preparer: Loving and Return Preparation*, 139 Tax Notes 767, 769 (2013).

section 7206 provides that it is a felony to willfully aid in the preparation of a fraudulent tax return.

At the time of this writing, four states have passed a regulatory scheme for tax return preparers: Oregon, California, Maryland, and New York. In all other states, there is no qualifying test, training program, or minimum competency requirement regulating tax return preparers. The only requirement is that these individuals obtain a Preparer Tax Identification Number (PTIN) from the IRS, which they must include on any return they prepare and submit for processing. Although this requirement helps the IRS trace returns to the preparer, it also presumes that a preparer will follow the rule and include their PTIN on the return.

Absent regulation, any individual can purchase tax software and charge people money to complete returns. Olson identifies this as both positive and negative:

> While there are clear benefits to commercial software, *e.g.* fewer omissions and transcription errors (and for the taxpayer user, the benefit of the question-and-answer format), there is no doubt that software has opened the doors to enable anyone, with good or ill intent, to present himself or herself as a return preparer.[44]

Unfortunately, many taxpayers are harmed by return preparers who are incompetent, unscrupulous, or both. In 2009, the IRS conducted a return preparer review and published a set of findings and recommendations.[45] The review describes two prior "mystery shopper scenario" studies: a Government Accountability Office (GAO) study of nineteen outlets of chain commercial tax return preparation firms; and a TIGTA study of twenty-eight unenrolled tax return preparers.[46] Although the sample sizes were small in both cases, the results were striking and disturbing. In the GAO study, all nineteen preparers made an error on the return. Some mistakes were in the taxpayer's favor, and others were in the government's favor. Of the ten preparers who were presented with an EITC scenario, only one "asked all of the required questions and half of the ten tax return preparers incorrectly reported that GAO's shopper was entitled to the earned income tax credit for two children when

[44] *Written Statement of Nina E. Olson, National Taxpayer Advocate, before the Comm. on Fin., S. Hearing on "Protecting Taxpayers from Incompetent and Unethical Return Preparers,"* 113th Cong. 4 (Apr. 8, 2014), www.irs.gov/pub/tas/Testimony_ReturnPreparerStandards_4-8-2014.pdf.

[45] *See I.R.S. Pub.* 4832, *Return Preparer Review* (Dec. 2009), www.irs.gov/pub/irs-pdf/p4832.pdf.

[46] *Id.* at 13–17.

the shopper was only entitled to claim the credit for one of her children."[47] In the TIGTA study, six of the twenty-eight return preparers "acted willfully or recklessly," inflating or inventing deductions in contradiction of information provided by the shopper.[48] These findings are consistent with those in similar studies conducted by consumer advocacy groups such as the National Consumer Law Center.[49]

After its 2009 report, the IRS proposed and established a comprehensive return preparer regulation scheme, which included mandatory return preparer registration, a suitability check, a competency exam requirement, continuing professional education requirements, and compliance with Treasury Department Circular 230 ethical standards. The IRS accomplished this regulatory scheme by amending and expanding Circular 230 to include a new category of practitioner in addition to attorneys, certified public accountants, and enrolled agents: "registered tax return preparers."

Three unenrolled tax return preparers challenged this expansion of Circular 230 and brought suit in *Loving* v. *IRS*.[50] The plaintiffs argued, among other things, that mandatory testing and continuing education would be burdensome and expensive to the preparers, and that, if required, these costs would be passed on to consumers in the form of higher fees.[51] The plaintiffs argued that the IRS had overstepped the authority delegated by Congress to the Treasury Department under 31 U.S.C. section 330(a)(1). The US District Court for the District of Columbia agreed that the IRS had overstepped its authority, and issued a permanent injunction barring the IRS from enforcing the registration scheme.[52] The IRS appealed and lost.[53] The only part of the regulatory regime that survived was the PTIN requirement, which was not challenged in *Loving*.

47 *Id.* at 14.

48 *Id.* at 16.

49 *See, e.g.*, Chi Chi Wu, *Riddled Returns: How Errors and Fraud by Paid Tax Preparers Put Consumers at Risk and What States Can Do*, Nat'l Consumer Law Ctr. (Mar. 2014), www.nclc.org/images/pdf/pr-reports/report-riddled-returns.pdf; Brief for Amici Curiae National Consumer Law Center and National Community Tax Coalition in Support of Defendants-Appellants and Arguing for Reversal of the District Court, Loving v. IRS, 742 F.3d 1013 (D.C. Cir. 2013) (No. 13-5061).

50 Loving v. IRS, 917 F. Supp. 2d 67 (D.D.C. 2013), *aff'd*, 742 F.3d 1013 (D.C. Cir. 2014).

51 Soled & Thomas, *supra* note 36, at 188–89 (presenting evidence from states with return preparer regulation to show that such costs to preparers are actually fairly low and would not result in significantly higher prices per return to consumers).

52 Loving v. IRS, 917 F. Supp. 2d 67, 80 (D.D.C. 2013).

53 Loving v. IRS, 742 F.3d 1013 (D.C. Cir. 2014).

Rather than appeal the appellate court decision, the IRS unveiled a voluntary "Annual Filing Season Program." Criticized as an end-run around *Loving*, the optional program awards a "Record of Completion" to preparers who elect to take an annual tax law refresher course and exam, so long as they also have a PTIN number and consent to be subject to Circular 230's ethical duties and restrictions. The IRS lists the names of preparers who are awarded a Record of Completion in its searchable online "Directory of Federal Tax Return Preparers with Credentials and Select Qualifications."

Many groups continue to oppose the idea of return preparer regulation, whether mandatory or voluntary, because they feel it imposes a burden and a barrier to entry upon independent preparers and increases end costs to consumers.[54] There is no easy solution to this problem. If Congress were to pass a law authorizing the IRS to regulate return preparers, testing and certification cannot cure all incompetence and wrongdoing. Even a well-designed and comprehensive regulatory regime presumes that taxpayers check for credentials. Taxpayers must be savvy enough to check a database, confirm that the preparer signed the return, and ensure that the information they provide the preparer is entered correctly.

Each filing season, the IRS issues press releases and engages in other outreach urging taxpayers to protect themselves against unscrupulous preparers. But many EITC-eligible individuals are not well equipped to do so. They are vulnerable for a host of reasons. Low-income taxpayers include the least educated members of society, and the least financially savvy. As the Congressional Budget Office (CBO) noted in its 2013 report on refundable credits: "relative to the rest of the filing population, a higher proportion of low-income filers are likely to be high school dropouts or to be from countries in which English is not the main language."[55] These filers rely on paid preparers because they depend on their know-how to complete the return, and they trust that it will be done correctly.

EITC claimants who use a paid preparer are most likely to select an unregulated and unenrolled preparer. Among taxpayers who use paid preparers, it is estimated that 44 percent of non-EITC claimants use a certified public accountant, whereas only 10 percent of EITC claimants use one.[56] An estimated 43 percent of EITC claimants have their return prepared by an

[54] *See, e.g.*, Michael Cohn, *Conservative Groups Oppose Licensing of Tax Preparers*, ACCOUNTING TODAY NEWS, (Mar. 8, 2016, 3:15 PM), www.accountingtoday.com/news/conservative-groups-oppose-licensing-of-tax-preparers.

[55] *Cong. Budget Office, Pub. No. 4152, Refundable Tax Credits 18* (2013), www.cbo.gov/publication/43767.

[56] I.R.S., *supra* note 11, at 24.

unenrolled and unregulated paid preparer, while another 35 percent use a paid preparer at a national tax return preparation firm.[57] There are likely many reasons for this, ranging from perceived cost to accessibility and advertising, especially given the proliferation of unregulated preparers in low-income neighborhoods.[58]

Though the IRS sponsors free tax return preparation sites throughout the country during filing season, including the Volunteer Income Tax Assistance (VITA) program and the Tax Counseling for the Elderly (TCE) program, the take-up rate for these programs is surprisingly low. Only 3 percent of EITC claimants take advantage of this free opportunity for assistance. VITA and TCE sites have also been found to have significant error rates. This counter-indicates the purported benefits of the IRS return preparer regulations program, given that these volunteers undergo IRS-approved annual training and testing before they are certified to prepare returns. The NRP compliance study found that the EITC overclaim rate on returns prepared by VITA or TCE was significantly lower than the overclaim rate on self-prepared returns or returns filed by paid preparers.[59] The NRP report, however, cautioned against drawing conclusions from that statistic, noting: "This does not necessarily imply that taxpayers or other kinds of preparers are either less capable or more unscrupulous. It may instead reflect the effect of selection bias arising from taxpayers' choice of preparer."[60] In other words, perhaps taxpayers believe or hear from others that a paid preparer knows how to get them a bigger refund, and are thus drawn to this type of preparer without giving thought to the preparer's credentials. Of course, a major advantage of using a VITA or TCE site is that there is no cost to the taxpayer. Another is that these preparers have nothing to gain financially from inflating refunds, so there is no reason to doubt their intentions.

On the other hand, every year there are egregious examples of unscrupulous paid preparers preying on EITC claimants. The next section explores the predatory lending practices of some of these preparers, which usually involve financial products. Some return preparers are simply stealing money from low-income taxpayers, and doing so on a large scale.

The US Department of Justice Tax Division, in conjunction with the IRS Criminal Investigation division, seeks civil injunctions against fraudulent

57 *Id.*

58 *See* Olson, *supra* note 43, at 769–70 (describing "the proliferation of return preparers . . . at check-cashing places, pawnshops, used car dealerships, furniture stores, and anywhere else you could receive a refund anticipation loan to apply immediately to purchases").

59 I.R.S., *supra* note 11, at 26.

60 *Id.* at 24.

return preparer chains and individuals to bar them from continuing to prepare returns. In some cases, preparers are sentenced to prison, and often they are ordered to pay restitution. The Department of Justice Tax Division website publicizes these injunctions and prosecutions, and maintains an online public list of enjoined preparers under the general heading "Program to Shut Down Schemes and Scams."[61] Similarly, the IRS provides information and resources to educate taxpayers about return preparer misconduct on its website, including tips for choosing a return preparer and a form to lodge a complaint about a return preparer.[62]

Fraudulent return preparer schemes involve all sorts of angles, not just refundable credits, but the Department of Justice website is replete with examples involving the EITC and CTC. It is easy for unscrupulous preparers to inflate income, claim false deductions, and falsely claim the EITC and CTC for taxpayers. A single unscrupulous preparer operating on a large scale can cost the federal government tens or hundreds of thousands of dollars; a return preparation chain can obtain millions in improper refunds in one tax season.[63] Some of these fraudulent preparers deliberately target taxpayers whose first language is not English.[64] Even when the return preparer is prosecuted, however, the taxpayer is generally held responsible for the contents of the return.[65]

It is not always easy to discern the motives of fraudulent return preparers and understand why and how they are inflating refunds. Some steal money by diverting part or even all of the refundable credit to their own account. Others may do it out of a desire to generate more business (and return preparation fees) by gaining a reputation as the preparer who produces big refunds for the taxpayer. Some base their fee on the size of the refund, structuring it as a

61 *See* US Dept. of Justice, *Program to Shut Down Schemes and Scams*, www.justice.gov/tax/program-shut-down-schemes-and-scams (last updated Oct. 3, 2018).

62 I.R.S., Tax Tip 2017-05, *Things to Remember When Choosing a Tax Preparer* (Jan. 30, 2017), https://www.irs.gov/uac/things-to-remember-when-choosing-a-tax-preparer.

63 *See, e.g.*, Press Release No. 14-879, US Dept. of Justice, Justice Department Sues to Stop South Florida Tax Return Preparer Engaged in Fraud and Earned Income Credit Schemes (Aug. 20, 2014), www.justice.gov/opa/pr/justice-department-sues-stop-south-florida-tax-return-preparer-engaged-fraud-and-earned; Press Release No. 17-357, US Dept. of Justice, Justice Department Seeks to Shut Down Chicago Area Tax Return Preparer (Apr. 4, 2017), www.justice.gov/opa/pr/justice-department-seeks-shut-down-chicago-area-tax-return-preparer.

64 *See, e.g.*, Press Release No. CAS17-0619-Cummings, US Dept. of Justice, Tax Preparers and Recruiter Who Preyed on Immigrants Sentenced to Prison (June 19, 2017), www.justice.gov/usao-sdca/pr/tax-preparers-and-recruiter-who-preyed-immigrants-sentenced-prison.

65 If taxpayers can demonstrate good-faith reliance on the preparer, they may avoid the additional 20 percent accuracy-related penalty, but will still be liable to pay the correct amount of tax (and return any overpayment received). *See* Treas. Reg. § 1.6664-4.

percentage, though the IRS takes the position that doing so is prohibited.[66] Still others have a more indirect but potentially more lucrative financial incentive: they have a financial product or consumer good to sell the taxpayer, and the preparer knows that a higher refund will be spent on loan fees that inure to the benefit of the payer. Another phenomenon is that of predatory lending, which is often related to return preparer misconduct but is distinct from theft.

REFUND-RELATED LENDING PRACTICES

It is a cruel irony that most EITC claimants pay money to receive their social benefit.[67] Under the best of circumstances, the taxpayer pays a modest fee and then receives the entire refund shown on the return. Under the worst of circumstances, the taxpayer is a victim of return preparation misconduct or is subject to examination by the IRS and never receives the refund. There are many permutations in between as well. The substantial lump-sum refund sets up EITC recipients to be taken advantage of by a consumer market. As Halpern-Meekin and her coauthors describe in their work, these taxpayers eagerly anticipate the lump-sum EITC for a variety of reasons, usually because they need part of it to pay off debt or make consumer durable purchases. In her scholarship, Francine Lipman described this demand as creating "an ever increasing profitable niche for tax practitioners," with the result that "the American marketplace is progressively undermining the anti-poverty effectiveness of the EITC."[68]

Paid preparers know just how vulnerable and eager these taxpayers are, and they provide a service that fills that need. Studies by the Progressive Policy Institute (PPI) show that paid preparer chain franchises proliferate in low-income neighborhoods: zip codes with the highest level of EITC filers have approximately 75 percent more preparers per filer than moderate EITC zip codes.[69]

66 Treas. Dept. Circ. 230 § 10.27(b) (June 2014), www.irs.gov/pub/irs-pdf/pcir230.pdf, generally prohibits charging a contingent fee; *but see* Ridgely v. Lew, 55 F. Supp. 3d 89, 97–98 (D.D.C. 2014) (holding that Circular 230 does not apply to ordinary refund claims, because that is not within the scope of "practice" before the IRS).

67 Many commentators have critiqued the EITC for having a hidden administrative cost borne by the recipient. *See, e.g.*, Anne Alstott, *The Earned Income Tax Credit and the Limitations of Tax-Based Welfare Reform*, 108 Harv. L. Rev. 533, 590 (1995).

68 Francine J. Lipman, *The Working Poor Are Paying for Government Benefits: Fixing the Hole in the Anti-Poverty Purse*, 2003 Wis. L. Rev. 461, at 467.

69 Paul Weinstein Jr. & Bethany Patten, *The Price of Paying Taxes II: How Paid Tax Preparer Fees Are Diminishing the Earned Income Tax Credit (EITC)*, Progressive Policy Inst.

Paid preparers typically charge a higher fee for EITC returns because there are extra forms and a higher level of due diligence to complete.[70] In an informal survey of preparer chains over a six-day period, the PPI found that in Washington, DC the fee for an EITC return ranged from $315 to $491, compared to an average tax return preparation fee nationally of $147 at H&R Block and $191 at Liberty Tax Service.[71] The PPI also discovered a degree of volatile variability in this informal survey of fees, with one chain representative quoting a normal EITC-return fee of $509, but offering a "one-day sale" price of $409.[72] (H&R Block criticized PPI's survey methodology, as well as the notion that H&R is "preying on the poor."[73])

Paid tax preparer chains have developed a number of financial products, and some nonfinancial ones, directed at low-income consumers. These products, including refund anticipation loans and refund anticipation checks, are controversial and have been widely criticized by consumer advocates as predatory, though that view is arguably paternalistic. Andrew Hayashi has argued that a taxpayer preference for an EITC-related financial product may not be irrational, either because the taxpayer is impatient (i.e., needs the money sooner) or because they are unbanked, and he raises the possibility that taxpayers benefit from the existence of refund anticipation loans.[74] Refund-related financial products are not predatory per se; the term is most applicable in the context of an unscrupulous preparer who deliberately inflates a filer's refund, or pushes a product with hidden fees. To the extent that associated fees are clearly disclosed to the tax filer, allowing for an informed decision, the preparers are providing the option of a much needed (even if costly) service. The existence of these products, and the taxpayer demand for them, highlight how time-sensitive the working poor are with respect to the EITC benefit.

(Apr. 2016), https://www.progressivepolicy.org/wp-content/uploads/2016/04/2016.04-Weinstein_Patten_The-Price-of-Paying-Takes-II.pdf.

70 I.R.C. § 6695(g), enacted in 1997, requires paid preparers to comply with due diligence requirements; these requirements are set forth in Treas. Reg. § 1.6695-2(b).

71 Weinstein & Patten, *supra* note 69, at 3.

72 *Id.* at 3, n. 13.

73 Michael Cohn, *H&R Block Objects to Report Claiming Tax Prep Chains Target Low-Income Workers*, ACCOUNTING TODAY (Apr. 14, 2016, 12:28 PM), www.accountingtoday.com/news/h-amp-r-block-objects-to-report-claiming-tax-prep-chains-target-low-income-workers.

74 Andrew T. Hayashi, *The Effects of Refund Anticipation Loans on Tax Filing and EITC Takeup* (Va. Law & Econ. Research Paper No. 2016-9, June 20, 2016, rev. Aug. 7, 2017), https://ssrn.com/abstract=2801591.

For many years, refund anticipation loans (RALs) were the most common tax-refund financial product.[75] A RAL operates somewhat like a payday loan: return preparers partner with banks to provide taxpayers their refund within 1–2 days; for an extra fee, some providers issue a same-day loan. The loan is satisfied when the IRS transmits the refund to the lender. Fees for both tax return preparation and the loan processing are subtracted from the proceeds. For taxpayers, this may be an attractive alternative to waiting a week or longer for direct deposit. RALs are less common today, after becoming the subject of great criticism, and then greater regulation, in the mid-to-late 2000s. Banks have exited the RAL market, though non-bank lenders continue to offer them.[76]

An alternative and lower-cost product that has become more popular than RALs are refund anticipation checks (RACs). Unlike a RAL, a RAC is not a loan, and it does not result in a faster receipt of money than would otherwise be available from the IRS; rather, it creates a temporary bank account into which the taxpayer can receive a direct deposit refund. RACs appeal especially to unbanked taxpayers, who would otherwise have to select the paper check refund option, which means a longer wait because the IRS processes direct deposit refunds much more quickly than paper checks. As with RALs, RACs provide a way for taxpayers who cannot pay tax return preparation fees up front to have them withheld from the refund. For this reason, RACs have been criticized as "nothing more than a disguised loan of the tax preparation fee."[77] The RAC provider charges a fee (typically around $30–35, but as high as $65) to set up the temporary account, which is then closed after the refund is delivered.[78] Consumer protection groups note that this fee is often in addition

[75] For a more detailed background and history of RACs and RALs, which is summarized in this paragraph, *see* Brett Theodos, et al., *Characteristics of Users of Refund Anticipation Loans and Refund Anticipation Checks*, Urban Institute (2010), https://www.treasury.gov/resource-center/financial-education/Documents/Characteristics%20of%20Users%20of%20Refund%20Anticipation%20Loans%20and%20Refund%20Anticipation%20Checks.pdf.

[76] Chi Chi Wu & Chantal Hernandez, *Minefield of Risks: Taxpayers Face Perils from Unregulated Preparers, Lack of Fee Disclosure, and Tax-Time Financial Products*, Nat'l Consumer L. Ctr. 5–6 (Mar. 2016), https://www.nclc.org/images/pdf/pr-reports/TaxTimeReport2016.pdf.

[77] *Id.* at 4. (citing two court opinions that have characterized RACs as loans of the fee: United States v. ITS Fin., No. 3:12-cv-95, 2013 WL 5947222 (S.D. Ohio Nov. 6, 2013); People v. JTH Tax, Inc., 212 Cal. App. 4th 1219 (2013)).

[78] *Id.* (pointing out that a fee of $35 to defer payment of a $350 tax preparation fee for three weeks is equivalent to an annual percentage rate of 174 percent); *see also* Chi Chu Wu, *Tax-Time Products 2018: New Generation of Tax-Time Loans Surges in Popularity*, Nat'l Consumer L. Ctr. 6 (Mar. 2018).

to "add-on fees," which can significantly add to the cost of return preparation.[79] In the 2014 filing season, 21.6 million taxpayers used a RAC; approximately 83 percent of these consumers were low-income, and approximately half were EITC recipients.[80]

Not surprisingly, EITC recipients have historically constituted the largest group of RAL and RAC consumers: "compared with non-EITC claimants with or without qualifying children, EITC claimants with a qualifying child are over 125 percent more likely to use a RAL and over 75 percent more likely to take out a RAC compared to using neither product."[81]

Unfortunately, such products diminish the amount of the social benefit these taxpayers were meant to receive. At the height of RAL usage, the National Consumer Law Center estimated that each year, taxpayers were losing between $738 million (in 2008, when 8.4 million RALs were made) and $1.24 billion (in 2004, when 12.38 million RALs were made) in RAL fees.[82] These figures did not include tax return preparation fees, expedited fees for "instant" loans, or other add-on fees, such as those for check cashing or data storage.[83] Bear in mind, this was during a decade in which the advance earned income tax credit (AEITC) option was available to taxpayers but severely underutilized.

When expressed as an annual percentage rate (APR), RAL fees and interest were sometimes equivalent to a triple-digit APR, particularly for loans on the relatively small side,[84] though taxpayers with larger refunds were more likely to use a RAL than those with smaller refunds.[85] Perhaps some taxpayers made a rational calculation that the expedited loan justified the high cost of the RAL, especially if they were behind on rent or utility payments. For some, the cost of expedited borrowing through a RAL was less expensive than borrowing on a credit card.[86] In examining RAL borrower motivations, the Urban Institute

[79] Wu & Hernandez, *supra* note 76, at 8–9.

[80] *Id.* at 3 (citing data from I.R.S. SPEC Returns Database for Tax Year 2013 – Returns Filed through June 30, 2014).

[81] Theodos et al, *supra* note 75, at 21.

[82] Chi Chi Wu & Jean Ann Fox, *Major Changes in the Quick Tax Refund Loan Industry*, Nat'l Consumer L. Ctr. & Consumer Fed. of America 6 (Feb. 2010), www.nclc.org/images/pdf/high_cost_small_loans/report-ral-2010.pdf.

[83] *Id.* at 7.

[84] *Id.* at 10: "the APR for a RAL of $300 is almost 500%. Conversely, the APRs for RALs of greater amounts are lower. The APR for a $10,000 RAL is about 50%." *See also* US Gov't General Accountability Off., GAO-08-800R, *Refund Anticipation Loans* (2008), https://www.gao.gov/new.items/d08800r.pdf.

[85] Theodos et al., *supra* note 75, at 21.

[86] *Id.* at 29.

identified "post-holiday financial strain," lack of money to pay tax return preparation fees, and lack of a bank account as among the reasons taxpayers relied on RALs and related products.[87]

At the height of the RAL era, many types of consumer businesses saw an opportunity to partner with tax return preparers and profit from the availability of the EITC. Auto dealers, pawn shops, rent-to-own furniture stores, and even shoe stores marketed tax return services and RALs to low-income communities.[88] As noted earlier, no regulations prohibit this, and many commentators have pointed out that these partnerships encourage preparer misconduct: If refunds are artificially inflated, then consumers have an opportunity and ability to spend more of their refunds on products that the preparers wish to sell.[89]

Until the 2011 filing season, RALs and RACs were relatively low risk for banks and tax return preparers. When a return was filed electronically, the IRS provided a debt indicator in its filing acknowledgment: This indicator alerted the preparer to whether the taxpayer had any outstanding federal debt against which the refund would be offset. This did not guarantee, however, that the refund would be paid in full or within the usual time frame: Taxpayers whose EITC claims were selected for examination might have their refund frozen until adequate substantiation was provided. This result could be potentially devastating to a taxpayer who would then owe money to the RAL provider, sometimes in addition to owing an accuracy-related penalty to the IRS.[90]

In response to criticism by consumer advocates, the IRS examined taxpayer use of, and need for, products such as RALs. In 2008, the Treasury

87 *Id.* at 28–31.

88 US Gov't Accountability Off., *supra* note 84, at 3, 6.

89 *See generally* Leslie Book, *Refund Anticipation Loans and the Tax Gap*, 20 Stan. L. & Policy Rev. 85 (2009); Danshera Cords, *Paid Tax Preparers, Used Car Dealers, Refund Anticipation Loans, and the Earned Income Tax Credit: The Need to Regulate Tax Return Preparers and Provide More Free Alternatives*, 59 Case W. Res. L. Rev. 351 (2009); and Nat'l Consumer Law Ctr. et al., Comments re: Advance Notice of Proposed Rulemaking, Guidance Regarding Marketing of Refund Anticipation Loans (RALs) and Certain Other Products in Connection with the Preparation of a Tax Return 20 (Apr. 21, 2008), https://www.regulations.gov/document?D=IRS-2008-0005-7351.

90 Generally taxpayers are responsible for what is on the returns they sign. However, in some cases the taxpayer is an unknowing victim of return preparer fraud; for example, if the preparer changes the return after it is signed so as to inflate the refund and divert it to the preparer's own account. In such a case, the IRS will not hold the taxpayer responsible for the stolen refund. *See, e.g., Written Statement of Nina E. Olson, National Taxpayer Advocate, before the Comm. on Fin., S. Hearing on "Protecting Taxpayers from Incompetent and Unethical Return Preparers,"* 113th Cong. (Apr. 8, 2014), https://www.irs.gov/pub/tas/Testimony_ReturnPreparerStandards_4-8-2014.pdf.

Department issued a notice of proposed rulemaking and sought public comment about the disclosure and use of tax return information by tax return preparers in connection with RALs.[91] Over 8,500 comments were received in response to the proposed rule.[92] Many of these comments were submitted by low-income taxpayers who were upset about the possible suspension of RALs. One respondent wrote, "As a single working mother, I really count on the fast refund I get from H&R Block. They are very helpful and the very idea our government is possibly preventing the loans is sad. Please stop this nonsense!"[93] Many comments objected to the proposed regulation as paternalistic and invasive, and at least one commenter seemed to take the proposed regulation as a personal affront:

> Well gee from the sounds of this law the IRS think that people who have low income that earn EITC are stupid and that they can't comprehend what is being explained to them by their tax preparers. So I guess their friends and families who ever received this tax credit are dumb also. This is just another way for government to control another aspect of our lives. Gee, keep coming up with these new laws and rules and we will be like old Russia in no time.[94]

As part of its 2009 return preparer review, the IRS studied the timing of refunds versus RALs and RACs. The IRS report acknowledged that consumer advocates opposed refund settlement products on various grounds, including (1) that such products "entice fringe tax return preparers, including payday loan stores, and check cashers"; (2) "that the presence of refund settlement products and their pricing structure encourages tax return preparers to take overly aggressive positions on returns to inflate the size of the expected refund and, therefore, the profits to be made from the refund settlement product"; and (3) that the industry engages in "misleading sales practices" and charges what critics "describe as high, unnecessary fees."[95]

[91] Guidance Regarding Marketing of Refund Anticipation Loans (RALs) and Certain Other Products in Connection with the Preparation of a Tax Return, 73 Fed. Reg. 1131 (Jan. 7, 2008).

[92] These comments are available for viewing online at regulations.gov, I.R.S. docket no. IRS-2008-0005.

[93] Sonia Espinal, *Comment on the I.R.S. Proposed Rule: Guidance Regarding Marketing of Refund Anticipation Loans (RALs) and Certain Other Products in Connection with the Preparation of a Tax Return* (Apr. 21, 2008), https://www.regulations.gov/document?D=IRS-2008-0005-6882.

[94] Dina Bardsley, *Comment on the I.R.S. Proposed Rule: Guidance Regarding Marketing of Refund Anticipation Loans (RALs) and Certain Other Products in Connection with the Preparation of a Tax Return* (Apr. 21, 2008), https://www.regulations.gov/document?D=IRS-2008-0005-6138.

[95] I.R.S., *supra* note 45, at 39.

Rather than pursue a ban on refund settlement products, the IRS chose to cease providing tax return preparers with debt indicator information beginning with the 2011 filing season. IRS Commissioner Doug Shulman explained: "We no longer see a need for the debt indicator in a world where we can process a tax return and deliver a refund in ten days. We encourage taxpayers to use e-file with direct deposit so they can get their refunds in just a few days."[96] This decision to remove the debt indicator greatly diminished the supplier market for refund-related financial products, because banks began to view the loans as too risky.

The decision to withhold debt indicator information coincided with certain other factors, including state regulation of the loans under consumer protection laws, which independently influenced many lenders to pull out of the RAL market. At least one bank, JPMorgan Chase, exited the RAL market after the 2010 filing season (and before the removal of the debt indicator), purportedly due to concern of a growing stigma that "the risk to its reputation from providing these high-cost loans outweighed their profitability."[97] H&R Block's lender, HSBC, quit making the loans in late 2010 after an order from the Office of the Comptroller of the Currency.[98]

But these products, and consumer demand for them, never fully went away. Banks and at least two major commercial tax preparation chains, H&R Block and Jackson Hewitt, stopped offering them for a time. But other tax preparation chains, including Liberty Tax, and fringe preparers partnered with nonbanks, such as payday lenders, continue to do so.[99]

More recently, these financial products have made a comeback in a far more consumer-friendly fashion. In the 2017 filing season, when legislation went into effect mandating a delay in issuing refunds so that the IRS would have time to match the income reported on third-party information returns with income reported on tax returns, national tax return preparation chains such as H&R Block and Jackson Hewitt began offering RALs with no fees or interest charges. This business move, quite curious on its face, was apparently motivated by the fact that the chains were losing business to self-preparation

96 I.R.S. News Release IR-2010-89 (Aug. 5, 2010).

97 Theodos et al., *supra* note 75, at 7.

98 Stacy Cowley, *Tax Refund Loans are Revamped and Resurrected*, N.Y. TIMES (Jan. 15, 2017), https://www.nytimes.com/2017/01/15/business/tax-refund-loans-are-revamped-and-resurrected.html.

99 Press Release, National Consumer Law Center & Consumer Federation of America, Consumer Advisory: Avoid Tax-Time Refund Traps Products (Jan. 17, 2013), https://www.nclc.org/images/pdf/pr-reports/pr-ral-11713.pdf.

on home software.[100] Thus, chains became willing to treat the loans as a marketing expense for their business.[101]

These chains have also created new types of financial products – for example, H&R Block's Emerald Card, which is a prepaid debit card onto which a tax refund and other direct deposits can be loaded. There is no fee to set up the card, and no fee if you actively use it, but fees apply to certain options such as ATM withdrawals and cash reload.[102] For an annual fee, certain Emerald Card users are eligible for an advance line of credit of up to $1,000, with the loan to be repaid from the tax refund and the balance subject to a high interest rate in the meantime. This type of loan is known as a "pre-season" or "paystub" loan.[103]

These tax-refund products remain controversial, but at the same time, consumer demand underscores the need for such products, or for access to loans, particularly among the unbanked. These needs should be evaluated in reimagining the delivery of social benefits.

TAX-RELATED IDENTITY THEFT

A different challenge at return time is the prevalence of tax-related identity theft. In addition to noncompliance and concerns about predatory lending, tax-related identity theft has plagued the IRS for several years. The IRS defines tax-related identity theft as "when someone uses your stolen Social Security number to file a tax return claiming a fraudulent refund."[104] Refundable credits such as the EITC and CTC attract identity thieves because of the easy availability of a large, one-time lump-sum refund. Identity theft is distinct from return preparer fraud, and the IRS response to it is also distinct. But both hurt low-income taxpayers: They negatively affect the taxpayer's ability to receive timely EITC and CTC benefits.

IRS Commissioner John Koskinen acknowledged that identity theft is perpetrated on a small scale and also by organized crime syndicates in

[100] Cowley, *supra* note 98; Leslie Book, *Refund Loans on the Comeback, with a Twist*, Procedurally Taxing (Jan. 24, 2017), http://procedurallytaxing.com/refund-loans-on-the-comeback-with-a-twist/.

[101] Cowley, *supra* note 98.

[102] H&R Block, *Emerald Card Fee Schedule*, https://www.hrblock.com/bank/pdfs/ec-fee-schedule.pdf (last visited Dec. 13, 2018).

[103] Wu & Hernandez, *supra* note 76, at 8.

[104] I.R.S. Pub. No. 5027, *Identity Theft Information for Taxpayers* (Rev. May 2018), https://www.irs.gov/pub/irs-pdf/p5027.pdf.

sophisticated large-scale operations.[105] Deceased taxpayers and nonworking taxpayers, including the elderly, are common targets of tax-related identity theft because those taxpayers have social security numbers that are not used for filing. The IRS has established an Identity Protection Specialized Unit to assist victims and has dedicated 3,000 of its employees to resolving these issues.[106]

Congress took an important step toward combating tax-related identity theft, and toward reducing the improper payment rate more generally, in the Protecting Americans from Tax Hikes Act of 2015 (PATH Act).[107] Among other things, the PATH Act simultaneously accelerated W-2 filing deadlines to January 31 and delayed EITC- and CTC-related refunds until at least February 15, effective with the 2017 filing season. (Previously, W-2 filing deadlines were the last day of February or, for electronic forms, March 31; and EITC- and CTC-related refunds were processed as soon as returns were filed.) This change in timing was intended to provide the IRS a window to match income with information reporting before issuing refunds. Previously, the IRS wasn't receiving wage and income information until long after refunds were issued. National Taxpayer Advocate Nina Olson credits the change as a possibly significant factor in the decline in identity theft cases reported in the 2017 filing season.[108]

Time will tell whether this change in information reporting deadline and refund release is effective. The Treasury Inspector General for Tax Administration reviewed the first filing year that this timing change was in effect (2017, when tax year 2016 returns were filed) and found that the IRS had held all refunds until February 15, but was unable to verify third-party reporting on all EITC returns: The TIGTA study found 1.4 million returns (out of 8.4 million

[105] *Written Testimony of John A. Koskinen, Commissioner, Internal Revenue Service, before the H. Oversight and Gov't Reform Comm., Subcomm. on Gov't Operations, on IRS Actions to Reduce Improper Payments*, 113th Cong. 1 (July 9, 2014), https://oversight.house.gov/wp-content/uploads/2014/07/Mr.-Koskinen-Testimony.pdf.

[106] *I.R.S., Fact Sheet 2014-2 Tips for Taxpayers, Victims about Identity Theft and Tax Returns* (Jan. 2014), https://www.irs.gov/uac/newsroom/tips-for-taxpayers-victims-about-identity-theft-and-tax-returns-2014.

[107] Consolidated Appropriations Act, 2016, Pub. L. No. 114-113, Division Q, Title II, § 201(b), 129 Stat. 2242, 3076 (2015) (codified at I.R.C. § 6402(m)).

[108] *Statement of Nina E. Olson, National Taxpayer Advocate, Hearing on IRS Oversight Before the Subcomm. on Fin. Services and Gen. Gov't Comm. on Appropriations, H.R.*, 115th Cong. 17 (May 23, 2017), https://www.irs.gov/pub/foia/nta_written_testimony_irs_oversight_5_23_2017.pdf; *but see Taxpayer Advocate Service, Fiscal Year 2018 Objectives Report to Congress* (Vol. 1) 88, https://taxpayeradvocate.irs.gov/Media/Default/Documents/2018-JRC/JRC18_Volume1.pdf (acknowledging that we do not know for certain the reasons for the decline, and providing statistics showing the decline began the year before the PATH Act changes became effective).

returns e-filed by February 15) for which approximately $6 billion in total EITC and CTC were allowed, but for which no Form W-2 was received or for which the Forms W-2 received did not match the wages reported on the return.[109]

Commissioner Koskinen and others recognize the difficult tension between combating identity-theft fraud and delivering social benefits to taxpayers in a timely manner. Refund delays can cause financial hardship for low-income taxpayers who depend on the annual lump sum to catch up on overdue bills and debt.

Tax-related identity theft is by no means limited to the EITC and CTC. The IRS is vulnerable both to cyberattack and identity thieves; Michael Hatfield argues that one reason for this is the sheer volume of refunds the agency issues per year: around $403 billion.[110] The EITC and CTC pay-outs constitute only a fraction of this total. Recognizing that the phenomenon of tax refunds stems not just from refundable credits but also from a culture of systemic overwithholding, Hatfield advocates moving to a pay-as-you-earn (PAYE) system so that refunds become the exception rather than the rule in the US tax system.[111] Ultimately, other types of social benefits are also susceptible to identity theft; this is not a problem unique to the EITC.[112]

SCREENINGS, EXAMINATIONS, AND SANCTIONS: GOVERNMENT RESPONSES AND CONSEQUENCES

For more than two decades, Congress and the IRS have reactively played defense to the challenges described in this chapter. Ultimately, each of these challenges – the stubbornly high improper payment rate, noncompliance, predatory lending practices, and identity theft – arises from the unique nature of the EITC and CTC design: the availability of a large annual lump sum of money through a process of self-declaration that can be submitted electronically.

[109] Treasury Inspector Gen. for Tax Admin., Ref. No. 2018-40-015, *Employer Noncompliance with Wage Reporting Requirements Significantly Reduces the Ability to Verify Refundable Tax Credit Claims before Refunds are Paid*, Treasury Dept. 5 (Feb. 26, 2018), https://www.treasury.gov/tigta/auditreports/2018reports/201840015fr.pdf.

[110] Michael Hatfield, *Cybersecurity and Tax Reform*, 93 Ind. L. J. 1161, 1167 (2018).

[111] *Id.* at 1194–96. I discuss PAYE in Chapter 5.

[112] Bob Carlson, *Protecting Your Social Security Benefits from ID Thieves*, FORBES (June 12, 2018, 11:50 AM), https://www.forbes.com/sites/bobcarlson/2018/06/12/protecting-your-social-security-benefits-from-id-thieves.

Most of the Congressional and agency responses have been aimed at reducing the improper payment rate through a combination of return screening, examination, and punitive sanctions. This has proved frustrating and difficult for the IRS because, as noted earlier, the two most common types of noncompliance are income misreporting and qualifying child errors. With both types, the IRS is at a disadvantage because of the difficulty of verifying factual requirements for eligibility, such as cash income earned and the qualifying child's residency.

Congress took a major step toward addressing income misreporting with passage of the PATH Act and its changes to third-party reporting dates and refund release dates. However, unless and until all sources of income are subject to third-party information reporting, taxpayers, their return preparers, or both can continue to manipulate the income reported on their tax return to qualify for the EITC (and in some cases, to maximize their EITC). Sometimes these cases can only be resolved by a Tax Court judge, who determines the veracity of the taxpayer's story.

Illustrative of this point is a recent case, *Lopez* v. *Commissioner*, which was resolved in favor of the taxpayer.[113] In the two tax years at issue, Ms. Lopez lived with her two minor daughters; this fact was not disputed by the IRS. In tax years 2012 and 2013, however, Ms. Lopez reported Schedule C income from an unlicensed hairdressing business. None of this income was subject to 1099 reporting, and it was all paid in cash. Ms. Lopez used a paid preparer. In 2012, her reported net self-employment income resulted in her receiving the maximum EITC available to an unmarried taxpayer with two qualifying children. In 2013, the amount she reported resulted in her receiving a few dollars below the maximum, though that year she also failed to report an unrelated $2,000 in nonemployee income that had been reported to the IRS on Form 1099. She reported business expenses for the hairdressing business in 2012 but not in 2013. Ms. Lopez's returns were selected for examination.

The IRS challenged her receipt of two years' worth of EITC and CTC, and asserted a deficiency of nearly $10,000. During the examination, the IRS discovered that Ms. Lopez had no formal training as a hairdresser, had no business license, did not maintain a bank account, was paid exclusively in cash, did not provide receipts to customers, and did not maintain any contemporaneous business records. Unsatisfied that she had actually earned the income stated from a hairdressing business, the IRS adjusted her return to

[113] Lopez v. Commissioner, T.C. Summ. Op. 2017-16, 2017 WL 1032772 (Mar. 16, 2017).

eliminate all Schedule C income. Additionally, the IRS took the relatively uncommon step of proposing a two-year ban on Ms. Lopez's future receipt of the EITC. The ban, authorized by I.R.C. section 32(k)(1)(B)(ii), can be imposed after a final determination that a taxpayer's claim was due to reckless or intentional disregard of rules and regulations, but without rising to the level of fraud.

After the examination was not resolved in her favor, Ms. Lopez exercised her rights and petitioned the US Tax Court. She obtained notarized written statements from her regular hairdressing clients to substantiate the income she had reported on her returns, and she testified that she had at least twelve regular clients.

The court was left to decide whether to accept Ms. Lopez's testimony. As the summary opinion noted:

> [The court] appreciate[s] respondent's suspicions in situations seemingly designed to maximize the refundable credits here in dispute, but respondent has not introduced any direct evidence casting doubt on petitioner's claim to have been in the cosmetology business during either year in issue. While we are not obligated to accept petitioner's testimony on her business practices [citation omitted], neither are we obligated to reject it.[114]

The court struck a middle ground and allowed gross Schedule C receipts of $10,000 each year, which meant she was entitled to some amount of EITC and CTC each year, though not as much as she had claimed on the original returns. This finding made the proposed two-year ban moot, because the EITC was not entirely disallowed, though Special Trial Judge Carluzzo cautioned in his opinion that "the failure to maintain adequate records to support items shown on a return can support a finding of negligence for purposes of section 6662(a)."[115] It seemed to be Judge Carluzzo's way of cautioning taxpayers about the importance of proper recordkeeping.

Noncompliance in the form of qualifying child errors presents a different challenge for the IRS. No third-party information about children is reported directly to the IRS, so the agency has to rely on other strategies. The IRS first screens all EITC returns for certain basic filing errors – confirming that a social security number is listed, that the qualifying child's social security number has not already been used on another return, and that the required schedules and forms are completed in full – and then uses data-driven filters to

[114] *Id.* at *2.
[115] *Id.* at *3.

identify possibly erroneous claims.[116] The filters use government data, such as the Dependent Database, to identity suspicious claims. (The Dependent Database incorporates data from other agencies, such as the National Prisoner File and child custody information from the Department of Health and Human Services.[117]) If a return is flagged based on those filters, the IRS may begin a correspondence examination, meaning it will mail an audit letter requesting the taxpayer to substantiate the claim. More often than not during the examination (in 80 percent of EITC audits and in 64 percent of CTC audits),[118] the IRS "freezes" the refund until the taxpayer responds with satisfactory documentation (or resolves the issue in Tax Court).

The IRS has evaluated the potential use of many national and state databases, but the GAO found that the "lack of available, accurate, and complete third party data complicates IRS's efforts to verify qualifying children eligibility requirements, increasing IRS's administrative costs and taxpayer burden."[119] The GAO cited the complexity of eligibility requirements and the differences in requirements between the EITC and CTC as being drivers of noncompliance; complicating the IRS's ability to administer the credits; and serving as a "major source of taxpayer burden."[120]

Because of limited resources, not all suspicious returns are selected for audit.[121] The audits that the IRS does conduct are highly automated and inefficient.[122] Audits are conducted entirely by mail correspondence, and no specific IRS employee is assigned to each one, so it can take many months for a taxpayer to resolve a frozen refund. Under the best of circumstances, the taxpayer is savvy enough to understand that he or she has been selected for audit, is able to secure the specific types of documents that the examiners prefer to substantiate the claims, and has the time and ability to respond quickly to the notice. The IRS estimates that responding to and participating in a correspondence examination costs the taxpayer thirty hours on average.[123] This is quite a burden for taxpayers who have children, often work inflexible hours, and have limited resources.

[116] US Gov't Accountability Off., GAO-16-475, *Refundable Tax Credits: Comprehensive Compliance Strategy and Expanded Use of Data Could Strengthen IRS's Efforts to Address Noncompliance* 16 (May 2016), https://www.gao.gov/assets/680/677548.pdf.

[117] *Id.* at 17.

[118] *Id.*

[119] *Id.* at 19.

[120] *Id.* at 21.

[121] *Id.* at 17.

[122] *See* Drumbl, *supra* note 3, at 132–39.

[123] US Gov't Accountability Off., *supra* note 116, at 23.

Free legal assistance is available for low-income taxpayers in nearly every state: Low-income taxpayer clinics, many of which are funded in part by a federal matching grant administered by a program overseen by the National Taxpayer Advocate,[124] routinely represent taxpayers in EITC audits. However, despite this free resource, the overwhelming majority of taxpayers are unrepresented during an EITC examination.[125] Though the IRS encloses contact information for these clinics with examination notices, and the Tax Court includes similar notices with trial information, many taxpayers go it alone and try to represent themselves. The outcomes for taxpayers represented by counsel are starkly different from those who are unrepresented. The national taxpayer advocate has highlighted findings from a 2004 study showing that "taxpayers who used a representative during the audit process were nearly twice as likely to be determined EI[T]C eligible when compared to taxpayers without representation."[126]

In most cases in which the outcome is adverse, taxpayers do not contest the result and the tax is assessed.[127] One sampling showed that a stunning 70 percent of taxpayers whose refunds are frozen do not respond to the audit inquiry letter;[128] the IRS cannot ascertain the reason for the silence, but the claim is denied. A cynic might posit that taxpayers are silent upon receiving an audit notice because they have been caught making a claim to which they were not entitled. However, further studies show a more concerning trend: a Taxpayer Advocate Service research study of audit reconsideration requests found that of cases closed because there was "no response" from the taxpayer, 43 percent of taxpayers prevailed at the follow-up audit reconsideration level; those who prevailed received, on average, 96 percent of the EITC that had been claimed on the original return.[129]

Studies show several enlightening, and quite troubling, trends with automated EITC audits. Among taxpayers surveyed about their receipt of an initial audit letter, more than 25 percent did not understand from the letter that the IRS was auditing their return; 39 percent did not understand what exactly the

[124] *See* I.R.C. § 7526.

[125] *See* Karie Davis-Nozemack, *Unequal Burdens in EITC Compliance*, 31 Law & Ineq. 37, 69–70 (2012); *see also* Taxpayer Advocate Service, 2007 Annual Report to Congress (Vol. 2) 94 (stating that in tax year 2004 only 1.8 percent of taxpayers audited on the EITC had representation during the audit, and noting that percentage was down from 3.5 percent in tax year 2002).

[126] Taxpayer Advocate Service, *supra* note 125, at 108.

[127] Taxpayer Advocate Service, 2012 Annual Report to Congress (Vol. 2) 82.

[128] Taxpayer Advocate Service, 2011 Annual Report to Congress (Vol. 2) 83.

[129] *Id.*

IRS was questioning about their EITC claim; and only 50 percent "felt they knew what they needed to do in response to the audit letter."[130]

With so many taxpayers confused by even the initial notice, it is not surprising that less than 1 percent of taxpayers who receive a statutory Notice of Deficiency after an examination respond by petitioning the US Tax Court.[131] In a separate study, the Taxpayer Advocate Service tried to understand why the IRS concedes so many of these cases instead of proceeding to trial.[132] In 20 percent of the study's sample of 256 docketed cases, the appeals officer or IRS Chief Counsel attorney accepted documents that the tax examiner had rejected at the audit level.[133] In 5 percent of cases, the IRS conceded after finding that the tax examiner had misapplied the law.[134]

Most frustrating for this small but persistent group of taxpayers who manage to pursue their EITC claim in the US Tax Court is that even when they prove they are entitled to the credit, it can take more than a year from the initial return filing to receive the EITC benefit. And they are a minority: Many others never receive a benefit intended for them because they do not understand that they are being audited or are unable to navigate the labyrinth of the examination and appeals process.

Congress has given the IRS certain punitive tools that can further frustrate taxpayers who are seeking their social benefits. In connection with the audit, some taxpayers are penalized an additional amount – 20 percent of the assessed deficiency – if the IRS imposes an accuracy-related penalty authorized under section 6662.[135] This penalty may be imposed when the taxpayer has underpaid tax attributable to one or more of several statutory grounds. One basis for the penalty is an underpayment resulting from the taxpayer's negligence or disregard of rules; the IRS bears the burden of proof in showing the penalty should apply.[136] Another ground for the accuracy-related penalty is

[130] Taxpayer Advocate Service, *supra* note 125, at 103–04.

[131] Taxpayer Advocate Service, *supra* note 127, at 82 (stating that the IRS Examination function issued more than 350,000 statutory notices of deficiency in FY 2012, and taxpayers filed a petition with respect to only 1,409 of those). These figures refer to all types of examinations, not just EITC examinations.

[132] *Id.* at 84.

[133] *Id.* at 89.

[134] *Id.* at 90.

[135] For a brief period following Rand v. Commissioner, 141 T.C. 376 (2013), the IRS did not impose the 20 percent penalty on refundable credits. However, Congress enacted legislation overriding Rand as part of the 2015 PATH Act. For a description of Rand and critique of the legislative override and its fallout, *see* Keith Fogg, *Chief Counsel Guidance on the Reversal of Rand*, Procedurally Taxing (Jan. 6, 2016), http://procedurallytaxing.com/chief-counsel-guidance-on-the-reversal-of-rand.

[136] I.R.C. § 6662(b)(1).

strictly computational: The penalty applies if the taxpayer makes an understatement of tax exceeding the greater of $5,000 or 10 percent of the tax that must be shown on the return.[137]

In cases involving a significantly sized refundable credit, the accuracy-related penalty can be justified by the IRS solely on the amount of EITC and CTC claimed, without factual development or a demonstration of negligence. Therefore, a taxpayer who fails to respond to an audit notice can be subject to the 20 percent penalty. As of the time of this writing, the IRS does not appear to be imposing the penalty on any portion of a refund that was frozen,[138] but only on refunds paid out to the taxpayer and then assessed as deficiencies. Even if the taxpayer successfully claims the EITC the following tax year, his or her refundable credit (that is, social benefit) is subject to offset to collect any outstanding balance on the 20 percent penalty. There is a defense to the accuracy-related penalty: If a taxpayer can show he or she acted with reasonable cause and in good faith in claiming the credit, the penalty will not apply. However, this an affirmative defense, and one the taxpayer would have to be aware of in order to raise it.[139]

Section 32(k), referenced above in connection with the Lopez case, is an even more severe sanction: It allows the IRS to impose a two-year ban on receiving the EITC if an improper claim is made due to reckless or intentional disregard of rules or regulations, and a ten-year ban if an improper claim is fraudulently made. When the ban applies, the individual will not receive the future years' EITC benefits even if otherwise entitled to it; for some, this makes the sanction a double penalty because they will not receive what they would have been entitled to and also must repay the EITC for the year in which they were not entitled to receive it but did.[140]

As part of the 2015 PATH Act, Congress enacted similar sanctions for CTC claims; section 24(g) provides the IRS the authority to impose two- and ten-year bans on CTC claims. At the time of this writing, the CTC ban provision was quite new, and it remains to be seen how often the IRS will pursue it. The

[137] I.R.C. § 6662(b)(2), (d)(1).

[138] IRM, Ex. 20.1.5-8, Underpayment Calculation with Frozen Refunds.

[139] I.R.C. § 6664(c). Thus, an irony emerges: Reasonable cause can include the taxpayer's lack of sophistication and tax expertise, but an unrepresented taxpayer who is unsophisticated and lacks tax expertise likely would not know of the availability of this defense. *See* Drumbl, *supra* note 122.

[140] Criticizing the ban as having "imprecise and blunt effects," Leslie Book points out that the consequences of the ban can also extend to a future spouse who may have not been implicated in the disallowance and would otherwise be entitled to the EITC. Leslie Book, *The Ban on Claiming the EITC: A Problematic Penalty*, PROCEDURALLY TAXING (Jan. 23, 2014), http://proceduralllytaxing.com/the-ban-on-claiming-the-eitc-a-problematic-penalty.

IRS has been somewhat sparing in its use of section 32(k) EITC bans, although the Taxpayer Advocate reports that at times it has been used inappropriately. In 2011, the IRS imposed the ban on 5,438 EITC claimants; of those banned, 2,121 (39 percent) were taxpayers who never responded to the audit notice.[141] This practice, which was even more frequent in 2009 and 2010, runs afoul of published IRS Chief Counsel guidance stating that a taxpayer's failure to respond (or failure to respond adequately) to a request for substantiation and verification does not, in and of itself, warrant a ban.[142] Of a sample of banned taxpayers that the Taxpayer Advocate examined more closely, the office found that 89 percent of the time the IRS did not provide the required explanation, either in its work papers or its letters to the taxpayer, of why the ban was imposed.[143] In response to the critical report from the Taxpayer Advocate, the IRS strengthened managerial oversight of the ban procedures, and the number of times the IRS imposed the two-year ban in 2015 decreased relative to the years prior.[144]

Regardless of whether a disallowance includes a two- or ten-year ban, the Code requires that in all cases in which a taxpayer has been disallowed the EITC or the CTC, the taxpayer must recertify eligibility on a special form the next time the taxpayer is eligible to claim either or both credits.[145]

Predatory loan products, stolen identities, delayed and denied refunds, and punitive outcomes for potentially innocent mistakes – these are all the very unfortunate costs of self-declaration and inexpensive administration of the EITC and CTC. And this is a very sad way to administer a social benefit program. The United States can do better. In this, EITC-like programs in other countries offer fertile ground to consider what the United States can do to reimagine its refundable tax credits.

[141] Taxpayer Advocate Service, 2013 Annual Report to Congress (Vol. 1) 103.
[142] *Id.* at 104–05, citing I.R.S. SCA 200245051 (Nov. 8, 2002).
[143] *Id.* at 104.
[144] US Gov't Accountability Off., *supra* note 116, at 24.
[145] See I.R.C. § 32(k)(2), 24(g)(2).

4

Importing Ideas

Case Studies in Design and Administrability

Nearly half of OECD (Organisation for Economic Co-Operation and Development) member countries have incorporated or experimented with using an EITC-like tax credit as a work incentive. Though not commonly referred to as such in the United States, transfer benefits conditioned on employment ("make-work-pay" policies) are generally known in other countries as "in-work benefits."[1] Different countries express different rationales for using in-work benefits, and the specific design features vary from country to country. Generally speaking, countries are motivated by two types of factors: (1) increasing employment among low-skilled individuals, and (2) strengthening safety nets, reducing poverty, and promoting self-sufficiency among low-income workers.[2] In some countries, the in-work benefit is a one-time payment or transitional program, while in other countries it is ongoing, like the Earned Income Tax Credit (EITC).

Differences in social policy, economic conditions, wealth distribution, and cultural norms influence the design features and framework for administering the credit. For example, past studies suggest that worklessness among single parents is a more prevalent issue in some countries than in others.[3] Differing ranges of income inequality among countries also would presumably influence policy goals and design. Culture and social policy differences in some cases make a side-by-side comparison of the United States and other countries

[1] For a report describing the policy rationale behind such benefits and summarizing different countries' approaches to in-work benefits, *see* Herwig Immervoll & Mark Pearson, *A Good Time for Making Work Pay? Taking Stock of In-Work Benefits and Related Measures across the OECD* (OECD Soc., Emp't and Migration, Working Paper, No. 81, 2009), http://dx.doi.org/10.1787/225442803245.

[2] *Id.* at 6.

[3] *Id.* at 32–33.

difficult. But accepting that as a given, there is still much to learn from what other countries are doing.

Among the sixteen OECD countries that have experimented with in-work benefit schemes, this book chooses two as in-depth case studies for administrability: New Zealand and Canada. These two countries provide useful points of comparison because their benefit schemes are similar to the refundable credits available in the United States in significant respects. First, in both New Zealand and Canada the revenue agency plays a role in administering the in-work benefit. Second, both countries include a family-based component in their tax credit design. Finally, Canada and New Zealand offer the benefits on an ongoing, recurring basis.

CASE STUDY 1: NEW ZEALAND

New Zealand calculates its in-work benefit as part of a comprehensive payment scheme known collectively as the Working for Families Tax Credits (WfFTC). Recipients can choose to have WfFTC benefits delivered weekly, fortnightly (i.e., every two weeks), or as an annual lump sum. Most recipients choose a periodic receipt rather than delaying payment to year's end.[4]

The WfFTC is not one credit. It is a benefits scheme that consists of several different types of possible payments for taxpayers with children. Each credit has independent eligibility criteria, as well as some common criteria.

At present, the credits that make up the WfFTC are (1) the family tax credit, which is based upon income and increases with each dependent child for whom the taxpayer cares; (2) the in-work tax credit, for families who are engaged in paid work; (3) the minimum family tax credit, which ensures that working parents reach a minimum family income each week; and (4) the Best Start tax credit, a payment for families with children three years or younger.[5] For the purposes of importing ideas to the United States, I focus my discussion primarily on the family tax credit and the in-work credit. These are the two most significant credits from a budgetary perspective in terms of total amounts

[4] Ctr. for Soc. *Research & Evaluation, Changing Families' Financial Support and Incentives for Working: The Summary Report of the Working for Families* package 33 (INLAND REVENUE DEP'T 2010), https://www.msd.govt.nz/documents/about-msd-and-our-work/publications-resources/evaluation/receipt-working-for-families/wff-full-report.pdf.

[5] Children born before July 1, 2018 are not eligible for the Best Start credit, but were eligible for the parental tax credit, which was available to new parents who didn't receive paid parental leave for the first ten weeks after a baby was born.

paid to families. They also provide useful examples for structuring separate work-support and family-support credits.[6]

Overview and Objectives

The WfFTC was enacted in 2004 "in recognition of the growing problem of child poverty in New Zealand and concerns about benefit dependency"[7] and was rolled out between October 2004 and April 2007. Before 2004, New Zealand had a family assistance program that included both a child tax credit and a family tax credit. Intended to make the overall benefits more robust but also to encourage work, the 2004 package introduced a new in-work benefit and provided a plan to replace the child tax credit over time. Unlike the child tax credit, the new in-work benefit required recipients to work a minimum number of hours per week. The child tax credit was "grandparented" so that families receiving it under the existing law who did not meet the new work hour requirement would not face a sudden reduction in benefits.

The WfFTC legislation had three objectives, as stated by the Cabinet Policy Committee in 2004:

1. Make work pay by supporting families with dependent children, so that they are rewarded for their work effort.
2. Ensure income adequacy, with a focus on low- and middle-income families with dependent children to address issues of poverty, especially child poverty.
3. Achieve a social assistance program that supports people into work, by making sure that people get the assistance they are entitled to, when they should, and with delivery that supports people into employment.[8]

The Cabinet Policy Committee proposal went on to describe two reasons why families with dependent children were a priority. The first reason relates to the economic transition from welfare to work: "many low income families

6 I acknowledge that, as with any politically driven program, the specifics of the program are subject to change, especially as political party changes occur over time. In fact the WfFTC specifics have changed since I started this book project. Because I am drawing upon these concepts and ideas, rather than importing specific statutory designs, I am observing the system at a high level and not concerned with the possibility that the specific details of this program will change in the future.

7 *CPAG in the Court of Appeal – The Case in a Nutshell*, Child Poverty Action Grp. (Aug. 5, 2013), https://www.cpag.org.nz/campaigns/cpag-in-the-court-of-appeal-4/the-case-in-a-nutshell-1.

8 Cabinet Policy Committee, Reform of Social Assistance: Working for Families Package 2.

with children are little or no better off in low paid work once work-related costs, benefit abatement and tax are taken into account." The second reason is to better support children given "the incidence of child poverty and the negative effects low living standards have on the well-being and development of children, particularly over time."[9]

The WfFTC credits are administered in collaboration by two agencies: Inland Revenue, which is New Zealand's tax agency; and Work and Income, a department of the Ministry of Social Development. There are four common eligibility criteria for the WfFTC: (1) recipients must have a dependent child in their care; (2) they must be responsible for the "day-to-day care" of the children (for this reason a recipient is referred to as "principal caregiver" or "carer"); (3) they must be at least sixteen years old; and (4) they must either be a New Zealand resident or claim a child who is a resident of and present in New Zealand.[10]

All credits, including the in-work benefit, are paid to the principal caregiver rather than the worker. The Cabinet proposal explains that "research supports the view that paying Family Income Assistance to the principal carer is in the best interests of the children."[11] For the in-work benefit, the proposal notes that "there may be a case in principle" for paying this benefit to the worker "to strengthen the link with work"; however, as a practical and administrative matter it is easier for the government to make all family income assistance payments in the same manner, and the principal caregiver payment structure was in place before the creation of the in-work tax credit.[12]

The family tax credit component is described as "ongoing family support for families." Families receive this component even if no one in the household is working. The in-work tax credit and minimum family tax credit, on the other hand, are designed for families "in paid work." This means they are available only to families in which at least one parent is working a minimum number of hours per week. Families receiving certain other social benefits, such an income-tested benefit, NZ Superannuation or Veteran's Pension, or student allowance, can receive the family tax credit, and this is the case even if they are not in paid work. Though the family tax credit is available in a broader set of circumstances than the in-work credit, it slowly begins to phase out (abate) at a lower annual family income level than does the in-work credit.

[9] *Id.*

[10] Income Tax Act 2007, pt MC 1 (N.Z.).

[11] Cabinet Policy Committee, *supra* note 8, at 5, app 1.

[12] *Id.*

The weekly amount of the family tax credit component varies according to the number of children in the family.[13] In 2018, the maximum weekly amount paid for the eldest child was $113, and $91 for each subsequent child.[14]

The in-work tax credit is fixed for up to three children, with an additional amount per child provided if the taxpayer has more than three children. The additional payment after the third child is "to ensure that the income from paid employment continues to make work pay for large families."[15] The amount is gradually reduced once a certain family income threshold is attained, and can vary according to the ages of the children. In 2018, families with one, two, or three children received a maximum in-work tax credit of up to $72 per week ($145 per fortnight), and families with additional children received an additional maximum of up to $15 more per child per week ($30 per fortnight).[16]

Unlike the family tax credit, the in-work tax credit requires work. It is conditioned on satisfaction of a "full-time earner" test based on number of hours in paid employment per week. In general, this full-time earner test is satisfied once one-parent families exceed twenty hours of paid work per week, and once two-parent families exceed a combined total of thirty hours of work per week.[17] The minimum hour thresholds were chosen to ensure the in-work tax credit "is targeted towards families with a significant level of participation in the labour market."[18] The in-work tax credit is more restrictive than the family tax credit as to what types of income qualify. An in-work tax credit recipient must receive at least one of the following types of income: a salary or wage; shareholder salary (if the recipient is a shareholder-employee in a "close company"); or business income.[19] Unlike the family tax credit, families receiving income-tested benefits or student allowance are not eligible for the in-work tax credit. For the minimum hour (full-time earner) requirement, the recipient must "normally" work the minimum hours. Exceptions apply if the worker becomes incapacitated or takes parental leave.[20]

[13] Income Tax Act 2007, pt MD 3(4) (N.Z.).

[14] For this and other monetary amounts, dollar figures refer to the currency of the country in question.

[15] Cabinet Policy Committee, *supra* note 8, at 3, app 1.

[16] Inland Revenue Department, *Working for Families Tax Credits: In-work tax credit*, https://www.ird.govt.nz/wff-tax-credits/understanding/all-about/iwtc.

[17] Income Tax Act 2007, pt MA 7(1) (N.Z.).

[18] Cabinet Policy Committee, *supra* note 8, at 4, app 1.

[19] Income Tax Act of 2007, pt MD 9 (N.Z.).

[20] Income Tax Act of 2007, pt MA7 (2) (N.Z.).

The minimum family tax credit is an additional "top-up" payment designed to guarantee a certain minimum net annual income for eligible families. The size of this credit does not vary by number of children, but it is available only to families with dependent children and has the same hourly work requirement as the in-work tax credit. It is not available to families receiving income-tested benefits. The work requirement is calculated based only on salaried or wage-related work; self-employment work is not eligible in calculating the minimum hours, though is included in the income calculation and does not disqualify the family from receiving the benefit.[21]

From a budgetary perspective, the family tax credit is by far the most significant in dollar amount: Of the total WfFTC paid in the fiscal year ended June 2015, the family tax credit constituted more than 76 percent of the cost of the WfFTC. The second most significant component was the in-work credit, which was nearly 22 percent. The total amounts of the other WfFTC benefits were insignificant by comparison.

Mechanics

To best understand the New Zealand structure and its usefulness for a reimagination of the US EITC, it is helpful to examine the particular mechanics of the program. Working taxpayers apply for the WfFTC by registering with the tax agency, Inland Revenue. This can be done online by filling out a registration form (Form FS1) on a secure website, or by completing the same form and mailing it to the agency.

The form is seven pages, plus a page of notes, and requires information about the "principal caregiver." *Principal caregiver* is defined in New Zealand's Income Tax Act as "the person, whether or not a parent of the child, who the Commissioner considers has the primary responsibility for the day-to-day care for the child, other than on a temporary basis."[22] If a "change in the arrangements for the care of the child" affects the person's status as a principal caregiver, the person is required to "notify the Commissioner immediately."[23]

Inland Revenue has published further clarifying guidance on who constitutes a principal caregiver, defining the term as the person who has the "main obligation or responsibility for ensuring that the health, welfare, maintenance and protection of the child are being provided for."[24] This is the person who

[21] Income Tax Act of 2007, pts ME 1, 2 (N.Z.).
[22] Income Tax Act of 2007, pt MC 10(1) (N.Z.).
[23] Income Tax Act of 2007, pt MC 10(6) (N.Z.).
[24] Inland Revenue Department Tax Information Bulletin, QB 16/01, (2016).

takes on the day-to-day responsibilities of caring for a child's needs, or arranges for these needs to be met. Examples of such needs include taking the child to and from school or childcare, preparing meals, supervising leisure activities, taking care of daily routines such a sleep and hygiene, and caring for the child when he or she is sick.[25] The same guidance clarifies what "temporary" means for purposes of the Income Tax Act; the agency defines a "temporary basis" to mean a "relatively short period" of less than three to four months during which time a caregiver has day-to-day responsibility that is either defined in advance or related to the fulfillment of a specific, passing purpose.[26]

For purposes of claiming WfFTC, there can be more than one principal caregiver – for example, when parents do not live together but share physical custody of a child. Under special provisions in the Income Tax Act regarding "shared care," in such cases more than one parent or caregiver can receive the WfFTC. In other words, the WfFTC does not operate as an all-or-nothing credit based on where the child spends more time. A parent who cares for the child for at least one-third of the year (on average) has full entitlement to the in-work tax credit for those weeks in which he or she also meets the minimum-hours test.[27] For example, if a child lives with one parent during twelve weeks of school holidays plus every second weekend, totaling 124 days, and lives with the other parent the remainder of the year, both parents meet the "shared care" criteria as caregivers.[28]

When registering by Form FS1, the principal caregiver must provide a range of information. This includes information about (1) the caregiver's spouse or partner, including a previous spouse or partner with whom the relationship ended within a certain period of the application, and his or her tax identification number; (2) the filer's citizenship or permanent residence status; (3) the names, dates of birth, and tax identification numbers of the children, as well as the date the child or children started living with the caregiver; (4) detailed information about shared-custody arrangements, if applicable; (5) an estimate of family income for the tax year; and (6) verification that the primary caregiver, spouse or partner, or both, worked the minimum number of hours per week. The applicant can check a box requesting that the agency check whether he or she might qualify to receive the WfFTC for the previous tax year. If requesting this, the applicant must either verify that the family details

[25] *Id.* at 126.
[26] *Id.* at 127.
[27] Income Tax Act of 2007, pt MC 10(3) (N.Z.).
[28] Inland Revenue Department, *Shared Care for Working for Families Tax Credits*, https://www.ird.govt.nz/wff-tax-credits/understanding/shared-care/shared-care.html.

(children, partner, shared care, and work hours) listed were the same for the prior year or fill out a separate "family details" form to provide those details for that year. Form FS1 must be signed by the applicant, and also by the spouse or partner if applicable.

Though the form is user-friendly, the information requested is comprehensive and not necessarily easy to provide. The information is, by its nature, subject to change throughout the year. After the form is submitted, applicants are required to notify Inland Revenue of any changes in income or family situation that arise during the year.

Inland Revenue and the Ministry of Social Development's Centre for Social Research and Evaluation jointly conducted an evaluation of the implementation and early impact of the Working for Families package, and published findings in a summary report in July 2010.[29] The report included a section on "lessons learnt from delivering the WFF changes."[30] The agencies evaluated the application process for all of the Working for Families benefits, which included non-tax benefits such as the Accommodation Supplement and Childcare Assistance. With respect specifically to the WfFTC, the agencies interviewed recipients and found that only 12 percent found applying for the WfFTC "difficult."[31] Those who found the application process difficult cited the amount of documentation required and the information provided by staff as making the process difficult. Many families who already received a form of social assistance were able to apply for WfFTC benefits in person at the Work and Income office, whereas only 13 percent of first-time applicants for WfFTC downloaded the application forms from the Internet. A significant percentage of first-time WfFTC applicants applied by calling the toll-free helpline, and this was a popular method among families who had never received a social assistance payment.[32] A small percentage – just 7 percent – applied for the WfFTC with the assistance of a tax agent or accountant.[33]

The evaluation addressed the issue of underpayment and overpayment of WfFTC, referring to both collectively as "an inevitable consequence of delivering weekly and fortnightly payments of an annual entitlement."[34] The agencies are less concerned with families who choose year-end delivery, stating in the evaluation that those families "are not overpaid or underpaid,"

[29] Ctr. for Soc. *supra* note 4, at 33.
[30] *Id.* at 35–39.
[31] *Id.* at 36.
[32] *Id.*
[33] *Id.*
[34] *Id.* at 37.

because they receive the lump sum after a reconciliation process.[35] In the first two years of the WfFTC, a higher percentage of recipients were overpaid (38–40 percent) or underpaid (43–45 percent) than were paid the correct amount (17 percent).

In the early years of the program, Inland Revenue introduced several initiatives aimed at minimizing the incidence of overpayment. These included "accumulative adjustments," which is a process to readjust the WfFTC payment amount after a recipient notifies Inland Revenue of a change in household circumstances; monitoring of actual family income against estimated income; automated information exchange of family and benefit data with the Ministry of Social Development; and a process called "protected family credit," which protects family tax credits made while recipients move into work, ensuring that those individuals are not later faced with a debt for family tax credits received while on an income-tested benefit.[36] By 2007, the overpayment rate had been reduced (to 27 percent) and the underpayment rate increased to 50 percent, reflecting an agency preference for taxpayers to underestimate their credits so as not to be in the position of owing at the year's end. Moreover, between 2004 and 2008, the percentage of families with large overpayments were reduced.[37] The agencies accomplished an impressively high take-up rate of the WfFTC benefits, reporting that by 2007, 95–97 percent of eligible families were receiving them.[38]

Critiques Raised by Domestic Scholars and Stakeholders

The WfFTC is praised for creating an incentive to come off government benefits, but others have critiqued it for its complexity and its impact on the poorest families. An early analysis authored by Gregory Dwyer, who had previously served as director of tax policy of the New Zealand Treasury, was skeptical about its incentive structure. Dwyer posited that, overall, the Working for Families welfare package (all elements, including the WfFTC) "does little to make the taking up of work or additional work more rewarding than nonwork and is therefore unlikely to have a noticeable (if any) net positive effect on aggregate employment."[39] Specifically, Dwyer noted that sole parents are encouraged to work a minimum number of hours, but once

[35] *Id.* at 37, 38.
[36] *Id.* at 37, 54, 58–59.
[37] *Id.* at 38.
[38] *Id.* at 47.
[39] G. E. Dwyer, N. Z. Business Roundtable, Dissecting the Working for Families Package 27 (2005).

that minimum is met, there is no additional incentive to work more or seek promotion.[40] For families with two parents, the in-work benefit required at least thirty hours per week; it did not include a specific incentive for the second parent to work and "may well discourage secondary earners from engaging in paid work."[41] Indeed, a working paper on labor supply responses to the WfFTC, published in 2014, found a slight increase in labor supply and labor force participation of sole parents and a decrease in the employment rate of secondary earners.[42]

The most controversial aspect of the WfFTC has been the in-work tax credit and its requirement to work a minimum number of hours. Economist Susan St. John argued that the work requirement was especially harsh and perhaps discriminatory for sole parents: "Ironically, the In Work [Tax Credit] makes it easier for one parent to stay home where there is a full-time breadwinner, while essentially implying that a sole parent should work at least twenty hours a week, no matter what their children's needs or how many children they have."[43] St. John criticized the original 2004 version of the in-work tax credit for leaving out the poorest children – those children who live in households ineligible for the credit because there is no worker present – and she was even more critical when in 2005 the income test threshold was raised and the abatement rate reduced, meaning that higher-income families became eligible for the in-work tax credit.[44] Similar to Dwyer's critique of the package as "poorly targeted," St. John argues that the "2005 changes extended the [In Work Tax Credit] to high income families who did not need an incentive to stay in work, and had no impact on child poverty."[45] St. John shares Dwyer's critique of the minimum-hours structure. While Dwyer questions the work incentive structure, St. John challenges it on fairness grounds: "A partnered woman working twenty hours, whose partner is unemployed, does not qualify for the IWTC, yet, even though her paid work hours are zero, a woman whose partner works for thirty hours may receive the IWTC."[46]

40 *Id.* at 28.

41 *Id.*

42 Penny Mok & Joseph Mercante, *Working for Families Changes: The Effect on Labour Supply in New Zealand,* New Zealand Treasury Working Paper 14/18 (N.Z. TREASURY, Nov. 2014), http://purl.oclc.org/nzt/p-1695 (showing overall that the WfFTC reform reduced the incidence and intensity of poverty as well as income inequality).

43 Susan St. John, *New Zealand's Financial Assistance for Poor Children: Are Work Incentives the Answer?* 8 EUROPEAN J. SOC. SEC. 299, 311 (2006).

44 Susan St. John & Margaret Dale, *The New Zealand Experience of Child-Based Work Incentives,* 12 EUROPEAN J. SOC. SEC. 216, 223 (2010).

45 *Id.*

46 *Id.* at 224.

St. John also objects to the connection between child poverty and work-based incentives. She believes such a policy connection raises human rights implications for children in nonworking households. She points out that the in-work tax credit design is aimed only at a subset of the population that experiences child poverty: Approximately 25 percent of New Zealand's children do not benefit from it because they are in families supported by other benefits that preclude them from eligibility for the in-work credit.[47]

St. John and others worked with the Child Poverty Action Group (CPAG) for several years to raise legal challenges to the design. In 2008, CPAG brought a class action suit against the government challenging the in-work tax credit. CPAG invoked the Human Rights Act 1993 and New Zealand's obligations under the United Nations Convention on the Rights of the Child, arguing that "it was wrong and unlawfully discriminatory to tie a child poverty alleviation measure to a work incentive."[48] CPAG opposes the rule that parents on income-tested benefits are excluded from receiving the in-work tax credit. It highlights the fact that children in families receiving income-tested benefits experience "significantly higher levels of poverty when compared to children in working families."[49] The Human Rights Review Tribunal wrote a 100-page judgment that acknowledged the discriminatory effect on income-tested families but held that such discrimination was not illegal.[50]

After nine years of litigation in ten separate hearings on this issue, CPAG decided to end its legal appeals and instead make political appeals. In 2016, the organization launched the Fix Working for Families (FWFF) campaign, urging the abolishment of paid work requirements and the addition of $72.50 per week (the amount of the current in-work tax credit) to the first child family tax credit.[51]

[47] *Id.* at 233.

[48] Frances Joychild, *Child Poverty Action Group, Child Poverty Action Group v. Attorney General – What Did We Gain* (2014), https://www.cpag.org.nz/assets/Articles/140326%20CPAG%20v%20AG%20-What%20did%20we%20gain%20260314.pdf.

[49] *Id.*

[50] St. John & Dale, *supra* note 44, at 236. *See also CPAG in the Court of Appeal – The Case in a Nutshell*, Child Poverty Action Grp. (Aug. 5, 2013), www.cpag.org.nz/campaigns/cpag-in-the-court-of-appeal-4/the-case-in-a-nutshell-1.

[51] At the time of writing, New Zealand had not abolished its paid work requirements, but CPAG praised the fact that the government increased WfFTC rates and added the Best Start tax credit, effective July 1, 2018. *See CPAG Welcomes Working for Families Increases on July 1*, CPAG.org (June 29, 2018), https://www.cpag.org.nz/news/?m=201806.

Takeaways for the US Context

The WfFTC package is quite different from the US EITC and Child Tax Credit (CTC), and there are a number of interesting takeaways that can be imported into a conversation reimagining family tax credits in the United States. One striking thing about the WfFTC package of tax credits is its complexity. The scheme involves several separate credits, each of which factors in different variables in different ways (or not at all): number of hours worked, number of children, and household income. The registration form (Form FS1) asks about more than twenty different potential sources of income. It requires a determination, which can be quite factual, of who a child's primary caregiver is. It requires a determination, often easily made but sometimes not, of whether the caregiver has a partner in the household whose sources of income counts toward determining family income for calculating credits. Somewhat invasively, Form FS1 also requires details on an ended relationship, including the "end date."

Chapter 3 described the challenges the United States faces with administering the EITC and CTC, and it might well be counterproductive to introduce greater complexity to the US system. This must be borne in mind when examining other systems. At the same time, there are a number of design distinctions that are worth considering as part of a broader conversation about improving tax credits for the working poor in the United States.

In particular, the WfFTC design contrasts with the US system in several notable ways that can inform a conversation about an EITC and CTC redesign. First, although the credit is administered by the revenue agency, the process for claiming it is divorced from the tax return itself. Even if one opts for the annual lump sum, one must still register using the separate Form FS1. This contrasts with the US EITC, for which a taxpayer can use return preparation software to see what amount of EITC would result from various income entries. As discussed earlier, this design invites taxpayer noncompliance. For example, a self-employed taxpayer like Ms. Lopez (whose Tax Court case was discussed in Chapter 3) could experiment with inflating the amount of income received in cash or with adjusting business deductions to achieve the maximum EITC and CTC. The proliferation of home preparation software makes this an enticing form of noncompliance. Kathleen DeLaney Thomas and Jay Soled point to tax software's "pre-payment position status bar" as problematic because "taxpayers might experiment with multiple variations of reporting until they achieve the outcome they desire."[52]

[52] Jay Soled & Kathleen DeLaney Thomas, *Regulating Tax Return Preparation*, 58 B.C. L. Rev. 151, 181 (2017).

Soled and Thomas cite two studies of tax evasion, reporting that some taxpayers engage in income manipulation when they are able to view the amount of tax due instantaneously on the software's prepayment positions status bar.[53]

Second, certain parts of the WfFTC (the in-work tax credit and the minimum family tax credit) require the recipient to work a minimum number of hours per week. In contrast, the EITC is based on income earned during the entire tax year, not on the number of hours worked in any given period. As noted, this aspect of the WfFTC is controversial and is criticized as economically inefficient. In his study of the New Zealand credits, Nick Johnson of the US-based Center on Budget and Policy Priorities echoed Gregory Dwyer, observing that the WfFTC "creates an expectation that sole parents will work twenty hours per week: no more and no less . . . [It] rewards the transition from no-work to part-time work far more than it rewards the transition from part-time work to full-time work."[54] The in-work credit has also been criticized as unfair to sole parents, to those who work seasonal jobs, and to those who have periods of no work in between jobs.

Third, the WfFTC is paid to the caregiver and not the worker. This is quite different from the US model, in which the working member of the household claims the child as a dependent even if that person is not the primary caregiver. Unlike New Zealand and most other countries, the United States requires married taxpayers who wish to claim the EITC to file a joint income tax return and determines both the tax liability and any refundable credits based on joint spousal income. With a married couple, it is highly likely that the caregiver is one of the spouses on the joint return. Marriage becomes an artificial dividing line in the US system, because unmarried cohabitating parents each file as "single" or, if applicable, "head of household"; these US taxpayers have the choice to allocate their dependent children however they wish to maximize the tax credits, and the household income is not aggregated for purposes of determining income eligibility. Thus, there may be no relationship between who claims the credit and who actually cares for the children; by extension, the person claiming the credit may not choose to prioritize the child when deciding how to spend the money. In New Zealand

53 *Id.* (citing William D. Brink & Lorraine S. Lee, *The Effect of Tax Preparation Software on Tax Compliance: A Research Note*, 27 BEHAV. RES. ACCT. 121, 130–31 (2015) and Susan C. Morse, Stewart Karlinsky, & Joseph Bankman, *Cash Businesses and Tax Evasion*, 20 STAN. L. & POLICY REV. 37, 59 (2009)).

54 NICK JOHNSON, FULBRIGHT N. Z., WORKING FOR FAMILIES IN NEW ZEALAND: SOME EARLY LESSONS 35 (2005).

(and Canada, as the next section explains), family tax credit benefits are calculated based on household income – whether of single-parent household, of a married couple, or of cohabitating partners. This is not without its own complications: While marriage may serve as an arbitrary dividing line or proxy measure in the United States, it can be tricky to determine what constitutes a partner relationship. St. John and her co-authors from the CPAG raise the concern that Inland Revenue "peers into the bedrooms of the poor" to determine what constitutes a relationship.[55]

Fourth, the WfFTC scheme provides a mechanism to split the in-work credit when custody is shared. There is no such mechanism for this in the United States, and it is an idea that the United States should study closely. In the United States, only the parent or guardian with whom the child lives for more than half the year can claim the tax credits, even if the child lives with the other parent for 182 nights. Robert Nassau evokes the story of King Solomon in describing the one exception to this rule: One can split the child for tax benefits purposes if the custodial parent agrees to waive the right to claim the child as a dependent, in which case the custodial parent can still claim EITC but the noncustodial parent can claim the CTC.[56] But even then, the EITC cannot be transferred or shared between the two parents, and this is true even if the noncustodial parent is paying significant child support to the custodial parent.

New Zealand's approach to family support benefits offers intriguing ideas for the US context. Certain of these takeaways also provide an interesting comparison to Canada's experience with administering social benefits through its revenue agency.

CASE STUDY 2: CANADA

Canada's in-work benefit and closest analog to the EITC is called the Working Income Tax Benefit (WITB). Introduced in 2007, it is a refundable credit based on earned income. Like the EITC and New Zealand's in-work tax credit, it is intended to encourage individuals to enter the work force and to support low-income earners. It is also intended to support working families: the WITB is higher if the taxpayer has children. The WITB is claimed on an

[55] Susan St. John, et al., Child Poverty Action Group, The Complexities of 'Relationship' in the Welfare System and the Consequences for Children (2014).

[56] Robert G. Nassau, *How to Split the Tax Baby: What Would Solomon Do?*, 61 Syracuse L. Rev. 83 (2010).

individual's tax return and is received annually. The taxpayer can opt to receive up to 50 percent of the benefit as four advance payments throughout the tax year.

In addition to the WITB, there is a separate credit for families that is not contingent on work. The current iteration of this credit is the Canada Child Benefit (CCB), unveiled in 2016 by the Trudeau administration; it is not a new concept in Canada, however. The CCB was designed to consolidate and replace a trio of child-related benefits – the Canada Child Tax Benefit (CCTB), the National Child Benefit Supplement (NCBS), and the Universal Child Care Benefit (UCCB). The family benefit long predates the WITB: Canada's tax system has included a refundable child tax credit in some form or fashion since 1978.[57]

The CCB is a nontaxable monthly payment to Canadian parents of qualified dependents. The payment is calculated, and then recalculated each July, based on information from the prior year's income tax return. Unlike the WITB, the CCB has no work requirement: a household with no income to report in the prior year will receive the maximum available benefit.

Similar to the US EITC and CTC, the Canadian WITB and CCB are housed within Canada's Income Tax Act and administered by the Canada Revenue Agency (CRA). An individual must file an income tax return, even if otherwise not required to do so, to receive either benefit.

Overview and Objectives

When the WITB was introduced in 2007, the budget report framed it as a work incentive: "A WITB will help make work more rewarding and attractive for an estimated 1.2 million Canadians already in the workforce, thereby strengthening their incentives to stay employed. In addition, it is estimated that a WITB will encourage close to 60,000 people to enter the workforce."[58]

Specifically, the budget plan referred to the WITB as a plan to help move taxpayers over the "welfare wall." The term *welfare wall* refers to social policies that unintentionally deter one's entry into the work force because of the accompanying sudden loss of welfare benefits:

[57] For a history of tax treatment of children in Canada, *see* Kevin Milligan, *The Tax Recognition of Children in Canada: Exemptions, Credits, and Cash Transfers*, 64 CAN. TAX J. (2016) 601. In summarizing the history, Milligan notes: "the size of the child benefits has grown substantially through time to become a major feature of the tax and transfer system." *Id.* at 611.

[58] DEPT. OF FIN. CAN., ASPIRE TO A STRONGER, SAFER, BETTER CANADA 78 (2007).

> For too many low-income Canadians, working can mean being financially worse off than staying on social assistance. For example, a single parent who takes a low-income job can lose a large portion of each dollar earned to taxes and reduced income support. In addition, he or she could also lose in-kind benefits such as subsidized housing and prescription drugs, and can often take on new work-related expenses.[59]

In general, a taxpayer must have "working income" (total income from employment and business, excluding losses) of over CAD$3,000 to claim the WITB.[60] The basic eligibility criteria for the WITB are age and residence: Generally one must be nineteen years of age or older by the end of the year and a resident of Canada (as defined for income tax purposes) throughout the tax year.[61] A taxpayer under age nineteen might still be eligible if he or she has a spouse or common-law partner or an eligible dependent.[62] Certain individuals are statutorily ineligible, including those exempt from paying Canadian taxes (e.g., diplomats); those incarcerated for ninety days or more of the year; and certain full-time students who do not have an eligible dependent.[63] An eligible dependent, for purposes of the WITB, is a child who, at the end of the tax year, resides with the taxpayer, is under nineteen years old, and is not him- or herself eligible for the WITB.[64]

The WITB is calculated based on marital status, income, and whether the taxpayer has an eligible dependent. In cases in which the taxpayer is also eligible for a disability supplement, the benefits are delivered together and the income thresholds are different. For simplicity's sake, this chapter provides information only on the basic WITB and not the disability supplement. The dollar amounts, including maximum benefit and income phase-in and phase-out amounts, vary a bit by province and territory. Except for in Alberta, Quebec, British Columbia, and Nunavut, the maximum benefit for an unmarried person with no eligible dependents in tax year 2017 was $1,043,

59 *Id*. Even prior to the WITB, the National Child Benefit Supplement, which was introduced in 1998, was intended to ease the "welfare wall" for low-income earners with children. *See* Milligan, *supra* note 57, at 609.

60 British Columbia, Nunavut, Alberta, and Quebec operate using different figures. In British Columbia, working income must exceed $4,750; in Nunavut, $6,000; and in Alberta, $2,760. In Quebec, single taxpayers (with or without children) are eligible if working income is $2,400 or higher, and families (meaning married or common-law couples, with or without children) are eligible if working income is $3,600 or higher.

61 Income Tax Act, R.S.C. 1985, c. 1 § 122.7(1)(Can.) (defining "eligible individual").

62 *Id*.

63 Income Tax Act, R.S.C. 1985, c. 1 § 122.7(1)(Can.) (defining "ineligible individual").

64 Income Tax Act, R.S.C. 1985, c. 1 § 122.7(1)(Can.) (defining "eligible dependant").

whereas the maximum benefit for a family (defined as a single parent with eligible dependent or a couple with or without eligible dependents) was $1,894. The income level at which the WITB began to phase out (known as the "base threshold") in tax year 2017 was $11,838 for a single person with no children and $16,348 for a single parent or a couple. In tax year 2017, the WITB was reduced to zero when a taxpayer's income reached $18,792 (if single with no children) and $28,975 (for single parents and couples).[65]

The CCB, meanwhile, was introduced in the 2016 budget as representing "the most significant social policy innovation in a generation."[66] Introduced as a better alternative to the previous child-related benefits, the budget plan hailed the CCB as "simpler, tax-free, better-targeted, and much more generous" than the scheme it replaced.[67] The CCB "gives Canadian families more money to help with the high cost of raising their children"[68] and is intended to "play a leading role in supporting poverty reduction."[69]

The CCB is delivered as a monthly payment; it is not delivered annually as a tax refund the way the EITC is in the United States. In 2017, families earning less than $30,000 net income per year received a maximum of $6,400 per eligible child ($533.33 per month) under the age of six and up to $5,400 per eligible child ($450 per month) aged between six and seventeen.[70] The CCB eligibility criteria differ from the WITB criteria. Most significantly, there is no minimum income requirement. The CCB is not an in-work benefit, even though it is administered by the revenue agency. Also different is that the person claiming the CCB must live with a child under the age of eighteen and be either "the parent who primarily fulfils the responsibility for the care and upbringing of the qualified dependant and who is not a shared-custody parent

65 Unlike the other provinces, which differentiate only between single individuals with children and – confusingly – "families" (a category that includes couples without eligible dependents), Quebec varies the amount of the benefit across four categories: single individuals without eligible dependents; single parents; couples with eligible dependents; and couples without. Under the Quebec structure, taxpayers with no children are eligible for a higher maximum benefit than single parents or families with children. In 2017, the maximum benefit in Quebec for a single parent was $972.72, as compared to a single taxpayer without an eligible dependent who could receive up to $1,661.73. Similarly, a couple with children could receive a benefit of up to $1,011.84, while a couple without an eligible dependent could receive more than double: $2,592.84

66 Dept. of Fin. Can., Growing the Middle Class 57 (2016).

67 *Id.*

68 *Id.*

69 *Id.* at 62.

70 *Id.* at 58.

in respect of the qualified dependant," or is a "shared-custody parent in respect of a qualified dependant."[71]

What constitutes "care and upbringing" of the qualified dependent? The Income Tax Regulations provide a list of factors to be considered in making this determination.[72] These include supervising daily activities and needs; maintaining a secure residence for the dependent; ensuring that regular medical care needs are met; arranging for educational, recreational, or athletic activities; caring for the dependent when he or she is ill; regularly attending to hygiene needs; providing guidance and companionship; and the existence of a court order about the qualified dependent.

Outside the shared-custody context, there is a rebuttable statutory presumption – assumed unless proven otherwise – that where the dependent resides with a female parent, she is presumed to be the one primarily responsible for the care and upbringing of the dependent.[73] Therefore the female parent is presumptively the parent who is eligible for the CCB. The Income Tax Regulations state that this presumption does not apply in four specific circumstances: (1) if a female parent declares in writing that the male parent, with whom she resides, is primarily responsible for the care and upbringing; (2) if a female parent is herself a qualified dependent of an eligible individual, and each of them claims the benefit for the same child; (3) if more than one female parent lives with the child and each parent claims the benefit for the same child; and (4) when parents living in different locations both claim the benefit for the same child.[74] This presumption in favor of the mother is not at all uncontroversial, as will be discussed later in this chapter.

These CCB requirements, including the presumption that the female parent is the caregiver, largely carry over from the requirements for the CCTB, which the CCB replaced. Notably, the dollar amounts currently available under the CCB are more generous than what was provided by the CCTB.

Whereas the WITB requires the claimant to be a resident of Canada for tax purposes throughout the year, the CCB requires that the claimant or the claimant's spouse or partner be either a Canadian citizen, a permanent resident, a protected person as defined in the immigration law, an Indian within the meaning of the Indian Act, or a temporary resident (as defined in

[71] Income Tax Act, R.S.C. 1985, c. 1 § 122.6 (Can.) (defining "eligible individual").
[72] Income Tax Regulations, C.R.C., c. 945 § 6302 (Can.) (last amended on July 1, 2017).
[73] Income Tax Act, R.S.C. 1985, c. 1 § 122.6(f) (Can.) (defining "eligible individual").
[74] Income Tax Regulations, C.R.C., c. 945 § 6301(1) (last amended on July 1, 2017).

immigration law) with a valid permit who has lived in Canada for the previous eighteen months.

The amount of the CCB varies according to the number of eligible children, their ages, and their eligibility for the disability tax credit. The CCB is based on the claimant's prior year adjusted family net income and is adjusted every July. Thus, a claimant and his or her spouse or partner must file a tax return every year in order to continue receiving the CCB, even if neither person has income.

The CCB is reduced once the adjusted family net income exceeds a base amount, which for the 2017 tax year was CAD$30,450. Because the credit is calculated as an amount for each eligible child, it is also reduced by a different percentage of excess income based on the number of children.

In addition to the annual readjustment according to the prior year's income, the CCB is adjusted if there is a change in marital status or number of children in the care of the claimant. Claimants are responsible for promptly reporting these changes and will owe a balance back for any overpayment that is determined. As with the WITB, CCB claimants can report changes by telephone, by mailing in a form, or by updating their account online or via a mobile app.

The CRA also administers several provincial and territorial child tax benefits, which are paid in addition to the CCB.

Mechanics

Taxpayers claim the WITB on line 453 of their individual T1 income tax return form, which must be accompanied by Schedule 6, "Working Income Tax Benefit." The Schedule allows taxpayers to indicate whether they had an eligible spouse, an eligible dependent, or both, and provides the calculation worksheet for "working income" and "adjusted family net income" so that taxpayers can calculate the basic WITB and, if applicable, the WITB disability supplement.

In Canada (as in most countries), married taxpayers file individual returns; there is no joint filing status as in the United States. Filers with a spouse who is also eligible for the WITB must choose between them who will claim the basic WITB, because only one individual in the couple can do so. Similarly, only one individual can claim the basic WITB for a specific eligible dependent.

Taxpayers who wish to elect the advance WITB must complete and submit a separate application form. The form provides information about the claimant's marital status and expected household income for the current tax year, including the name of any employers and a certification signed by both the claimant and, if applicable, the spouse or partner. Taxpayers who wish to receive advance payments must submit the form every year any time after January 1, but no later than August 31. There are four advance payment dates, and these generally are on the fifth day once per quarter, in April, July, October, and January of the following year. The Revenue Canada website states: "Our goal is to issue your notice and payment, if applicable, within eleven weeks of receiving your paper benefit application." Thus, to receive a payment in April, the first quarterly payment date, one must submit the form in January. This requires taxpayers to project expected income and deductions at the very start of the year if they wish to receive quarterly payments. If the application for advance payments is submitted or processed after the first or second payment date, the benefits are issued in equal installments on the remaining payment dates (e.g., if the application is processed in May, the claimants will receive the allowable advance payments in three equal installments in July, October, and January).

An advance claimant must notify the CRA of any change of address, marital or partner status, significant change in income, or WITB eligibility requirements. This can be done by calling, submitting a paper form, or updating information by logging into the CRA website or mobile app.

If the agency determines that it overpaid a claimant's advance payments, the agency will notify the taxpayer and collect the amount overpaid via the next year's income tax and benefit return. Until the overpayment is repaid, the CRA can keep future WITB payments and tax refunds, as well as goods and services/harmonized sales tax credits that are due to the taxpayer.

When distributed quarterly, the WITB advance payment is not a significant sum, especially relative to the CCB. In most provinces, the maximum for a family in 2017 was $1,894. Advance payments can only total up to half of the WITB; in 2017 that was a maximum of $947. Divided into quarterly payments, the most a family could have received via the advance WITB was $236.75 every three months. Of course, many recipients received less because they do not qualify for the maximum, meaning the amounts are even less significant.

There are two ways to apply for the CCB. One is automated: A mother of a newborn can fill out and sign the child's birth registration form, give consent to the vital statistics office to share information, and provide her social insurance number. The other way to apply is to fill out Form RC66, the Canada Child Benefits Application. This form is simpler to fill out than the tax form used to claim the WITB; the applicant must provide information about him- or herself, including marital status, information about a spouse or partner, and information about the child. The form specifies that if both a male and a female parent live in the same home, "we usually consider the female parent to be the applicant." The instructions note that if male and female parents live together and the male parent is primarily responsible, he can apply if he "attaches to his application a signed note from the female parent that states he is primarily responsible for all of the children in the household."

With respect to the child, the CCB applicant must enter the date on which she or he became "primarily responsible for the care and upbringing" of the child, and must indicate whether there is a shared-custody situation. The Income Tax Act defines a "shared-custody parent" as one of the two parents who live apart but "reside with the qualified dependant on an equal or near equal basis, and primarily fulfil the responsibility for the care and upbringing" of the child when the child is with that parent.[75] In a shared-custody situation, each parent gets 50 percent of the benefit he or she would have otherwise received (according to net household income).[76]

For new applicants, there is a section to provide information as to "change of recipient" if the child was previously living with another caregiver or an agency. At the end of the form, the applicant (and, where applicable, the applicant's spouse or partner) signs a certification stating that the information is correct and complete. Below the signature line, the form states: "It is a serious offence to make a false statement." The applicant does not need to provide any information about estimated income, because the benefit is based on the previous year's income.

While it is not required with the application, the CCB form notes that the applicant may be asked later to provide supporting documents to prove responsibility for the child, such as a signed statement from the day care or school confirming the child's address and guardian of record; a signed statement from "a person in a position of authority (such as a lawyer or a social worker)"; a registration form from an activity or club in which the child is enrolled; or a court order, decree, or separation agreement.

As in the United States with the EITC, in a certain percentage of cases the CRA later asks recipients to verify eligibility. Benefits are suspended during this verification period while the recipients find documents to substantiate marital status, relationship, and primary caregiver status.[77] The same challenges existed under the predecessor program to the CCB – the CCTB – and

[75] Income Tax Act, R.S.C. 1985, c. 1 § 122.6 (Can.) (defining "shared-custody parent").

[76] Income Tax Act, R.S.C. 1985, c. 1 § 122.61(1.1) (Can.).

[77] J. Paul Dubé, Taxpayers' Ombudsman, Proving Your Status: Establishing Eligibility for the Canada Child Tax Benefit 1 (Gov't of Canada Oct. 2010).

the Taxpayers' Ombudsman studied the problem and issued a report.[78] Substantiation problems often result from a change in status, and, ironically, can result from a recipient timely reporting a change. The Ombudsman report provides the example of a mother who separated from her common-law partner and advised the CRA of the change. The agency began sending a higher benefit because the household income was lower, but two years later the CRA asked her to substantiate the end of the relationship. She provided bills and a lease listed in her name only, as well as the contact information for her ex-spouse. The CRA was not persuaded by this proof, and retroactively denied her change in marital status, requiring her to repay $4,200.[79] The Ombudsman report contains other, different examples in which recipients were denied benefits or asked to repay them because of substantiation challenges. The CRA implemented some changes because of the Ombudsman's systemic review, but problems persisted, and continue to persist under the CCB.

As in the United States, the self-declaration of eligibility for the CCB (and the CCTB before that) reduces administrative costs. The CRA estimated that if all recipients were required to provide documents up-front showing eligibility, the cost to the CRA would be approximately seven times higher.[80]

Critiques Raised by Domestic Scholars and Stakeholders

The WITB receives praise across party lines for its role in reducing the welfare wall, and policy makers and scholars alike have called for the WITB to be expanded.[81] Public policy contributors to the non-partisan Canada 2020 initiative have mentioned the WITB as one important part of addressing income inequality, and have argued for it to be further enhanced.[82]

Economics professor Kevin Milligan has argued that the WITB is too meager and lacks salience.[83] He suggests that because it is embedded in the income tax form, Canadians are less aware of it and are not likely to "plan

78 *Id.*

79 *Id.* at 2–3.

80 *Id.* at 10.

81 Rob Gillezeau & Sean Speer, *The Cross-Party Case for the Working Income Tax Benefit*, Policy Options (Dec. 7, 2016), http://policyoptions.irpp.org/magazines/december-2016/the-cross-party-case-for-the-working-income-tax-benefit.

82 *See* Mark Cameron, "Why Canadians Should Care about Income Inequality," and Sherri Torjman & Ken Battle, "Inequality Is Not Inevitable," Can. 2020, *The Canada We Want in 2020* (Nov. 2011), http://canada2020backup.see-design.com/canada-we-want/reducing-income-disparities-and-polarization.

83 Kevin Milligan, *Improve the WITB* (hard copy on file with author).

their work year around it."[84] In other words, if workers are not cognizant of the credit and how it operates, it cannot serve as a work incentive.

Regarding family benefits, Milligan has written that children, as human beings, deserve recognition in the tax system regardless of their parent's or parents' income level. By this he means that there should be universality: A child should not disappear from the return because the child's parents have relatively higher income. Milligan thus favors universal recognition of children coupled with "strong redistribution toward those with lower incomes."[85] Canada has moved away from universal recognition of children in phasing out benefits to the highest earners.

Milligan argues: "The best way to deliver child benefits is the refundable tax credit, paid frequently. For those on low incomes, paying out benefits once a year when taxes are filed is too infrequent – funds are needed on a more continuous basis throughout the year."[86]

The WITB does not increase according to the number of children the taxpayer has, and has less generous income thresholds, leading scholars Rob Gillezeau and Sean Speer to note that the EITC coverage is much broader than that of the WITB. They rightly add that an "apples-to-apples" comparison of the WITB and EITC is not possible because of the robust CCB and other means-tested child benefits in Canada.[87] When combined with the much more generous CCB, total benefits to low-income working families are more robust than the equivalent US programs. Nonetheless, Gillezeau and Speer identify sound policy reasons for increasing the scope of the WITB to improve labor market incentives for low-income workers, including the "critical need for a positive policy agenda that addresses the needs of workers dislocated by automation, trade, and other factors."[88]

Political management professor Jennifer Robson raises important concerns about how single parents who remarry or have a new common-law partner are disadvantaged by a system that bases benefits on household income. While Robson notes that this is "consistent with a principle of individual assessment for taxation and family assessment for benefits," she observes that this assumes "that the new spouse will be contributing all of his or her income to the

84 *Id.*
85 Kevin Milligan, *A Reset for the Child Tax Benefit System*, 34 INROADS J. 57 (2013).
86 *Id.* at 59.
87 Gillezeau & Speer, *supra* note 81.
88 *Id.*

welfare of the reconstituted family" even though the new spouse may have "no ongoing legal obligation toward the children of the prior marriage."[89]

The CCB has been criticized in online forums, parenting blogs, and in newspaper articles as "sexist" and "antiquated" for its statutory presumption that the mother is the parent who primarily cares for the child. A father named Jason Beaudoin made headlines when he spoke out about how the CRA assumed that his live-in partner, who was not the mother of his children, was the primary caregiver of his boys. Beaudoin said that the CRA required him to seek permission from his common-law wife even though he had full legal custody and he is their primary caregiver: "Frankly it made me a bit angry . . . I make the lunches, I do the suppers, I get them ready for school. I give them showers and baths . . . They told me whether she has legal custody or is a stepmom or not, I still have to get that permission."[90]

The CCTB operated upon the same statutory presumption in favor of the female parent, so this is not a new requirement specific to the CCB. In a 1998 case, *Cabot* v. *The Queen*, the Tax Court of Canada examined the circumstances in which the presumption is rebutted. In analyzing the presumption question, the court commented:

> The child tax benefit is to benefit the child. The child tax benefit provides the parent who primarily fulfils the responsibility for the care and upbringing of the child with funds to bring up the children . . . To put the child tax credit benefit in the hand of a parent who is not fulfilling the responsibility for the care and upbringing of the child defeats the purpose of the child tax benefit.[91]

The court noted that the "child tax benefit is to benefit the child."[92] It underscored that this purpose of benefiting the child is the reason why the benefit is not subject to bankruptcy, cannot be set off under the Financial Administration Act, and is not garnishable under the Family Orders and Agreements Enforcement Act. The Income Tax Act provides that the child

89 Jennifer Robson, *The Problem of Child Benefits in Shared Custody*, MACLEANS.CA (May 30, 2016), www.macleans.ca/economy/economicanalysis/the-problem-of-child-benefits-in-shared-custody.

90 Julie Ireton, *Ottawa Dad Urges Canada Revenue Agency to Rethink 'Sexist' Child Benefit Policy*, CBC NEWS (Oct. 20, 2016, 5:00 AM ET), www.cbc.ca/news/canada/ottawa/canada-child-benefit-by-default-goes-to-woman-1.3812520.

91 Cabot v. The Queen, 4 C.T.C. 2893 (1998).

92 *Id.*

benefit cannot be applied against a taxpayer's liability unless the liability arose from an overpayment of a child tax benefit.[93]

Takeaways for the US Context

From a US perspective, the presumption in favor of paying the CCB to the female parent is somewhat striking. No such gender presumption exists for the EITC or CTC, which are paid to the worker who claims the qualifying child.

More relevant and interesting than the presumption, however, is the explicitly recognized notion that the benefit belongs to the child rather than the adult. Family support benefits are not framed this way in the United States, but perhaps policy makers ought to consider whether they should be, at least in part. In the next chapter, I discuss how the way benefits are framed might influence the way in which a recipient spends the benefit. Perhaps framing the benefit as for the child (as opposed to a reward for work) could influence the recipient to prioritize the money for uses that benefit the child's interests.

In this regard, however, it is also crucial to remember that there is no work requirement connected to the CCB. This is consistent with New Zealand's family tax credit, and strikingly different from the refundable credit regimes in the United States, which require a minimum earned income.

The WITB design has more in common with the US system than the CCB design does. As with the EITC, the WITB is designed to transition taxpayers back into work. It requires a minimum threshold of income and phases out as income rises. The maximum WITB available is far less generous than the EITC, and it does not increase by number of children. For the most part, the WITB is claimed on the tax return and delivered as a refund, though taxpayers can elect an advance WITB that allows quarterly delivery of a portion of the benefit.

Like New Zealand's WfFTC, the WITB has a shared-custody rule. This is a much friendlier rule for divorced parents, and US policy makers should study this design feature carefully. It better reflects the economic realities of divorced parents and can reduce incentives for EITC noncompliance. I address this idea further in the next chapter as part of my reimagination of the EITC.

Stepping back and viewing social benefits more holistically, there is a more subtle but very significant takeaway. The combination of the WITB and the CCB addresseses two distinct needs, and each program's design reflects its

[93] *Id.* (citing Income Tax Act §§ 122.6(4) and 164(2.2)). These same provisions remain in place currently with respect to the CCB (*see* Income Tax Act §§ 122.61(4) and 164(2.2)).

distinct objective. The objective of the WITB is to "make work pay" and "lower the welfare wall."[94] Given its mission to reward work, it makes sense that it does not fluctuate by number of children. Furthermore, its default delivery at tax time is as a refundable credit: It reduces the tax burden on wages, or rather, increases the net return from work. The budget plan provided an example to illustrate this objective:

> In 2007, a typical single parent, with two children, in receipt of social assistance in Nova Scotia will receive approximately $19,100 in combined federal and provincial benefits. If that person were to take a full-time job at $8.25 per hour and leave social assistance, he or she would earn about $14,500 per year and receive an additional $8,435 in government support. That family's disposable income would be $22,935, so that the net return from work would be only about $3,835 per year, which does not account for additional work-related expenses nor the loss of in-kind benefits. A WITB will increase the net return to work by about 25 per cent to $4,835, and bring the family's total disposable income to about $23,935.[95]

Because the WITB boosts the earnings of the worker, it lowers the so-called welfare wall by providing an extra incentive to work.

The CCB, on the other hand, is explicitly tied to the cost of raising children: "Poverty is particularly challenging in the case of children, and its effect can be long term. When children are lifted out of poverty, they are better able to develop to their fullest potential, an opportunity that every Canadian deserves."[96]

The US EITC no longer has a coherent policy objective. What started as a credit to offset regressive payroll taxes and incentivize welfare recipients to join the work force became an antipoverty program to support families into the middle class. As a low-income supplement, it vastly outsizes the CTC. Its most generous benefits go to taxpayers with children, yet politicians from both parties have called to increase the EITC amounts available for childless workers.

The takeaway is that Canada has given thought to what these social benefits are, and has structured them differently. The work incentive is distributed on the tax return (in whole or, at a minimum, 50 percent of it is), while the family benefit is distributed monthly so that families can incorporate that amount into a budget of monthly expenses. The work incentive does not vary by size of family, but the family benefit does.

94 Dept. of Fin. Can., Aspire to a Stronger, Safer, Better Canada 78 (2007).

95 *Id.* at 79.

96 Dept. of Fin. Can., Growing the Middle Class 57 (2016).

The next chapter builds on this takeaway by proposing that the EITC be split into a work-based component and a family-based component in order to convey a more coherent policy to the public. As I argue, this bifurcation would be good for both those who receive the social benefits and those who do not, as it would allow taxpayers to understand what the refund represents.

If one understands the WITB as an incentive to work and the CCB as a support for families near the poverty line, then it is important to highlight another key distinction of delivery (apart from timing): The WITB is paid to the worker and the CCB is paid to the person primarily responsible for the care and upbringing of the child. Contrast that to the United States, which pays both the EITC and CTC to the worker. This distinction perhaps becomes significant if the carer and the worker are not the same person and the two have different priorities as to how the money should be allocated.[97]

Another difference US policy makers should study is how the rate for the WITB varies among the provinces and territories. The United States could consider a similar adjustment. Both the cost of living and wage levels are very different in Wyoming, for example, than in New York City, yet the EITC is calculated the same way across all locations. This affects taxpayers most in higher-cost urban areas, because they need more money to cover necessities such as housing, but their EITC benefit does not stretch as far.

NO UTOPIA

Of course, no social benefit design functions perfectly; there are benefits and burdens to all approaches. The designs implemented in Canada and New Zealand certainly have critics. Compliance is imperfect, with overpayments resulting just as in the United States. Taxpayers cannot always provide perfect income estimates, and the benefit design must account for this reality. Timing will always be imperfect, because benefit delivery will not always match need. Finally, benefit take-up remains a concern across all approaches. Like the old adage that the grass is always greener on the other side, it is human nature that policy makers from one country may look at another and think that the other has a better system.

Accepting that each approach has advantages and disadvantages, my reimagination for the United States focuses on broad ideas drawn from Canada and

[97] *See, e.g.*, Robson, *supra* note 89 (pointing out that a new spouse may have no ongoing legal obligation toward the children of the prior marriage).

New Zealand. Despite cultural and social differences among the countries and population size disparities between the United States and these two nations, there are interesting takeaways to glean from these case studies. The next chapters will build upon these takeaways, importing ideas back from two of the countries that drew inspiration from the US EITC.

5

Reimagining the Credit

Why and How to Restructure the EITC

The benefits that the US Earned Income Tax Credit (EITC) provides to the working poor are undeniable. The EITC has assumed a central role in the social safety net for millions of Americans, and studies show it benefits these families. Yet as previous chapters illustrate, its implementation is far from ideal. While it is true that most families experience no problems with delivery each year, and that studies show recipients express a preference for a lump-sum annual benefit, it is not without its downsides. These downsides, which animate my critique, can be categorized into different tiers. One tier is the immediate financial hardship individual claimants face when their EITC is delayed or denied. Another tier, perhaps less urgent but applicable to a broader number of filers, includes issues of income smoothing, cost shifting, and unfavorable lending practices. A third tier includes broader policy questions: How should we measure income as an eligibility factor? Why do we insist on a work requirement? What type of work do we wish to encourage?

Congress can and should reform both the EITC and the Child Tax Credit (CTC) to better serve low-income families. This chapter lays out a reimagination of how the EITC might be structured and delivered. I first make the case for *why* we should reimagine the delivery. One benefit is that a reimagination allows an opportunity to conceptualize and convey a more coherent tax policy to all taxpayers, both those who receive the credit and those who do not. A second benefit is that such a reimagination provides an opportunity for a simplification of the refundable credit structure, which boosts coherence and may thus reduce noncompliance.

In the remainder of the chapter, I broadly imagine *how* to reconfigure the EITC to better reflect its purpose. I propose two categories of ideas: those that restructure the credit while staying mostly within the existing parameters, and others that consider more radical shifts from the current structure. Both reimaginations retain a few of the credit's basic parameters. First, although there are good policy reasons to provide greater social benefits to individuals who do not meet a minimum earned income level, my reimagination retains the work requirement that has always been a part of both the EITC and CTC. While I believe the government should provide robust support for nonworking families, as they are among the most vulnerable members of society, this reimagination assumes that support for nonworking families will continue to come from other social programs, as it has for decades.[1]

My initial reimagination rests primarily on reforming the *administration* and *delivery* of the credit. In this, I do not propose any changes as to *who* is eligible for the credit. In this regard, this proposal is a modest reimagination. However, in the final section of this chapter, I make the case for some of the elements seen in Canada and New Zealand that would represent a more transformative reimagination. These proposals would require statutory amendments and fundamental changes to eligibility. I recognize that we cannot simply transplant another country's system into the United States. There are significant differences between the sizes, cultures, and histories of the United States and Canada and New Zealand that surely underlie some of the reasons for delivering social benefits differently. But there are elements of how these countries have structured their work and family tax credits that deserve serious consideration for refundable credit reform in the United States. I propose three systemic differences that the United States would do well to consider: changing the way income is measured; splitting benefits between parents who are separated or divorced; and making regional adjustments to the amount of the EITC.

In all, I set forth a number of specific ideas for a reconceptualization of the EITC, some of which have been proposed before and some of which are my own. The ideas in this chapter are not necessarily interdependent, a panacea, or the only path forward. This chapter adds to broader conversation about what EITC reform should look like, and is intended to infuse that conversation with some specific ideas inspired by and drawn from what other countries have done.

WHY RESTRUCTURE THE CREDIT?

The EITC has lost its coherence, to the extent it ever had any. Lawrence Zelenak, who has proposed restructuring the EITC as a minimum wage

[1] It also assumes, somewhat pessimistically, that neither Congress nor the White House would support an increase in public benefits for nonworking individuals through the Code, an idea I take up further in the final chapter.

adjustment based on family size, suggested that the "somewhat incoherent nature of current law might be the result of a compromise between conflicting visions of the credit's purpose, rather than the lack of any clear vision, but it is difficult or impossible to find attractive accounts of the purpose of the [EITC] even in the academic literature."[2]

The EITC has only grown more incoherent as it has expanded in scope and structure. Its original function as a credit to incentivize work and ease the regressive nature of social security taxes has long since been overshadowed by its role as an antipoverty program benefiting families. I am not suggesting that this is a bad outcome; it is merely an impetus for reexamining how the EITC is marketed and delivered. A reimagination must be grounded within a coherent and clearly stated policy rationale.

Currently, the value of the benefit rises dramatically for taxpayers depending on whether they have children at all, and then rises significantly again according to whether they have one, two, or three children. The fact that the credit varies by number of children signals that the credit is meant to help supplement the cost of raising children. Further, it is commonly framed (including by the Internal Revenue Service [IRS]) as an "antipoverty" program.

Indeed, studies show that the EITC has a "substantial effect on reducing poverty on average among all recipients and particularly those with children."[3] But the goal of reducing poverty is not limited to those with children: Those who advocate for an expanded EITC for childless workers note that doing so could decrease the overall percentage of taxpayers living in poverty.[4]

As for the credit's function as a work incentive, empirical evidence shows that the EITC has a strong effect on labor force participation for some claimants (single mothers in particular) and "much less, if any" effect on hours worked for those who are already employed.[5] Studies are inconclusive about the effect of the EITC on labor force participation for childless workers

[2] Lawrence Zelenak, *Redesigning the Earned Income Tax Credit as a Family-Size Adjustment to the Minimum Wage*, 57 Tax L. Rev. 301, 346 (2004).

[3] US Gov't Accountability Off., GAO-16-475, *Refundable Tax Credits: Comprehensive Compliance Strategy and Expanded Use of Data Could Strengthen IRS's Efforts to Address Noncompliance* 72 (2016), https://www.gao.gov/assets/680/677548.pdf.

[4] *Id.* at 53.

[5] *Id.* at 53, 71. *See also* Laura Tach & Sarah Halpern-Meekin, *Tax Code Knowledge and Behavioral Responses among EITC Recipients: Policy Insights from Qualitative Data*, 33 J. Policy Analysis and Mgmt. 413, 414–15 (2014).

or secondary workers in the household; some studies show no effect or even a decline in participation.[6]

Meanwhile, the separate CTC, which as of 2018 is up to $2,000 per child (but only refundable up to $1,400), has no upper limit on the number of children in the household. Many low-income taxpayers are eligible for both the EITC and the CTC, and most probably give no thought to why they receive two distinct credits for their children (assuming they are even aware that their refund includes two distinct credits). In fact, there is no coherent reason for this; it is merely the result of the political patchwork of legislation that was enacted at different times, and then expanded at different times, to support families. The CTC, to be sure, benefits families with a far wider range of income, and it reaches more families in the middle class (and beyond – at least between 2018 and 2025, the tax years for which the phase-out threshold was increased to an adjusted gross income of $400,000 for married filing jointly and $200,000 for all other filing statuses).

The incoherence of the EITC, and its inconsistency with the CTC, negatively affects the delivery, efficacy, and public perception of the credit. My reimagination seeks to provide coherence and realignment by splitting the EITC in two to align with its dual purpose as a work-incentive and antipoverty supplement. While I am far from the first to suggest splitting the credit in this manner, I further propose that the income support (or "antipoverty") element that results from claiming one or more qualifying children be reconfigured as a "family support" credit that is delivered separately from any tax refund. This family-support portion would be divorced, so to speak, from the tax return filing process. The portion of the EITC that offsets payroll taxes (one might call this the "work support" credit) should remain with the tax return filing process, where the CTC also would remain. As I explore in the following pages, these shifts would simplify and communicate a more coherent tax policy, leading to improved compliance and taxpayer perceptions.

The Social Science of Signaling: How Benefits Are Framed Matters

How should the family-support portion of the EITC be framed and presented to the public? This is a significant question in part because I envision that the family-support portion would constitute the larger percentage of the reimagined EITC.

[6] US Gov't Accountability Off., *supra* note 3, at 53, 71.

As noted, I propose maintaining the work requirement; as such, the benefit remains, in part, a reward for work. But this portion is also intended to be an antipoverty supplement. Does framing such as this impact the way in which the recipients view and, ultimately, spend the benefit?

Social science research suggests that such framing does matter, though most of the research is not particular to the EITC. Nicholas Epley and Ayelet Gneezy argue that the framing of financial windfalls can "dramatically influence their consumption."[7] They define windfalls as "a temporary boost in income" rather than a "permanent increase in one's standard of wealth," and they include stimulative tax rebates within their description of what might constitute a windfall. Epley and Gneezy have found a small but substantial difference in how recipients respond to money they perceived as a "bonus" as opposed to a "rebate," with a recipient more likely to spend the former and more likely to save the latter. One example cited by Epley and Gneezy involved reconstructing memory about how money was spent: A sample of the public was asked whether they recalled receiving the 2001 tax rebate, and how they spent it. Some participants received a questionnaire framing the 2001 rebate program as "bonus money" – a check was issued because of the budget surplus after the government spent less than expected; other participants received a questionnaire framing the rebate as "withheld income" that resulted from the government collecting more than it needed. When asked to recall how much of the rebate they spent versus how much they saved, those in the "bonus money" group recalled spending 87 percent of the rebate, while those in the "withheld income" group reported that they spent, on average, 25 percent.[8] Of course, the working poor rarely have the luxury of deciding whether to save or spend: These families are simply trying to keep up with life's necessities.

Sociologist Viviana Zelizer has written about the "social meaning" of money, analyzing and categorizing the "different meanings and separate uses" we assign to particular monies.[9] In line with the idea that windfall income and bonuses are viewed differently, even if the same sums are involved, Zelizer assigns a separate category to the social interaction of "establishing or

[7] Nicholas Epley & Ayelet Gneezy, *The Framing of Financial Windfalls and Implications for Public Policy*, 36 J. SOCIO-ECONOMICS 36, 36–47 (2007). As discussed in Chapter 2, Sykes *et al.* discuss Epley and Gneezy's work, and that of Viviana Zelizer, discussed *infra*, in their qualitative EITC study. *See* Jennifer Sykes, Katrin Križ, Kathryn Edin, & Sarah Halpern-Meekin, *Dignity and Dreams: What the Earned Income Tax Credit (EITC) Means to Low-Income Families*, 80 AM. SOCIOLOGICAL REV. 243 (2015).

[8] *Id.* at 44.

[9] VIVIANA ZELIZER, THE SOCIAL MEANING OF MONEY 5 (Basic Books 1994).

maintaining inequality." This category includes monies earmarked as welfare payments for the poor and monies for children.[10] Zelizer asserts that how money is distributed sends a signal: She traces how, dating to the nineteenth century, American welfare experts declared that "in the hands of the morally incompetent poor . . . money could turn into a dangerous form of relief, easily squandered for immoral purposes."[11] Thus certain forms of charitable payments were offered as in-kind payments (such as grocery orders or food stamps) with superimposed moral guidelines, as a way of supposedly protecting poor people from themselves.[12] This trend has not reversed over time. In the decades since the 1960s, restricted in-kind assistance to the poor (for food, housing, and medical care) has increased relative to cash assistance.[13]

Zelizer also provides the counterexample of early twentieth-century social workers (such as home economist Emma Winslow) who advocated for cash relief to the poor as a way of promoting self-respect and independence, and as a way for recipients to learn the buying power of money.[14] This more radical concept – of empowering the needy through cash – resonates with the form of today's refundable credits, which are paid in cash with no restrictions.

In addition to how money is *distributed*, the way a social assistance program is framed also sends a signal. Zelizer writes that when Social Security was enacted, its framers drew a distinction between social security, which was seen as a payment for services, and other types of public assistance, which were means tested and considered a "more undignified 'gratuity'."[15] In other words, certain types of public assistance are seen as earned or deserved, while others are seen as a handout.

At its heart, the EITC is a hybrid, much like social security: It is a payment for services that is also meant to provide social assistance. The EITC is popular among recipients precisely because it is not seen as a gratuitous handout. Previous studies note how EITC recipients perceived the income boost as "earned" money, and this made them feel proud.[16] Although the EITC is the government's largest cash-based assistance benefit, one of its defining

[10] *Id.* at 26.
[11] *Id.* at 120–21.
[12] *Id.* at 124–25.
[13] *Id.* at 195.
[14] *Id.* at 122–23.
[15] *Id.* at 193.
[16] *See* Sarah Halpern-Meekin, Kathryn Edin, Laura Tach, & Jennifer Sykes, It's Not Like I'm Poor, 69 (University of California Press 2015); *see also* Celia J. Gomez, *It's Not Like I'm Poor: How Working Families Make Ends Meet in a Post-Welfare World, Editor's Review*, 86 Harv. Educ. Rev. 1 (2016).

characteristics is that it has no superimposed moral guidelines – the IRS does not direct, advise, or even suggest to recipients how to spend it. IRS promotional materials use phrases such as "Life's a little easier with EITC."[17] One IRS bulletin refers to it as a "tax break,"[18] which contradicts the reality that many people who receive it do not owe federal income taxes.[19] The EITC Awareness Day toolkit suggests promoting awareness of the credit with the tweet "You earned it. Now file, claim it and get it."[20]

Is it misleading to characterize the credit as "earned"? The *earned* modifier refers to the fact that one must have earned income (as opposed to passive investment income or no income at all) to qualify for the credit. At the same time, one "earns" the EITC by working. Yet, borrowing terminology from Sara Sternberg Greene, the EITC is "at the heart of the public safety net."[21] I very much like her terminology, but the EITC is not marketed to recipients as a "safety net." What if the IRS explicitly promoted it as such, while emphasizing that it is earned and not a handout? If one goal of the EITC is to provide a safety net to the working poor, then perhaps promoting it as such would nudge recipients to mentally earmark the funds that way.

It seems a starting point for a reimagination should be a question of framing: What is it that Congress wants recipients to do with the refundable credit? Should it be framed as a reward for work, as a safety net, or as a program to lift children out of poverty? If Zelizer is correct in her theory that people earmark different types of money for different purposes, then perhaps the framing of the benefit influences perceptions and uses for the benefit. Without being paternalistic or undermining the dignity of recipients, framing the credit both as "earned" and as a "safety net" seems like an appropriate signaling to recipients: like social security, it is not simply a gratuitous handout, but it is intended to help support the household.[22] Additionally, if the credit were split in two as I reimagine it, Congress could frame the work-support portion as a reward for work and the family-support portion of the

[17] I.R.S. Pub. No. 962 (Rev. Nov. 2016), https://www.irs.gov/pub/irs-pdf/p962.pdf.

[18] I.R.S., Tax Tip 2017-04, *Claim the Earned Income Tax Credit* (Jan. 27, 2017), https://content.govdelivery.com/accounts/USIRS/bulletins/1834a57.

[19] The overwhelming annual cost of the EITC is due to outlays (the term for the refundable portion of the credit) rather than reduction in revenues. *See* Cong. Budget Office, Pub. No. 4152, Refundable Tax Credits 8 fig. 3 (2013).

[20] I.R.S., Outreach Sample Tweets (2018), https://www.eitc.irs.gov/partner-toolkit/basic-marketing-communication-materials/sample-tweets/sample-tweets.

[21] Sara Sternberg Greene, *The Broken Safety Net: A Study of Earned Income Tax Credit Recipients and a Proposal for Repair*, 88 N.Y.U. L. Rev. 515, 519 (2013).

[22] I am appreciative of my former student Arthur Vorbrodt for helping me articulate this suggested signaling.

credit explicitly as a credit intended to benefit children. This would reflect Canada's approach to its tax credits: The more modest Working Income Tax Benefit is clearly intended to incentivize work, while the larger Canada Child Benefit is framed explicitly as a benefit for children that is intended to lift children out of poverty.

Framing also influences perceptions of those members of the public who are *not* receiving the benefit, because the EITC is a form of wealth redistribution. For this reason it seems politically important to emphasize that the benefit is conditioned on work, and is part of the so-called American Dream. When President Bill Clinton advocated for expansion of the EITC in 1993, he framed it as part of a national work ethic: "We will reward the work of millions of working poor Americans by realizing the principle that if you work forty hours a week and you've got a child in the house, you will no longer be in poverty."[23] In writing about perceptions of tax fairness and wealth redistribution, economist Steven Sheffrin suggests that evolutionary behavior may play a role in why the American public insists on work as a condition for benefits: because "prospects for survival could be adversely affected by group members who shirk in critical settings," there has emerged a "social bias for full participation."[24]

Recall that in the 1970s discussion leading up to the enactment of the original EITC, Senator Russell Long and the Senate Finance Committee chose a benefit that did not vary by family size, because they did not want to provide economic incentive for having additional children.[25] Indeed, researchers have studied whether the EITC affects childbearing rates; most studies find that the EITC has no or very small effects.[26] Laura Tach and Sarah Halpern-Meekin concluded that the EITC recipients they interviewed are rational actors in this regard: they understand there is a link between more children and a higher EITC, but "they report that the rewards for doing so are far outweighed by the costs of childrearing."[27] Further countering Long's

[23] *Clinton's Economic Plan: The Speech; Text of the President's Address to a Joint Session of Congress*, N.Y. TIMES (Feb. 18, 1993), www.nytimes.com/1993/02/18/us/clinton-s-economic-plan-speech-text-president-s-address-joint-session-congress.html?pagewanted=all.

[24] Steven M. Sheffrin, Tax Fairness and Folk Justice 16 (Cambridge University Press 2013).

[25] I discuss this in Chapter 1.

[26] Tach & Halpern-Meekin, *supra* note 5, at 416 (2014). Tach and Halpern-Meekin note that other researchers have "shown somewhat larger fertility effects" when factoring in the EITC, CTC, and the other family-based Code provisions such as the deduction for dependency exemptions.

[27] *Id.* at 418.

concern about incentives is that EITC expansions have consistently been linked with increased labor participation among single mothers.[28]

Another framing issue arises due to the sheer percentage of taxpayers who receive the EITC, and how that intersects with their overall tax liability. In tax year 2016, approximately 44 percent of households (tax units) had zero or negative federal income tax.[29] Of course, this includes nonworkers, and retirees comprise a significant portion of this 44 percent figure. Yet a majority of these households with no federal income tax liability include someone who works; many of those workers pay payroll taxes – withholdings for programs such as Social Security and unemployment. The Tax Policy Center estimated that of those individuals who work and owe no federal income tax, two-thirds will have payroll tax liability in excess of their total refundable income tax credits.[30] In other words, because the payroll tax is due on the first dollar earned, there are many taxpayers who owe payroll taxes but no federal income tax, and this remains true even when factoring in refundable credits (which, if high enough, can offset both income taxes and payroll taxes). By these same estimates, however, approximately one-third of workers who pay no federal income tax get net refundable credits that fully cover their payroll taxes, including their employer's share.[31] That figure attracts some attention.

Conservative columnist George Will describes the "moral hazard" created when a majority of households pay nothing or less than 5 percent of their income in taxes: "an already large … American majority has a vanishingly small incentive to restrain the growth of a government that they are not paying for through its largest revenue source."[32] While recognizing that this might result from "defensible tax and social policies," Will emphasizes the 40 percent of earners who are net recipients of the income tax because of the EITC and the CTC.[33] Bruce Bartlett, who served as domestic policy advisor to Ronald Reagan, has acknowledged that, in principle, having so many citizens free of

28 *Id.* at 415.

29 T16-0121 *Tax Units with Zero or Negative Income Tax under Current Law, 2011–2026*, Tax Policy Ctr. (July 2016), www.taxpolicycenter.org/model-estimates/tax-units-zero-or-negative-income-tax-july-2016/t16-0121-tax-units-zero-or-negative.

30 Roberton C. Williams, *A Closer Look at Those Who Pay No Income or Payroll Taxes*, Tax Policy Ctr. (July 11, 2016), www.taxpolicycenter.org/taxvox/closer-look-those-who-pay-no-income-or-payroll-taxes.

31 *Id.*

32 George F. Will, *Here's an Idea, Republicans: Repeal and Replace the Tax Code*, Wash. Post (Nov. 10, 2017), https://www.washingtonpost.com/opinions/heres-an-idea-republicans-repeal-and-replace-the-tax-code/2017/11/10/03352606-c57e-11e7-84bc-5e285c7f4512_story.html?utm_term=.229e5dabbod2.

33 Will is using a different and slightly higher figure than the Tax Policy Center 2016 estimates.

taxation is a threat to democracy because they can vote themselves larger benefits "at the expense of the taxpaying class."[34] This critique, of course, ignores the disparate influence and access that the wealthy can employ by way of campaign contributions and legislative lobbies. It also presumes that non-taxpaying individuals are monolithic, which is hardly the case; for example, elderly retirees constitute a significant slice of those who pay no income tax, and those voters' interests do not necessarily align with those of low-income families.

Other critics have emphasized the EITC overpayment rate while dismissing the meaningfulness of the work requirement. Stuart Varney, a conservative pundit and Fox Business anchor, argued that "this is a direct transfer payment from this group of people who pay taxes ... to this group of people who have never paid a dime in their lives but they get a check from the government."[35] This assertion is incorrect: many EITC recipients have paid taxes in the past, and many pay payroll taxes while receiving the EITC. In the same segment, Varney repeatedly referred to the EITC program as "corrupt," referring in his remarks to the improper payment rate and asserting that many recipients have "off-the-books" income and thus are receiving a benefit by making themselves look poor when they are actually not.

In no small part because of these perceptions (and in some cases, misperceptions), the overpayment rates on these benefits matter. If the public perceives the program as being rife with fraudulent claims, or believes that it leads to wastefulness, this can trigger resentment among nonrecipients and corrode their attitude toward the tax system more broadly.[36] After all, why should they be compliant in paying their taxes if there is widespread noncompliance about how public money is redistributed as a social benefit? There are many theories and models about what drives tax compliance. One body of research about general taxpayer compliance involves community norms, including group identity, and attitudes toward government, including a sense of systemic fairness or unfairness.[37] In general, it is thought that taxpayers who

[34] Bruce Bartlett, *Republicans and the Earned Income Tax Credit*, TOWNHALL (June 13, 2003, 12:00 AM), https://townhall.com/columnists/brucebartlett/2003/06/13/republicans-and-the-earned-income-tax-credit-n868045. Bartlett refers to the EITC and the CTC as "bad ideas that have come back to haunt [Republicans]." *Id.*

[35] Ellie Sandmeyer, *Fox Business Host Admits He's 'Being Mean to Poor People'*, MEDIA MATTERS (June 5, 2013), http://mediamatters.org/blog/2013/06/05/fox-business-host-admits-hes-being-mean-to-poor/194360.

[36] Michelle Lyon Drumbl, *Beyond Polemics: Poverty, Taxes, and Noncompliance*, 14 EJOURNAL OF TAX RESEARCH 253 (2016).

[37] *See* Susan C. Morse, Stewart Karlinsky, & Joseph Bankman, *Cash Businesses and Tax Evasion*, 20 STAN. L. & POLICY REV. 37, 40–41 (2009).

believe that most other taxpayers comply with the laws are more likely to reciprocate by complying themselves.[38] Conversely, it follows that if taxpayers believe that money is being redistributed in a manner that is unfair or improper, they may be likely to reciprocate by finding their own ways to cheat the system. For example, a small business owner who feels that his hard-earned money goes to waste by the government may be more likely to understate cash income or overstate business expenses.

The public at large, including those who support the idea of the EITC, is prone to making its own moral judgments. While data suggests that the large annual windfall is more often than not spent with good judgment, would the public at large view the EITC more favorably if it were delivered monthly and perceived generally as a wage supplement? This is worth studying.

Simplicity Begets Coherence – and Compliance

Economist Kevin Milligan, writing about the numerous tax credits available a few years ago to families in Canada, critiqued the complexity of Canada's Working Income Tax Benefit. The complexity, he writes,

> obscures the labour market incentives many of these tax credits are designed to create. Evidence suggests a great deal of success for initiatives like the National Child Benefit in improving labour market attachment of lower-income parents. Yet it is hard to believe that a complex, narrowly targeted tax credit like the Working Income Tax Benefit, when added to the stew of other programs, and delivered once a year as a footnote to the tax forms, would readily be incorporated into the decisions of many families. However precisely designed the incentives may be, they are obscured from view.[39]

The complexity of the refundable credits in the US system obscures incentives here too, and also creates problems with compliance due to the nature of self-declaration of eligibility.

Laura Tach and Sarah Halpern-Meekin, who write about the dignity that comes from self-declaring EITC eligibility (in contrast to the stigma associated with obtaining benefits through the welfare office), concluded from their interviews of EITC recipients that those recipients did not understand what portion of the refund came from the EITC. "The opaqueness of the credit destigmatizes this government cash transfer, but it also limits recipients'

[38] Taxpayer Advocate Service, 2012 Annual Report to Congress (Vol. 2) 1. This survey's focus was on Schedule C filers (sole proprietors).

[39] Kevin Milligan, *A Reset for the Child Tax Benefit System*, 34 Inroads J. 58 (2013).

knowledge of the program's incentive structures."[40] Tach and Halpern-Meekin found that recipients are thus not able make decisions about work schedules in a fashion that would maximize their EITC. This supports Milligan's theory that labor market incentives are obscured by the complexity of the credits. As discussed in Chapter 2, this lack of understanding of how the EITC is determined goes hand in hand with the phenomenon of overwithholding – maximizing the refund one is due at tax time at the opportunity cost of receiving a bit more money in each paycheck.

For two decades (1998–2017), the US tax system had four different Code provisions that impacted a family's tax liability: filing status, personal exemption deductions for the taxpayers and dependents, the EITC, and the CTC. These intersecting provisions were referred to collectively by National Taxpayer Advocate Nina Olson as the "family status" provisions.[41]

The Tax Cuts and Jobs Act of 2017[42] changed the world of low-income taxation in significant respects, though no changes were made to the EITC. The Act temporarily suspended the personal and dependency exemptions, effective for tax years 2018–25, so only three of the family status provisions are in effect for the foreseeable future.[43] If history is an indicator, there is some chance these changes will be made permanent by a future Congress. But we know that at least for this eight-year period, low-income taxpayers will benefit from a higher standard deduction while losing their personal and dependency exemptions. At the same time, the CTC has been increased to $2,000 per child, with a cap of $1,400 for the refundable portion. The impact of this increase may feel arbitrary: Some low-income taxpayers will fare better, while others, depending on marital status and the number of children in the household, would have been better off under the pre-2018 structure.

These intersecting family status provisions (both before and after the 2017 tax reform) do not convey a coherent tax policy, because the eligibility requirements are overlapping but not consistent. Parents can claim a qualifying child for the EITC until the child reaches age nineteen, or until age twenty-four so long as the child is a full-time student. But for the CTC, that same child can only be claimed until age seventeen, regardless of student status. Why is the CTC cut-off earlier? There is no coherent reason for this,

[40] Tach & Halpern-Meekin, *supra* note 5, at 414.

[41] *See, e.g.*, Taxpayer Advocate Service, 2016 Annual Report to Congress (Vol. 1) 325.

[42] Act of Dec. 17, 2017, Pub. L. No. 115-97, 131 Stat. 2054 (2017) (providing for reconciliation pursuant to titles II and V of the concurrent resolution on the budget for fiscal year 2018).

[43] The definition of dependent remains in the Code, however, and is still relevant for other purposes, including the new $500 nonrefundable credit for dependents other than qualifying children.

and taxpayers are often unaware of the difference. Furthermore, what is the rationale for allowing the EITC to parents of a college student: Is it to support educational costs? If so, why not extend CTC eligibility to the same age? In all, the credits would be easier to understand if a common age were used.

When the dependency exemption was in effect before 2018, the term *dependent* was broad enough to encompass individuals who had no formally recognized relationship to the taxpayer, a category that included children of a taxpayer's live-in partner. However, for the EITC and CTC, a relationship is required, either by blood, adoption, foster-child status, or marriage (in the case of stepchildren). One might imagine that this complexity disappeared when Congress suspended the personal and dependency exemption deduction. However, it did not; the Tax Cuts and Jobs Act introduced a new $500 nonrefundable credit for dependents who are not qualifying children.

The rules applicable to divorced parents are particularly complex[44]: When the deduction for dependency exemption was in effect, it could be waived by the custodial parent such that the noncustodial parent could claim the deduction, regardless of with whom the child resided for most of the year. Taxpayers generally understood this rule. However, many did not understand that there was no such residency exception for the EITC: Only the custodial parent could claim the child for the EITC, regardless of who claimed the dependent exemption. The same rule applies for filing status: The parent with whom the child resides is the one who is entitled to claim head of household status, even if the claim for the dependency exemption is waived. This understanding was further clouded by the fact that the CTC followed the dependency exemption – whoever claimed the child as a dependent was entitled to claim the CTC, regardless of the actual custody arrangement.

One might anticipate that this, too, would be simplified by the suspension of the personal and dependency exemption deductions. To the contrary, the definition of qualifying child for CTC purposes still follows the rule for divorced parents, meaning the noncustodial parent can claim the child for the CTC if the custodial parent waives the right, but only the custodial parent can claim the child for the EITC. This is, perhaps, the most incoherent possible result, especially given the very different income phase-out levels for the two credits.

If simplification can increase coherence, taxpayers may be more likely to respond to underlying incentives in the Code provisions, and can incorporate their understanding into their decision making. For example, divorced parents

44 *See* I.R.C. § 152(e).

might better understand the connection between their custody arrangement and tax benefits. Of greater possible significance, simplifying the family status provisions such that there is a clear and coherent set of rules may help to reduce noncompliance.

The Treasury Department has identified complexity as one of several factors that contribute to EITC noncompliance and present difficulties for reducing the rate of EITC overclaims.[45] In Chapter 3 I discussed the complexity of the four family status provisions (currently three, after the suspension of the personal exemption deductions) and how misaligned eligibility requirements contribute to unintentional noncompliance. Nina Olson describes the complexity of the family status provisions as "mind-numbing," and she recommends simplification to minimize both taxpayer burden and the risk of noncompliance or fraud.[46] In several of her annual reports, Olson has advocated for Congress to consolidate the numerous family status provisions into two simplified credits: a refundable family credit, reflecting the cost of maintaining a house and raising a family, and a refundable EITC, which would provide a work incentive and a subsidy for low-income workers.[47]

RESTRUCTURE THE CREDIT WITHIN THE CURRENT PARAMETERS: A MODEST REIMAGINATION

Nina Olson joins a number of scholars and policy makers who have proposed splitting the EITC into a family credit and a work credit.[48] These ideas are not new: The conversations have been happening for more than twenty years, and have included some very well thought-out proposals to Congress, which has not acted on them.[49] My reimagination adds to this ongoing conversation,

[45] US Dept. of Treasury, Agency Financial Report: Fiscal Year 2013 214 (Dec. 16, 2013).

[46] Taxpayer Advocate Service, 2016 Annual Report to Congress (Vol. 1) 334.

[47] *Id.* at 328. *See also* Taxpayer Advocate Service, 2008 Annual Report to Congress (Vol. 1) 363.

[48] *See also* Elaine Maag, *Investing in Work by Reforming the Earned Income Tax Credit*, Tax Policy Ctr. (May 2015), www.taxpolicycenter.org/sites/default/files/alfresco/publication-pdfs/2000232-investing-in-work-by-reforming-the-eitc.pdf; George K. Yin, John Karl Scholtz, Jonathan Barry Forman, & Mark J. Mazur, *Improving the Delivery of Benefits to the Working Poor: Proposals to Reform the Earned Income Tax Credit Program*, 11 Am. J. Tax Policy 225, 279 (1994); George K. Yin & Jonathan Barry Forman, *Redesigning the Earned Income Tax Credit Program to Provide More Effective Assistance for the Working Poor*, 59 Tax Notes 951 (1993).

[49] President's Advisory Panel on Federal Tax Reform, Simple, Fair, and Pro-Growth: Proposals to Fix America's Tax System (Nov. 2005) (proposing to replace the standard deduction, personal exemptions, CTC, and head of household filing status with a family credit, and to replace the EITC and the refundable Child Tax Credit with a working credit); *see, e.g.*, *Written Testimony of George Yin, Hearing before the Subcomms. on Select Revenue*

using as a framework the challenges described in Chapter 3 and the comparative perspective set forth in Chapter 4's examination of non-US programs.

My reimagination is similar to Olson's in certain respects. Like Olson, I argue that Congress should split the EITC into two distinct parts: a refundable credit for all workers that helps offset the regressive nature of payroll or self-employment taxes for the lowest earners (a work-support credit); and an expressly antipoverty element, which would be income-based and would vary by household size (a family-support credit). The work-support credit would be calculated as part of the tax return, as it always has been. The family-support credit would be administered separately, for reasons I describe below.

Work-Support Credit

The work-support credit would be administered according to income and would not be adjusted for household size. If the reimagination is to be approximately revenue neutral (i.e., not an expansion of the current benefit), the work-support credit would necessarily be quite modest. It would incentivize work at the lowest income levels, but it would not serve an antipoverty function. It would look much like the current "childless" EITC, which helps offset the regressive nature of payroll taxes for the poorest workers, but does not serve an antipoverty function.

In tax year 2017, the maximum EITC amount available to a worker without a qualifying child was $510; for a single taxpayer, it began to phase out at an income level of $8,350. The childless EITC fully offsets the regressive nature of the payroll tax only at very low income levels: A childless taxpayer earning $6,650 per year will receive the maximum EITC, and at that income level the maximum EITC fully offsets the 7.65 percent payroll tax. Assuming a single childless worker earns the federal minimum wage of $7.25, the payroll tax is *fully* offset only if the taxpayer works less than half-time (approximately 920 hours per year). This represents a policy determination (and perhaps a political compromise) that payroll taxes are most regressive for those earning the lowest annual wages (currently less than $6,650), and this is the population of workers that receives the maximum level of support when they enter or remain in the work force.

The current EITC is not available to childless workers who work full-time, even at a minimum wage. For a single taxpayer, the childless EITC is fully

Measures and Human Resources of the H. Comm. on Ways and Means on Selected Aspects of Welfare Reform, 103rd Cong. 215–18 (1993) (proposing the EITC be split into a "working poor" benefit and a "family allowance" benefit).

phased out (meaning it is not available at all) at $15,000, which is the approximate amount that a single taxpayer earning the federal minimum wage and working full-time would earn in one year. A taxpayer earning $15,000 is subject to a payroll tax of $1,153. In 2017, a single childless taxpayer earning $15,000 who claimed the standard deduction would have had a federal income tax liability of $460. That individual's after-tax income (that is, income remaining after paying federal income tax and the 7.65 percent payroll tax) for the year thus would have been $13,387.[50] If one accepts the Department of Health and Human Services annual poverty guidelines as the standard definition for "poverty," this individual's after-tax income is above the poverty line.[51] While $13,387 is not a robust amount to live on for a year, it does exceed the minimum threshold for poverty as defined by the United States.

There has been bipartisan talk of expanding the childless EITC. In the early 2010s, House Speaker Paul Ryan supported this idea, as did President Obama. Both advocated for a more robust EITC for childless workers earning up to full-time minimum wage, though neither of their proposals would have offset the payroll tax by 100 percent at that income level. Ultimately, the childless EITC was not expanded during the comprehensive 2017 tax reform.

Splitting off and promoting a "work support" portion of the EITC would emphasize its intention to offset the regressive payroll taxes. If Congress chooses in the future to bolster the benefit for childless workers, all the better. Either way, this portion will retain its incentive for all individuals to work, in the same manner that Canada's Working Income Tax Benefit lowers the welfare wall and provides an incentive to enter the work force.

Family-Support Credit

Splitting off a "family-support" portion of the EITC will better emphasize the credit's function as an antipoverty supplement to support working families. The family-support credit should vary according to household size, reflecting the fact that each additional person in the household requires additional support. Splitting off this portion is also an essential step to transitioning to a periodic payment distribution. In the next chapter, I detail what a periodic

[50] Note that this individual will fare slightly better after the 2017 tax reform takes effect; because of the higher standard deduction in effect beginning in 2018, his federal income tax liability for 2018 would be only $300.

[51] In 2017, the federal poverty line for a household of one was $12,060. In 2018, it was increased to $12,140.

payment distribution might look like in the United States and why I favor that approach.

As part of this reimagination, I propose that the process for claiming the family-support credit be decoupled from the tax return filing. Though the work requirement would remain part of the eligibility determination, the family-support credit would not be distributed as part of the tax refund. The family-support amount should be delivered periodically throughout the year, and packaged as a safety net or social benefit for families, rather than in an annual lump sum as a "tax break."

While I advocate for splitting off the family-support element of the EITC, I simultaneously envision leaving the CTC with the tax return filing process for several reasons. First, the CTC reaches families at much higher income levels, especially after the 2017 tax reform (though only through 2025, as this is, at the time of writing, a temporary provision). Thus, the CTC needs to stay on the return in order to reach those families, many of whom receive it as a credit offsetting their tax liability rather than a refundable benefit. It would be far too complicated to move it off the income tax return only for a subset of eligible families. Second, leaving it on the return provides a cushion for lower-income families, as well as the possibility of a tax-time lump-sum refund to provide a resource boost. Without the EITC in the tax refund, the lump sum will be much smaller for most families, but it can play an important role in offsetting tax liabilities, especially for self-employed individuals who are not subject to income tax withholding and additionally owe a self-employment tax liability. Third, leaving the CTC on the tax return amplifies its distinction from the EITC, and therefore may provide greater clarity of purpose to recipients.

What would decoupling look like? Claims for the family-support portion of the EITC would be administered as an entirely separate process that occurs after the tax return is filed. This process must be simple; if not, taxpayers will be deterred from filing it themselves and the take-up rate will decrease, which is entirely counterproductive to this reimagination.[52]

Using a separate form would have several advantages. Again, it lends itself to more policy coherence: Taxpayers would no longer conflate a refund of their own withholding with receipt of an antipoverty supplement. The separate form should clearly indicate that the family-support credit is based on income, and that work is a prerequisite. The form can also be used to signal this credit as an income-based social benefit – a safety net that is earned – for working

[52] *See, e.g.*, Margot Sanger-Katz, *Hate Paperwork? Medicaid Recipients Will be Drowning in It*, N.Y. TIMES (Jan. 18, 2018), https://www.nytimes.com/2018/01/18/upshot/medicaid-enrollment-obstacles-kentucky-work-requirement.html.

families. In its current form as one lump-sum refund, the messaging is unclear. Imagine an unmarried taxpayer, Michael, who has one child and earns $18,000. Michael would file using the head of household status; in 2018, when the standard deduction for taxpayer filing head of household was increased to $18,000, he would owe no income tax. He would have payroll taxes of $1,377 withheld, resulting in net income of $16,623, which by only a very modest amount exceeds the 2018 HHS poverty line of $16,460 for a household of two. Yet he is due a total tax refund of $4,800 (CTC of $1,400 and an EITC of $3,400). How should Michael understand this sizable refund? He may think of it as his own money coming back to him because too much has been withheld by his employer. How are we to understand it? Is it a refund of his payroll taxes, an antipoverty supplement, or both? Technically, his household was not below the poverty line (if Michael is even aware of what HHS declares to be the poverty line). And if a childless worker with the same income does not receive payroll tax relief, it stands to reason that this is not payroll tax relief. For Michael, certainly this additional $4,800 will benefit his household. The $4,800 is his "family support." But it is not messaged clearly – it is simply a tax refund, with no explanation. If a portion of it were decoupled from the tax return, it could be explicitly messaged as family support.

Another benefit of having workers claim the family-support credit on a separate form rather than a tax return is that it would give the IRS even more time to verify the claimant's past-year income, which may in turn reduce EITC noncompliance. As discussed in Chapter 3, income misreporting is the most common error, and frequently the only error, associated with EITC overclaims.[53] Beginning in the 2017 filing season, the PATH Act legislation simultaneously accelerated W-2 filing deadlines to January 31 and delayed EITC- and CTC-related refunds until February 15. Before that change, the IRS did not receive wage and income information until after refunds were issued. I revisit the timing of income reporting and verification when discussing periodic payment structures in the next chapter.

A third benefit to decoupling the family-support credit from the tax return is that it would cut out the middleman who plays a role in most EITC claims – the tax return preparer. This, in turn, will reduce the incentives and opportunities for tax preparer misconduct, identity theft, and high-interest lending practices such as refund anticipation loans. While filing a return will still be required as a prerequisite to claiming the credit, the return would be much

[53] I.R.S., Pub. No. 5162, *Compliance Estimates for the Earned Income Tax Credit Claimed on 2006–2008 Returns* 17 (Aug. 2014), https://www.irs.gov/pub/irs-soi/EITCComplianceStudyTY2006-2008.pdf.

simpler, because the complex EITC qualifications and calculations would no longer be part of the tax return. Taxpayers wouldn't be lured in by promises of large, fast refunds, because the credit would not come through the tax filing process. Again, the separate form to claim the family-support benefit must be as simple as possible; a more complicated form will only invite the middleman into this separate process.

Separating tax returns and the claim process for the family-support benefit also removes incentives for taxpayers to engage in noncompliance. In the current system, taxpayers can log onto tax software and watch their refund go up or down depending on how much income is reported. This creates a powerful temptation to manipulate the return by reporting cash income that doesn't exist or by omitting cash income or inflating deductions. Taxpayers can watch the bottom line – the amount of the refund – go up or down until they achieve the highest number. This form of reverse engineering is not uncommon.[54] The IRS is well aware that some taxpayers do this, which is why it routinely requests self-employment income substantiation as part of its EITC audits.

This doesn't mean the IRS should not publicize the income levels related to the EITC benefits. To build on the thinking of economist Kevin Milligan, if we want taxpayers to respond to work incentives, they must have full access to information. This would include access to earning thresholds and phase-out levels so that taxpayers can understand the incentives. It would be better, however, if it were easy for taxpayers to look into that question separately and plan work accordingly, instead of discovering the connection in the actual moment of reporting income on the tax return. To the extent that some people are manipulating their income in the moment to maximize their tax refund, this is not accomplishing the credit's work-incentive goals.

I envision that taxpayers would apply for the family-support benefit on a separate, short, very simple form (either in hard copy or electronically) that would include questions about their household composition. The agency could then match the form with the income amounts from the claimant's most recent tax return. The form would not show the family-support EITC benefit due to the claimant – that amount would be calculated by the government agency after the form was submitted. In the next chapter, I discuss what I envision on this form in more detail, drawing upon what is done in Canada and New Zealand.

[54] I have seen examples of this on self-prepared tax returns as well as returns completed by paid preparers. *See also* Jay Soled & Kathleen DeLaney Thomas, *Regulating Tax Return Preparation*, 58 B.C. L. Rev. 151, 180 (2017).

A MORE RADICAL REIMAGINATION: THINKING BEYOND TODAY'S EITC

The framework for my initial reimagination leaves current EITC eligibility and calculation rules largely intact. However, programs in other countries provide inspiration for a more radical reimagination. As before, I retain work as a precondition for the credit, but the variations I propose here would allocate the credit quite differently than the current system. In that sense, these ideas offer both a reimagination and a critique of the current structure.

Calculate Credits by Household Income, Not Marital Status

The United States imposes taxation on the marital unit as opposed to the individual taxpayer. Married couples in the United States have the choice of two filing statuses: they may elect to file a joint return, with joint liability for the income tax liability, or they may choose to file using the "married filing separate" status. Nearly 95 percent of US married filers choose joint filing.[55] There are many incentives for those who elect joint filing status, including administrative convenience and, for taxpayers with disparate incomes, income splitting. At the same time, there are many structural disadvantages to choosing the married filing separate status.[56] Married taxpayers who file separately are statutorily ineligible for several tax benefits they might otherwise receive, including the EITC. Section 32(d) provides: "In the case of an individual who is married (within the meaning of section 7703), this section shall apply only if a joint return is filed for the taxable year under section 6013." Whether the taxpayer otherwise meets all EITC eligibility requirements is irrelevant. The rule has been in place since 1975, but nowhere in the legislative history is there a coherent policy reason for denying the EITC to married taxpayers filing separately. One can speculate that it relates to administrability concerns with calculating the income threshold and phase out. Legislative history from the 1975 enactment of the EITC provided:

> The credit is to be calculated on a return-by-return basis. Individuals who are married and filing a joint return are eligible for only one credit on the combined income of both individuals. Married individuals filing separate returns are not eligible for the credit. A married individual who is treated as not being married (under sec. 143(b)) for return-filing purposes (i.e., a head of

[55] I.R.S., PUB. NO. 1304, INDIVIDUAL INCOME TAX RETURNS 2014 tbl. 1.6 (2016).

[56] *See generally* Michelle Lyon Drumbl, *Joint Winners, Separate Losers: Proposals to Ease the Sting for Married Taxpayers Filing Separately*, 19 FLA. TAX REV. 399 (2016).

> a household whose spouse has not been a member of the household for the entire year) is eligible for the credit in the same manner as a single individual (and any of the absent spouse's income attributed to him under State community property laws is to be disregarded).[57]

Curiously, the Internal Revenue Code does not contain a similar rule for the CTC: Married couples filing separately can still claim the CTC, subject to different income threshold numbers than married couples. Through tax year 2017, the CTC began to phase out at an adjusted gross income of $110,000 on a married filing joint return; a married filing separate taxpayer could claim the CTC, with the phase-out beginning at $55,000 for those individual filers, whereas the phase-out began at $75,000 for unmarried filers. A degree of consistency was enacted with the 2017 Tax Cuts and Jobs Act, albeit temporarily. As noted previously, for tax years 2018–25, the CTC income phase out was increased to $400,000 for married filing joint returns and $200,000 for all other taxpayers (including both unmarried and married filing separately).

Unlike the United States, Canada and New Zealand (and most OECD countries) have a system in which the individual, and not the marital unit, is the unit of taxation. Whereas in the United States income tax is calculated on the aggregate income of a married couple, in these other countries, tax is calculated based on the incomes of each individual regardless of marital status or domestic situation.[58] However, although tax liability is computed on individual income, both Canada and New Zealand determine their refundable credits based on household income. This determination considers not just marital status, but also whether a taxpayer has an unmarried cohabitating partner.

The United States, meanwhile, relies on marital status as a rigid proxy for measuring family income for EITC (and CTC) eligibility. There are good reasons for this, one of which is that marriage conveys legal rights to income and property that do not exist in relationships which lack formal recognition. This is especially true in the nine states that follow the community property system, wherein each spouse generally owns an undivided one-half interest in property acquired during the marriage. However, the result of this is that unmarried cohabitating parents in the United States can receive a higher EITC, or receive EITC despite a higher household income, than married

[57] H.R. REP. NO. 94-19, at 30–31 (1975). Senate Report 94-36 contains nearly identical language with no further elaboration. S. REP. NO. 94-36, at 35 (1975).

[58] For a summary of trade-offs of each approach and description of which countries have adopted each approach, *see* Org. for Econ. Co-operation & Dev., PF1.4, *Neutrality of Tax-Benefit Systems* (2016), www.oecd.org/els/soc/PF1_4_Neutrality_of_tax_benefit_systems.pdf.

TABLE 5.1 *EITC income phase outs for tax year 2017*

	Qualifying children claimed			
Filing as	Zero	One	Two	Three or more
Single, head of household or widowed	$15,010	$39,617	$45,007	$48,340
Married filing jointly	$20,600	$45,207	$50,597	$53,930

couples. This is because the EITC income phase outs for married couples filing jointly are less than double those for unmarried parental units who file individually (Table 5.1).

As a result, unmarried cohabitating parents raising children together receive more favorable tax treatment than similarly situated married parents. One of the parents can file as single, and the other as head of household; because each is subject to an individual income phase out, they may collectively earn more than a married couple and still remain eligible for the EITC. Alternatively, one parent may be "low-income" and the other high-income, but because their incomes are not aggregated, the low-income earner will receive the same benefit as a single parent who does not benefit from living with a high-income partner. As I have written elsewhere,[59] I believe this structure runs contrary to the policy rationale of the EITC as an antipoverty measure.

Furthermore, cohabitating parents of multiple children can split the children between themselves to maximize the EITC benefit in a way that married couples cannot. In tax year 2017, the maximum EITC available for one qualifying child was $3,400; for two children, $5,616; and for three or more qualifying children, $6,318. A married couple claims their children on a joint return; an unmarried couple can divide the children between them. As a simple example, imagine an unmarried couple with three children, and with each individual having an adjusted gross income of $25,000: Using the applicable tables for tax year 2017, one parent could claim two of the children and receive $4,208, the other parent could claim the third child and receive $2,332. Collectively, the unmarried parents would receive a total of $6,540 in EITC benefits. Meanwhile, a married couple filing jointly would receive only $822 for their three qualifying children based on their joint income of $50,000.

[59] *See* Drumbl, *supra* note 56, at 449.

This gaping inconsistency of treatment between married and unmarried parents is unfair and illogical. It also creates structural incentives for noncompliance, such as if married taxpayers realize that they can claim a significantly larger EITC by portraying themselves as unmarried and filing separate returns. Filing status errors are the third-largest category of EITC overclaims, after income misreporting and qualifying child errors.[60] The most recent IRS study of EITC noncompliance estimated that approximately one million EITC claimants incorrectly chose single or head of household as their filing status, resulting in estimated overclaims of $2.3–3.3 billion annually.[61] The IRS report elaborates: "[m]ost of these overclaims come from married taxpayers who file separately from their spouse and incorrectly claim either single or, more frequently, head-of-household filing status. This practice tends to overstate the amount of the credit on one or both returns by splitting household income."[62]

As I have argued elsewhere,[63] I believe family-support credits should not be categorically denied to married taxpayers filing separately; the determination should rest on household income. Likewise, family-support credits should be calculated on the basis of household income without regard to marital status. This is a significant departure from our current system, but would result in greater horizontal equity as between households with children.

Unlike the United States, Canada's income tax law provides a federal definition for common-law partners for purposes of determining family-support credits. Claimants who are married or have a common-law partner must report this status and their family net income. For this purpose in Canada, a common-law partner is someone who is not one's spouse, but with whom one is in a conjugal relationship if one of three criteria are met: (1) the couple has lived together for at least twelve continuous months without a relationship "breakdown" of ninety or more days; (2) the couple has a child together, by birth or adoption; or (3) the partner has custody and control of the claimant's child and the claimant's child is wholly dependent on that person for support.[64]

60 I.R.S., *supra* note 53, at 20.
61 *Id.* at 19, tbl. 5.
62 *Id.* at 20.
63 *See* Drumbl, *supra* note 56, at 444–55.
64 Income Tax Act, R.S.C. 1985, c.1 § 122.6 (Can.) (defining "cohabitating spouse or common-law partner"); *id.* § 252(1) (defining "extended meaning of child"); *id.* § 248. *See also Form RC66 – Canada Child Tax Benefits Application*, CAN. REVENUE AGENCY (2017), https://www.canada.ca/en/revenue-agency/services/forms-publications/forms/rc66.html.

To claim the Canada Child Benefit (CCB), both the claimant and the spouse or partner must file a tax return, even if otherwise not required to do so.[65] The claimant must provide the spouse or partner's taxpayer social insurance number on the benefit application. Recipients are required to notify the Canada Revenue Agency (CRA) if there is a change in marital or relationship status resulting in a separation of ninety days or more due to a breakdown in the relationship. Recipients can report this change on a simple one-page form, and are required to do so by the end of the month after the month in which the status changed. Upon receiving this notification, the CRA adjusts the benefit amount, effective the following month, based on the change in family net income.[66] In some cases, the CRA will later request documentation substantiating the change in marital or common-law partnership status.[67]

As in Canada, in New Zealand the individual (not the married couple) is the taxable unit, and Working for Families Tax Credits (WfFTC) benefits are calculated based on relationship status. Individuals are considered to be "in a relationship" if they are married, in a civil union, or in a "de facto relationship." While marriage or civil union status is readily ascertainable, whether one is in a "de facto relationship" is a facts-and-circumstances determination, the parameters of which are set forth by statute. A de facto relationship occurs when two persons, both aged eighteen or older, live together as a couple, but are not married or in a civil union. To determine whether two persons "live together as a couple," the following circumstances may be considered: relationship duration; nature and extent of the common residence; existence of a sexual relationship; degree of financial dependence or interdependence; ownership, use, and acquisition of property; degree of mutual commitment to a shared life; care and support of children; performance of household duties; and reputation and public aspects of the relationship.[68] Of course, not all these factors are easily measurable or verifiable.

The Child Poverty Action Group (CPAG) in New Zealand has written about the "disjunction between the marriage-neutral treatment of the

[65] *See* Income Tax Act, R.S.C. 1985, c.1, § 122.61(1) (Can.).

[66] *See Update Your Marital Status with the Canada Revenue Agency*, Gov't of Can., https://www.canada.ca/en/revenue-agency/services/child-family-benefits/update-your-marital-status-canada-revenue-agency.html (last updated Apr. 17, 2018); Form RC65 – Marital Status Change, Can. Revenue Agency (2017), https://www.canada.ca/content/dam/cra-arc/formspubs/pbg/rc65/rc65-18e.pdf.

[67] *See* J. Paul Dubé, Taxpayers' Ombudsman, Proving Your Status: Establishing Eligibility for the Canada Child Tax Benefit (Gov't of Canada Oct. 2010).

[68] Property (Relationships) Act 1976, pt 2D 1(2) (N.Z.) ("Meaning of de facto relationship").

individual in the tax system and the marital unit basis in the welfare benefit system."[69] Furthermore, CPAG has identified the complications that arise from the reliance on using the presence or absence of a relationship or marriage to determine benefit entitlement.[70] CPAG also notes that different agencies have conflicting interests: In New Zealand, Inland Revenue pays WfFTC benefits to the principal caregiver, sometimes based upon the partner's demonstrated minimum work hours. Thus Inland Revenue scrutinizes whether the recipient is "in a relationship" to determine eligibility for benefits and payment rate; because minimum work is required, it may be to the WfFTC applicant's advantage to be considered to be in a relationship with a worker. In contrast, the Work and Income agency administers a variety of social safety net benefits, including those for unemployed individuals; in those cases, being in a relationship may reduce eligibility for the social safety net. The CPAG authors write:

> A serious confusion about relationships in our system needs to be acknowledged. There are so many combinations and permutations of co-habitation, financial interdependence, emotional commitment, forward plans, and sexual/family patterns, it is no wonder that no one simple clear definition can be found. So much is at stake for those whose lives are already complex, stressed and difficult.[71]

CPAG's observations and critiques provide a useful consideration for reconfiguring the US system. As between Canada and New Zealand, the Canadian definition of a common-law partner seems easier to administer than New Zealand's "de facto relationship" definition. In Canada, there is a bright-line temporal element: unmarried parents who live together are common-law partners, and couples who live together for at least twelve months are common-law partners, regardless of whether they have a child together. This is not to suggest that administration is perfect in either country. The Office of Taxpayers' Ombudsman has studied complaints from taxpayers about the difficulty they face documenting relationship changes to the CRA, whether it involves a separation or status as primary caregiver.[72] Periodic media reports have highlighted stories of individual struggles with the CRA, both under the

69 Susan St. John, Catriona MacLennan, Hannah Anderson, & Rebecca Fountain, *The Complexities of 'Relationship' in the Welfare System and the Consequences for Children*, Child Poverty Action Grp. 6 (2014).

70 *Id.* at 2.

71 *Id.* at 37.

72 *See* Dubé, *supra* note 67.

old Canada Child Tax Benefit (CCTB) and its successor, the CCB.[73] It seems that, just as in the United States, some Canadian taxpayers struggle to satisfy the agency that they are in fact entitled to benefits. The same is true in New Zealand.

No matter what the benefit criteria are, substantiation challenges will exist in some form. No system will produce perfect compliance or be burden free to recipients. A savvy couple who wishes to cheat the system could use a different address, such as a friend's or family member's address, on one partner's tax return to preserve income eligibility for the other partner, who could then claim to live alone. Ultimately, there is no way to eliminate this sort of benefit fraud for residence-based credits. Take the example of the Netherlands: all residents are required to register their home address with the local municipality, and the information is cross-checked when residents apply for benefits. This level of affirmative reporting of one's whereabouts to a government agency would make most Americans bristle, not to mention that it would require a level of coordination between federal and local municipalities that doesn't currently exist. Moreover, it doesn't fully solve the problem of benefit fraud. In one Dutch village, authorities discovered that dozens of young fathers had falsely registered as living at their parents' address even though they lived with their partner; this was done so that the mother would appear in the system as a single mother, making her eligible for a higher benefit.[74]

While it seems inevitable that no structure can avoid every substantiation challenge or ensure perfect compliance, we can create a system that more fairly and realistically measures income and family structure. To return to the question of how household income should be measured for EITC purposes, the United States could adopt a new standard that borrows from the Canadian

[73] *See, e.g.*, Stephanie Taylor, *'It's a joke': Woman Battles CRA to Change Marital Status for Child Benefits*, CBC NEWS (Dec. 21, 2017, 5:37 PM CT), www.cbc.ca/news/canada/saskatchewan/cra-saskatchewan-1.4461490; Jennifer Quesnel, *Low-income, Indigenous Families Feel Weight of Child Benefit Reviews*, CBC NEWS (May 25, 2017, 5:00 AM CT), www.cbc.ca/news/canada/saskatoon/low-income-indigenous-families-feel-weight-of-child-benefit-reviews-1.4120221; David Shield, *'Why do we have 4 car seats?': Saskatoon Man Uses Family Pictures, Sarcasm to Respond to Federal Tax Review*, CBC NEWS (Aug. 29, 2016, 10:30 AM CT), www.cbc.ca/news/canada/saskatoon/four-carseats-respond-canada-revenue-audit-1.3739740; David Shield & Jennifer Quesnel, *Sask. Women Struggling after Canada Child Benefit Payments Cut*, CBC NEWS (Aug. 24, 2016, 6:29 PM ET), www.cbc.ca/news/canada/saskatchewan-women-struggle-canada-child-benefit-cut-1.3734486.

[74] Alexandra Gowling, *Benefit Fraud a Serious Problem in the Netherlands*, I AM EXPAT (Dec. 12, 2013), http://www.iamexpat.nl/expat-info/dutch-expat-news/benefit-fraud-serious-problem-netherlands; *see also 'We Do Take Housing and Child Benefit Fraud Seriously,' Says Minister*, DUTCHNEWS.NL (Dec. 10, 2013), www.dutchnews.nl/news/archives/2013/12/we_do_take_housing_and_child_b.

approach without going as far as the common-law partner standard. We could include parental cohabitation as a bright-line factor in determining income eligibility for refundable credits, just as marital status is currently a factor. In other words, two unmarried cohabiting parents would be "considered as married" solely for determining income eligibility for EITC and CTC benefits. At the same time, a parent who lives with a partner who is not the parent or stepparent of his or her child would be considered as single (or head of household) when determining income eligibility. This would be consistent with the notion that parenthood bestows legal obligations, just as marriage does. One has a moral and financial duty to one's child (and to one's spouse), whereas a boyfriend or girlfriend has no duty to financially support a partner's child if he or she is not the parent of the child.

This middle-ground approach would be relatively simple to administer, especially if family-support credits were calculated on a separate form from the tax return. In addition to requiring information about marital status, the family-support form would require information about whether the parents of the child live together. Requiring that taxpayers list a physical address (rather than a P.O. Box) on their tax return would allow addresses to be cross-referenced against the address listed on the request for family-support benefits.[75]

The idea of determining income eligibility based on either marital status or parental cohabitation segues quite naturally into the next: The United States should allow parents with shared custody to share the family-support benefits, as Canada and New Zealand do.

Allow Parents Who Share Custody to Share the Credits

As noted in earlier chapters, family-support benefits in the United States are generally calculated per child on an all-or-nothing basis. Parents who live apart but share custody cannot both claim the same qualifying child for the EITC and CTC. There is a mechanism for the custodial parent to waive his or her right to the CTC, allowing the noncustodial parent to claim the CTC despite not meeting the residency requirement. The EITC, however, goes entirely to the parent with whom the child resides for more than half the year.

[75] Currently, IRS Form 1040 requires filers to provide a home address; the instructions allow a filer to list a P.O. Box only if the post office doesn't deliver mail to the filer's home. Form 1040 could be changed to allow filers to list their physical address plus a mailing address, if different.

Many divorced parents have joint physical custody agreements, also known as shared parenting, in which the child spends at least 35 percent of the year with each parent. Shared parenting is an increasingly common arrangement in the United States and other countries.[76] Multiple studies on shared parenting arrangements have linked it to positive emotional, behavioral, and physical health measures for children of all ages.[77]

As Chapter 4 described, both Canada and New Zealand allow family-based credits to be split between parents who share physical custody of the children. New Zealand provides that a parent who cares for the child for at least one-third of the year (on average) has full entitlement to the in-work tax credit for those weeks in which he or she also meets the minimum hours test.[78] The Canadian Income Tax Act defines a "shared-custody parent" as one of the two parents who live apart but "reside with the qualified dependant on an equal or near equal basis, and primarily fulfil the responsibility for the care and upbringing" of the child when the child is with that parent.[79] In shared-custody situations in Canada, each parent gets 50 percent of the CCB that he or she would have received (according to net household income) if the child lived with the parent all of the time.[80] For example, imagine parents A and B, who share custody of a child, and assume the following scenario:[81] If parent A had primary (not shared) custody, he would be entitled to a $5,550 credit based on his net household income; alternatively, if parent B had primary (not shared) custody of the child, she would be entitled to a $14,400 credit based on her net household income. Under the shared-custody rules, both parents instead get 50 percent of what they would receive if they had primary custody: parent A gets $2,775 and parent B gets $7,200. Collectively, the total CCB is more than it would be if A had primary custody but less than if B had primary custody. Yet it appropriately reflects the shared-custody arrangement, because the child splits time between the households.

A similar shared-custody rule was in effect for the CCB's predecessor, the CCTB, as of 2010. The Tax Court of Canada has interpreted the shared-custody provision in several cases and has emphasized the facts and

76 Linda Nielsen, *Shared Physical Custody: Summary of 40 Studies on Outcomes for Children*, 55 J. Divorce & Remarriage 613 (2014).

77 *Id. See also* Richard A. Warshak, *Social Science and Parenting Plans for Young Children: A Consensus Report*, 20 Psychology, Pub. Policy, and L. 46 (2014).

78 Income Tax Act of 2007, pt MC 10(3) (N.Z.).

79 Income Tax Act, R.S.C. 1985, c.1, § 122.6. (Can.).

80 Income Tax Act, R.S.C. 1985, c.1 § 122.61(1.1) (Can.).

81 Tanya Budd & Trent Robinson, *The Canada Child Benefit and Child Custody*, 6 Can. Tax Focus (2016).

circumstances of the taxpayer behavior (for example, did each shared-custody parent demonstrate the characteristics of "care and upbringing" during the days the child lived with him or her?) over the formality of the separation agreement.[82] In one case, the Tax Court of Canada found that a 45/55 physical custody met the "shared custody" standard because it was "near equal" and both parents were involved in the care and upbringing of the children.[83]

In my work with low-income taxpayers, I see many custodial parents whose return is selected for EITC audit because their ex-spouse wrongly claimed the EITC but filed his or her tax return first. These parents are negatively affected because their badly needed refund proceeds are frozen for many months while the examination unit tries to sort out which parent is entitled to the EITC. In shared parenting arrangements, especially those that are approximately fifty–fifty, it can be exceptionally difficult to prove where the child lived for 183 nights. This is further complicated if the child spent time away from both parents (with a grandparent, for example) for some nights of the year. The examination process can devolve into a battle of "he said, she said," with each parent claiming more nights were spent with them. I have spoken to parents who think it is legally proper to alternate years of claiming the EITC, though this is technically only correct if the physical custody schedules are alternated such that the 183-night residency requirement is met in a given year.

Leslie Book, who has written extensively about EITC noncompliance, identifies particular concerns about the status of noncustodial parents. A low-wage worker may be the primary provider for his or her child and may spend significant time with the child, but not meet the 183-night residency requirement to claim the EITC. Book uses this as an example of a structural incentive to cheat, sometimes with the blessing of the custodial parent (who may not have any earned income, and thus be entirely ineligible for the EITC). At the same time, the noncustodial parent may be required to pay child support. Both Book and National Taxpayer Advocate Nina Olson have proposed creating a separate tax credit for noncustodial parents who pay child support.[84] Book argues this is one way to "lessen the existing structural incentive for individuals to borrow or lend children to enhance their EITC eligibility."[85]

82 *Id.*

83 Brady v. The Queen, 2012 D.T.C. 1204.

84 Leslie Book, *Freakonomics and the Tax Gap: An Applied Perspective*, 56 AM. U.L. REV. 1163 (2007); TAXPAYER ADVOCATE SERVICE, 2005 ANNUAL REPORT TO CONGRESS (VOL. 1) 398.

85 Book, *supra* note 84, at 1178.

Rather than create a separate credit for noncustodial parents (including parents who share in the parenting and live with the child on a near-equal basis but less than 183 days per year), why not allow parents who share physical custody to each receive half of the family-support benefit for which they would otherwise be eligible? This feature places the child at the center of the credit, in recognition that both parents spend money on and support the child, instead of turning the credit into a zero-sum game between the adults.

Adjust Credits Regionally for Cost of Living

The EITC benefit amounts are the same for recipients at the same income level across the United States, regardless of cost of living. This makes little sense for an antipoverty supplement, given how greatly the cost of living varies between urban and rural areas, and among different regions of the country. Why not adjust the credit regionally, perhaps by zip code or county?

At first blush, this sounds administratively complex. However, such regional variations exist for other purposes. For example, Temporary Assistance for Needy Families (TANF) and Supplemental Nutrition Assistance Program (SNAP) benefits vary in amount from state to state. One reason why is because the states are involved in funding and administering these programs.

In a sense, there is a regional EITC supplement in those states that have incorporated a state version of the EITC into their income tax. As of 2017, twenty-nine states and the District of Columbia had an EITC; in twenty-four of these jurisdictions, the EITC was refundable.[86] Generally the state EITCs are a percentage of the federal credit and are easy for taxpayers to calculate.[87]

However, not all states have an income tax system. Moreover, the cost of living can vary significantly across a state, particularly between urban and rural areas. But the IRS already has a readily accessible repository of data on housing and utilities costs by state and county level, and that information is updated annually. This information, which is derived from the US Census Bureau, American Community Survey, and Bureau of Labor Statistics data, is used by the IRS to determine monthly necessary expenses in the collections context. In determining family-support benefits, the IRS could use a multiplier based on the applicant's county (which would be provided on the simple, separate application form) and increase or decrease the standard benefit accordingly. This would increase the EITC benefit to taxpayers in high-cost

[86] Ctr. on Budget & Policy Priorities, Policy Basics: State Earned Income Tax Credits (2017).

[87] *Id.* at 2.

areas such as the Virginia suburbs outside Washington, DC (where housing and utility costs for a family of four exceed $3,000 per month), relative to less expensive rural southwest Virginia (where in some counties the housing and utility costs for a family of four are closer to $1,500).[88]

Varying EITC amounts by county would provide a more meaningful safety net to those who live in more expensive areas, and it can be done with information already compiled annually and readily available to the IRS.

In all, there are many ways to reimagine the tax credits for the working poor. There are compelling reasons to split the EITC into a work-support credit and a family-support credit, and to decouple the family-support portion from the tax filing process. These include simplification, clearer messaging, and reducing incentives for noncompliance.

Splitting the credit into two parts is a necessary prerequisite to moving delivery to periodic payments. The other proposals in this chapter are not prerequisites for a change in delivery. The next chapter describes why a move to periodic payments is desirable, and what that would look like. This change in frequency of delivery could be made without decoupling the family-support credit from the return filing process, although as the next chapter explains, periodic payments go hand in hand with decoupling the claim process from tax returns.

[88] I.R.S. SB/SE Research – Team #3, 2017 *Allowable Living Expenses Housing and Utilities Standards*, Internal Revenue Serv. (2017), https://www.irs.gov/pub/irs-utl/all_states_housing_standards.pdf.

6

Making a Case for Year-Round EITC Delivery

The previous chapter set forth a reimagination of the delivery and administration of the Earned Income Tax Credit (EITC), describing how and why Congress should reform these refundable credits. Among other things, I proposed splitting off the family-support component and decoupling it from the tax return filing process.

But regardless of whether EITC claims are decoupled from the return filing process, the working poor would benefit from a transition to periodic payment of the family-support component. As Chapter 4 described, year-round delivery of refundable tax credits is a norm in other countries. In New Zealand, recipients of the Working for Families Tax Credits (WfFTC) can choose among weekly or fortnightly benefits, or can opt for an annual lump sum. In Canada, taxpayers can elect to receive part of the Working Income Tax Benefit (WITB) as a quarterly advance, while the more sizable Canada Child Benefit (CCB) (which is not predicated on a work requirement, but is administered by the Canada Revenue Agency [CRA]) is delivered monthly.

In the United States, the Advance Earned Income Tax Credit (AEITC) provided an opportunity for periodic payments. As described in Chapter 2, for more than thirty tax filing seasons (1979–2010), taxpayers could elect this advance receipt option. Those who opted for the AEITC had to notify their employers, who then adjusted withholding. Taxpayers then received a portion of the EITC in advance, in the form of a slightly higher paycheck each pay period. Taxpayers were required to file a tax return at the end of the year to reconcile any difference. The AEITC option was chronically underutilized, with the take-up rate never exceeding single digits.

In Chapter 2, I considered the reasons for the AEITC's stunningly low take-up rate, and canvassed a few theories: (1) taxpayers did not like having their employer act as an intermediary for something so personal, and perhaps did not understand it as a social benefit because it came in a paycheck; (2)

taxpayers were reluctant to participate because it was based on projected earnings and they worried about owing something back at tax filing time; and (3) taxpayers prefer receiving the benefit as a larger sum because larger amounts of money are psychologically more meaningful.

The latter two theories derive from published experiments and also qualitative interviews conducted by other scholars.[1] With a fair amount of literature supporting the notion that taxpayers enjoy annual lump-sum delivery, is it paternalistic to propose a restructuring to periodic payments? This is a fair question, especially if the payments are deferred and paid over a period of twelve months instead of immediately when calculated. But program design is an administrative choice, and there are valid reasons to move to a periodic delivery of this benefit, which I set forth in the next section.[2] As a timing issue, taxpayers must balance annual lump-sum delivery with the reality of monthly billing cycles and the inevitability of unexpected expenses such as car repair (referred to in the literature as "financial shocks"[3]) that arise despite the most carefully planned monthly budget.

Several small-scale studies and pilot programs offer countervailing evidence, revealing that a sizable percentage of taxpayers would like the option to receive periodic payments, and that this is seen as empowering.[4] Most notably, in 2014, a Center for Economic Progress (CEP) pilot program made the EITC available in quarterly periodic payments; as I discuss elsewhere, subsequent interviews with those recipients revealed an overwhelming preference for periodic payment over a lump sum.

This chapter weighs the advantages of periodic payment against those of lump-sum payment. It outlines the pros and cons of different possible periodic payment structures. In addition to suggesting ways for the IRS to adapt to a periodic system, I also consider issues that would arise in a transition from lump sum to periodic distribution. Ultimately, year-round delivery offers advantages both to recipients and to the government, and can be structured in a variety of different ways.

1 *See* Sarah Halpern-Meekin, Kathryn Edin, Laura Tach, & Jennifer Sykes, It's Not Like I'm Poor, 69–72 (University of California Press 2015); Damon Jones, *Information, Preferences and Public Benefit Participation: Experimental Evidence from the Advance EITC and 401(k) Savings*, 2(2) Am. Econ. J.: Applied Econ. (2010), 147–49.

2 For an excellent discussion of paternalism and the cognitive implications of program design, *see* Brian Galle & Manuel Utset, *Is Cap-and-Trade Fair to the Poor? Shortsighted Households and the Timing of Consumption Taxes*, 79 Geo. Wash. U. L. Rev. 33 (2010).

3 *See* Sara Sternberg Greene, *The Broken Safety Net: A Study of Earned Income Tax Credit Recipients and a Proposal for Repair*, 88 N.Y.U. L. Rev. 515 (2013).

4 Steve Holt, *Periodic Payment of the Earned Income Tax Credit Revisited*, The Brookings Inst. 11–13 (Dec. 17, 2015), https://www.brookings.edu/research/periodic-payment-of-the-earned-income-tax-credit-revisited.

ADVANTAGES OF A PERIODIC PAYMENT STRUCTURE

As Chapter 2 detailed, scholars have highlighted certain advantages of the annual lump-sum structure. These advantages should be borne in mind when considering a change to delivery, but it is important to note that they are not tied to frequency of payment so much as to the stigma-free packaging of the benefit.

A major advantage highlighted by Sykes and her coauthors is that the lump-sum tax refund delivery reduces stigma: EITC recipients feel pride in having earned "a just reward for work,"[5] and receiving it "enhances feelings of social inclusion via consumption and fostering mobility goals."[6] In contrast, cash welfare "confers stigma and detracts from well-being."[7]

If the EITC were repackaged as a family-support credit for working families and distributed periodically instead of in a lump-sum tax refund, it would be important that recipients not feel stigmatized. This could be achieved by intentional messaging in order to reinforce the purpose of the EITC as a supplement for working parents. Earlier, I discussed the political need to maintain work as a condition of receiving the credit: The credit's connection to work is meaningful both to recipients and to non-recipients.

The same researchers who praise the lump-sum EITC delivery for its lack of social stigma also found that 90 percent of the recipients they interviewed had debt, whether credit card debt or overdue rent or utility bills.[8] The interviewees reported spending a significant amount – on average 25 percent of the total EITC received – to pay down debt.[9] Even so, recipients reported that they liked the large lump-sum benefit because "they found making so much progress on their debts all at once quite gratifying."[10]

Yet the debt accumulates throughout the year because the recipients live on a low wage and cannot make ends meet. Halpern-Meekin and her coauthors write about the financial strain these recipients feel throughout the year – racking up debt, accumulating interest and late fees – while waiting for their annual windfall.[11] It is farcical to view the lumpiness of an annual windfall as

5 Jennifer Sykes, Katrin Križ, Kathryn Edin, & Sarah Halpern-Meekin, *Dignity and Dreams: What the Earned Income Tax Credit (EITC) Means to Low-Income Families*, 80 Am. Soc. Rev. 243 (2015).

6 *Id.* at 260.

7 *Id.*

8 *Id.* at 251.

9 *Id.*

10 *Id.* at 252.

11 Halpern-Meekin *et al.*, *supra* note 1, at 71.

"progress" while ignoring the reality that families are borrowing for life's necessities.

Periodic payments would go far to assuage this cycle of debt and give recipients access to their family-support benefit more evenly throughout the year. This is the norm in Canada and New Zealand, where family benefits are distributed periodically. I favor this approach: Although empirical evidence shows that US taxpayers like "forced savings," my experience working with EITC recipients validates the notion that this population would benefit from access to the money more frequently – at least quarterly. In particular, there are three distinct advantages to a periodic payment structure: year-round delivery would reduce the use of unfavorable borrowing practices, would discourage third-party misbehavior, and would lower the stakes for overpayments and frozen refunds.

Reduce Reliance on Unfavorable Borrowing Practices

It is well known that the working poor face challenges making ends meet on a day-to-day basis. A majority of US households report having unstable work schedules, and employment instability can lead to income volatility and disruptions.[12]

When American workers can't make ends meet, they turn to various ways to get by. Some have credit cards, and often carry a balance from month to month, with high interest rates that make it a Sisyphean task to ever pay off the card in full. Others rely on short-term products such as payday loans and car title loans to get by in emergencies or make ends meet. These types of loans typically have triple-digit interest rates when expressed as an annual percentage rate (APR), yet demand for such products is high, especially among those who cannot access credit in a more traditional fashion.

Although states and the Consumer Financial Protection Bureau (CFPB) regulate these loans in a variety of ways, the industry argues that such regulation may create "credit deserts for many Americans"[13] because the borrowers

[12] Dylan Bellisle & David Marzahl, *Restructuring the EITC: A Credit for the Modern Worker*, Center for Economic Progress 2 (2015) (noting that 64 percent of US households report having unstable work schedules, and stating that "nearly half of Americans regularly experience significant fluctuations in their income, and 55% either break even or spend more than they make in a typical month"), https://www.economicprogress.org/assets/files/Restructuring-the-EITC-A-Credit-for-the-Modern-Worker.pdf.

[13] Stacy Cowley, *Payday Lending Faces Tough New Restrictions by Consumer Agency*, N.Y. TIMES (Oct. 5, 2017) (quoting Edward D'Alessio, executive director of Financial Service Centers of America), https://www.nytimes.com/2017/10/05/business/payday-loans-cfpb.html.

who use payday loans cannot access credit from banks or credit unions. There is no doubt that many Americans rely on these products and need the access to money they provide. In a study of 3.5 million records of car title loans, the CFPB found high levels of "reborrowing," meaning borrowers repaid the loan but took out another shortly thereafter; it was unusual for borrowers to take out a loan, repay it, and not take out another.[14] The study found that 80 percent of vehicle title loans were reborrowed on the same day a previous loan was repaid, and nearly 90 percent were reborrowed within sixty days. Among those who engaged in vehicle title loan sequences, the default rate was high: Approximately one-third of the loan sequences experienced a default, and one in five resulted in the repossession of the borrower's vehicle.[15]

Some employers have begun experimenting with payroll options that provide relief to low-income earners. For example, both Lyft and Uber offer drivers the option to access their earnings immediately instead of waiting for a paycheck. Lyft says that its drivers prefer this option: "Express Pay began after drivers backed the initial concept. They believed the instant access would help make their lives easier by having quick cash for life expenses such as groceries and rent, covering emergencies, and keeping gas in their cars."[16] Start-up companies FlexWage and Activehours partner with companies to allow workers to access their wages as earned, either directly from the employer or as an advance from the third party, in which cases wages are withdrawn from the worker's bank account after the employer deposits them.[17] While many of these products are fee-based, Walmart partnered with an app called Even to allow its employees advance access to a portion of wages up to eight times a year, free of charge. (Walmart pays a small fee to Even, and no interest is charged because it is a payday advance, not a loan.)[18]

The timing of social benefits has salience to recipients. Economists who study household budgeting refer to the concept of "consumption smoothing" as the desire for stable consumption over time. Consumption smoothing is more difficult for low-income households than for high-income households,

[14] *Single-Payment Vehicle Title Lending*, CONSUMER FINANCIAL PROTECTION BUREAU (2016).
[15] *Id.*
[16] Lyft (Dec. 21, 2016), https://blog.lyft.com/posts/get-paid-quickly-express-pay. A transfer fee of $0.50 applies each time drivers cash out their earnings. *Id.*
[17] Stacy Cowley, *New Payday Options for Making Ends Meet*, N.Y. TIMES (July 4, 2016), https://www.nytimes.com/2016/07/05/business/dealbook/new-payday-options-for-making-ends-meet.html.
[18] Michael Corkery, *Walmart Will Let Its 1.4 Million Workers Take Their Pay Before Payday*, N.Y. TIMES (Dec. 13, 2017), https://www.nytimes.com/2017/12/13/business/walmart-workers-pay-advances.html.

because the former are relatively more budget sensitive.[19] Economists have found that SNAP (Supplemental Nutrition Assistance Program) benefits, which are distributed monthly, have a "first of the month" effect: Food stamp recipients spend more on food in the first three days after benefits are received, and food expenditures in these households decline later in the month.[20] One study found that the "average caloric intake of members of [food stamp] recipient households declines by 10 to 15 percent over the food stamp month."[21] Researchers have even found a link between the timing of benefit distribution and crime levels: When Illinois changed its policy in 2010 and distributed food stamp benefits more evenly throughout the month, researchers found a reduction in shoplifting in Chicago grocery stores.[22]

By the time the annual lump-sum EITC benefit is in sight, many recipients are so desperate for the cash infusion that they buy a financial product from their return preparer to obtain the refund the same day the return is filed. Although this comes at a cost, recipients do not want to wait a week or two for the Internal Revenue Service (IRS) to process the return and direct deposit the refund into their account (for those who do not have a bank account, the wait time for a paper check is even longer). Paid preparers offer a variety of financial products. The details and names of these products shift from year to year, but typically there are fees or hidden costs attached. I discussed these products in detail in Chapter 3: Refund anticipation checks (RACs) allow filers to pay for tax return preparation out of their refund proceeds. The National Consumer Law Center estimates that 20.5 million taxpayers spent over $500 million on RACs in 2017.[23] "No fee" refund anticipation loans (RALs) are loans secured by the refund: The tax return filer does not pay a fee

[19] For a survey of economic studies discussing low-income households and liquidity restraints, and the limited ability of these households to engage in consumption smoothing, *see* Galle & Utset, *supra* note 2, at 48–52.

[20] Justine Hastings & Ebonya Washington, *The First of the Month Effect: Consumer Behavior and Store Responses*, 2 AMER. ECON. J. 142 (2010); Parke E. Wilde & Christine K. Ranney, *The Monthly Food Stamp Cycle: Shopping Frequency and Food Intake Decisions in an Endogenous Switching Regression Framework*, 82 AMER. J. AGR. ECON. 200 (2000).

[21] Jesse Shapiro, *Is There a Daily Discount Rate? Evidence from the Food Stamp Nutrition Cycle*, 89 J. OF PUB. ECONOMICS 303, 304 (2005).

[22] Jillian Carr & Analisa Packham, *SNAP Benefits and Crime: Evidence from Changing Disbursement Schedules* (Miami U. Farmer Sch. of Bus., Working Paper No. 2017-01, Mar. 2017), www.fsb.muohio.edu/fsb/ecopapers/docs/packhaam-2017-01-paper.pdf; Sahil Chinoy, *Shoplifting in Chicago Dropped after a Change in the Food Stamp Program*, WASH. POST (July 13, 2017), http://www.washingtonpost.com/news/wonk/wp/2017/07/13/shoplifting-in-chicago-dropped-after-a-change-in-the-food-stamps-program/?utm_term=.c6a8d840e0b2.

[23] Press Release, Nat'l Consumer Law Ctr., Tax Time Consumer Issues: New Risks, Old Problems (Jan. 29, 2018), www.nclc.org/images/pdf/taxes/tax-consumer-advisory-2018.pdf.

for the loan; the lender charges the return preparer a fee. Of course, nothing stops preparers from passing these costs along in the form of tax return preparation fees. (A taxpayer who uses a free return preparation service such as the IRS Volunteer Income Tax Assistance [VITA] program, as well as a taxpayer who chooses to self-prepare, will not have access to a RAC or RAL. As noted, a minority of EITC filers chose either of these filing methods.)

Periodic payment frequency is a significant design question. It is not necessarily desirable – or necessary – for the EITC to be available weekly. However, moving to a periodic model, whether quarterly or monthly, would provide low-income workers a smoother path to make ends meet and could reduce reliance on the high-interest or high-fee stopgap products that they regularly turn to in today's market.

Reduce Incentives for Third-Party Misbehavior

Chapter 3 detailed the problems of return preparer misconduct and identity theft, and drew a connection between these practices and the administration of refundable credits. I also described how tax-time EITC delivery shifts the costs of the administration to the recipient, since so many EITC filers rely on a paid preparer. The National Taxpayer Advocate Nina Olson has called for better tax return preparer regulation, noting that

> Taxpayers who are the beneficiaries of [the EITC and CTC] are often the least educated and least financially sophisticated in the United States today. Thus, they become easy targets for marketing schemes of unregulated and unqualified so-called return preparers whose real interest in the tax return process is to push high-interest loans . . . and charge high fees.[24]

The IRS has acknowledged that the sheer size of the refundable credits attracts fraud and fraudulent preparers, creating compliance challenges.[25]

[24] Nina E. Olson, *More Than a 'Mere' Preparer: Loving and Return Preparation*, 139 Tax Notes 767, 769 (2013).

[25] Treas. Inspector Gen. for Tax. Admin., Ref No. 2011-40-023, *Reduction Targets and Strategies Have Not Been Established to Reduce the Billions of Dollars in Improper Earned Income Tax Credit Payments Each Year*, Treasury Dept. 29 (Feb. 7, 2011), https://m.treasury.gov/tigta/auditreports/2011reports/201140023fr.pdf; *see also Written Statement of J. Russell George, Treasury Inspector General for Tax Administration, Hearing before the H. Comm. on Ways and Means, Subcomm. on Oversight, H.R.*, 112th Cong. 2 (May 25, 2011), https://www.treasury.gov/tigta/congress/congress_05252011.pdf. ("Although [each of the EITC and CTC] provides benefits to individuals, the unintended consequence of these credits is that they are often the targets of unscrupulous individuals who file erroneous claims for these credits.")

Decoupling the family-support benefit from the tax refund would not solve all tax compliance challenges, but it would remove one of the most sizable refundable credits from the tax return filing process. As Michael Hatfield has argued, "Reform that made refunds the exception rather than the rule, making the IRS less like an ATM[,] would reduce its appeal to financial thieves."[26]

It is possible, perhaps likely, that some return preparers would seek to become involved in the family-support credit claim process. This type of rent-seeking seems to emerge wherever there is a market for it, and it is easy to imagine return preparers promoting it as an add-on service. But if the form were simple, asking only for demographic information and not income calculations, few claimants would require assistance. Canada, for example, uses a simple two-page form for its CCB application. The IRS could provide and support opportunities for free assistance with the application, along the lines of its VITA program.

Shifting to a two-step process – a tax return reporting income, and a separate, subsequent application for the family-support benefit – would hopefully reduce the incentives and opportunities for third-party misbehavior. As I will discuss, if the benefit is claimed through a process separate from a tax return, there are ways that the IRS can improve on the eligibility determination.

Lower the Stakes for Overpayments and Frozen Refunds

EITC recipients who receive an overpayment may know or suspect that they are not entitled to the benefit, in whole or in part. Some may mistakenly believe that if the refund was issued, the IRS has verified the claim. Some may choose to be willfully blind to the question. Still others may be wholly unaware that they were not entitled to the EITC.

Whatever the recipient's understanding may be, it is rare for the refund to remain unspent in the recipient's checking account. When a return is questionable, the IRS can freeze the refund pending substantiation through the examination process, but this is not always the case.[27] If an individual receives an overpayment before being selected for an examination and it is later

[26] Michael Hatfield, *Cybersecurity and Tax Reform*, 93 IND. L. J. 1161, 1194 (2018).

[27] As noted in Chapter 3, up to 80 percent of questionable EITC claims are frozen pending taxpayer substantiation. US Gov't Accountability Off., GAO-16-475, *Refundable Tax Credits: Comprehensive Compliance Strategy and Expanded Use of Data Could Strengthen IRS's Efforts to Address Noncompliance* 17 (2016), https://www.gao.gov/assets/680/677548.pdf.

determined that they owe money back, the government is unlikely to receive a direct return of the overpayment: In my experience representing taxpayers in EITC audits, I cannot recall ever working with a taxpayer who had not used the refund, in whole or in part, almost immediately upon receiving it. The debt may eventually be recouped through the IRS's collection process, with interest and applicable penalties, and until that happens, the liability becomes part of the taxpayer's cycle of debt.

Delayed or frozen refunds present their own challenges: Filers who were counting on that refund to pay bills or cover other expenses must wait an uncertain period of time – typically six months or longer, and in some cases more than a year – while trying to resolve the issue.[28]

If the benefit were distributed as a periodic payment, particularly one based on income already earned, the stakes would be lower in either case. If the recipient receives an overpayment, less money will be owed to the government when the error is caught. If the benefit is frozen pending additional substantiation, the filer will still be short money to pay the bills, but they will not have been expecting such a large sum to begin with. In both cases, this assumes a system in which overpayments are also detected and audited periodically, rather than evaluated only in a year-end reconciliation process. This would be most effectively done if coupled with real-time income reporting, which I discuss later in this chapter.

WAYS TO STRUCTURE PERIODIC PAYMENTS

Moving to periodic EITC payments would be a radical shift for the United States. Beyond the pros and cons of making such a shift lie fundamental questions of what it would look like. There are two crucial design questions. The first involves frequency: Should the periodic payment be monthly, quarterly, or some other frequency? Here a reimagination must strike a balance between practical considerations and recipient preferences, as

[28] I have seen refunds frozen for as long as six months to a year when the taxpayer has prevailed at the examination level. If the taxpayer must appeal the examination outcome in Tax Court, it is not unusual for it to take more than a year to resolve the issue. For my clients, this is exacerbated by the reality that the Tax Court typically only has one calendar call a year in Roanoke, Virginia, which is the closest place of trial for most of my clients. However, a National Taxpayer Advocate study reveals that such delays are common in many Tax Court cases: It reported that in 99 out of 256 cases in the research sample, or almost 39 percent of the sample, taxpayers waited an average of almost a year and a half to get the refunds the IRS conceded they were entitled to. *See* TAXPAYER ADVOCATE SERVICE, 2012 ANNUAL REPORT TO CONGRESS (VOL. 2) 77.

understood through empirical research and evidence from prior experiments. Second, should the periodic benefit be based on projected future earnings, as the WfFTC is in New Zealand and as the AEITC was here in the United States? Or should it be based on the past year's earnings, like the current US EITC and the CCB?

In addition to these fundamental design considerations are questions of how income would be reported and reconciled. I consider different approaches and their implications. A shift to a periodic payment structure would be a significant change from the current design, but the design options offer intriguing possibilities for improving the delivery and efficacy of the United States' largest social benefit for working families.

Weekly, Monthly, Quarterly: What Payment Frequency Is Best?

The theory of consumption smoothing suggests that a weekly social benefit distribution may be ideal to help recipients budget effectively. However, that frequency would translate into a relatively small sum weekly of money. For example, in 2016 the maximum available EITC was $6,269; made available weekly, that would be an additional $120.55 per week. This disregards any cap that might be put on the benefit if the money were made available as an advance; Canada, for example, caps its advance WITB at 50 percent of the total. The US AEITC used a similar cap. In 2016, families with children received an average EITC of $3,176.[29] If distributed weekly, that would be an additional $61 per week. There is no doubt that these families could actually *use* an extra $61 per week, but this could diminish or undermine the perceived significance of the benefit.

The idea of distributing relatively small sums frequently runs contrary to the empirical evidence that social scientists such as Sarah Halpern-Meekin and others have collected, which suggests that receiving a larger sum instills pride in work and financial hope. The EITC recipients they interviewed were giddy with excitement about their large windfall. In contrast, working taxpayers interviewed after the 2017 tax reform, which modestly increased take-home pay for many workers by virtue of its reduction in tax rates, shrugged their shoulders at the idea of receiving a little bit extra in each paycheck.[30]

[29] Ctr. on Budget & Policy Priorities, *Policy Basics: The Earned Income Tax Credit* (2018), https://www.cbpp.org/research/federal-tax/policy-basics-the-earned-income-tax-credit.

[30] *See, e.g.*, Halpern-Meekin *et al.*, *supra* note 1, at 69–72 (interviewing taxpayers about lump-sum delivery); *but cf.* Michael Tackett, *Blue-Collar Trump Voters Are Shrugging at Their Tax Cuts*, N.Y. TIMES (Mar. 7, 2018), https://www.nytimes.com/2018/03/07/us/politics/tax-cut-offers-working-class.html.

For this reason, a weekly sum is perhaps too small to make a cognizable difference to taxpayers. Messaging matters in this regard. If a primary goal of the EITC is to motivate working parents to join or stay in the work force, we would want to choose a system that regularly reinforces the value of that choice by delivering amounts that are large enough to be noticeable.

To that end, a monthly benefit would be a more meaningful sum than a weekly benefit. Using the same 2016 tax year numbers as before (and disregarding any percentage caps), under this model a taxpayer receiving the maximum possible EITC would receive $522 per month, and the average working family would receive $265 per month. One advantage of using this monthly distribution model is the messaging: By normalizing the EITC as a monthly benefit, it could help reframe the benefit as a right, an entitlement for workers – rather than just a privilege. Notably, this is how social security benefits are distributed.

A monthly benefit would also mirror the rhythm of the monthly bill cycle. Yet, for that reason, perhaps it would not feel like "forced savings" or offer the hope of accumulating a larger sum that could be put toward debt or durable goods. Ironically, another downside of monthly delivery is that taxpayers may begin to plan on – *to depend on* – that extra monthly benefit in their budgeting. For example, they may rely on it to afford a nicer apartment, or a more expensive car. But if a change in circumstances resulted in a loss or reduction of the benefit – a reduction in income, a child who aged out of EITC, a change in who is the custodial parent – the recipient's budget would be disrupted. Even an examination of one's most recent tax return could potentially disrupt the benefit, since benefits can be frozen while awaiting examination results. Arguably, it may be better for families to budget based on actual income so that they can then apply their EITC to larger financial commitments – debt, unexpected expenses such as car repairs, and larger purchases (as evidence suggests they are doing under the current design).

If providing a safety net for these larger financial commitments is one benefit of the EITC, then perhaps the happy medium between an annual lump sum and a more frequent distribution would be quarterly delivery of the family-support benefit; it provides a significant sum on a regular but not too frequent basis. The 2014 CEP Chicago pilot program, first introduced in Chapter 2, provides some evidence about how taxpayers might perceive quarterly payments. The purpose of the pilot program was to rethink annual lump-sum delivery of the EITC in light of income volatility and debt patterns. As the CEP noted, "providing a large annual lump-sum refund, absent substantial income support during the year, creates an unhealthy and unproductive cycle of scarcity and abundance."[31]

The CEP pilot provided four periodic advances of the EITC to selected participants who it had determined would be eligible for an EITC of at least $600. Participants executed a no-cost loan agreement, with the loan to be repaid once the EITC was received after their 2014 tax return filing. Payments were based on estimated income for 2014; the CEP anticipated the amount of EITC that would be received when a return was filed. Due to concerns about creating an overpayment due at tax time, as well as a desire to preserve "a reasonably large tax refund for most EITC recipients," CEP limited the total periodic payment to 50 percent of the anticipated EITC, up to a maximum of $2,000 total.[32] Periodic payments ranged from $80 to $500 and were distributed in four installments: in May/June, August, October, and December 2014.

The CEP, in partnership with the University of Illinois at Urbana-Champaign, drew three key conclusions from the pilot: (1) 90 percent of participants expressed a preference for the periodic payment model over a single lump sum; (2) periodic payments diminish debt accumulation and late fees; and (3) periodic payments appeared to reduce financial stress and correlate with better mental health.[33] The CEP concluded that "spreading out a portion of the tax refund payment makes sense," and it recommended expanded pilot programs and future research on the issue, noting the importance of taxpayer feedback and input to any change in design.[34]

The question of delivery timing must weigh practical considerations and preferences, bearing in mind the purpose of the family-support benefit. Quarterly distribution offers a way to balance the benefits of regular delivery alongside psychologically significant sums.

Past or Future Earnings: Which Income Measure Is Best?

Currently, the EITC is calculated based on last year's earnings, without regard to the taxpayer's current financial circumstances. For example, a taxpayer who worked and was income eligible in 2017 would receive the benefit after filing a return in the early months of 2018. Notwithstanding compliance challenges and third-party information timing issues, this approach is the most accurate measurement of what the taxpayer earned for the prior calendar year. Because

[31] Bellisle & Marzahl, *supra* note 12, at 4.
[32] *Id.* at 5.
[33] *Id.* at 7–8.
[34] *Id.* at 9.

the measuring period has ended, there is no need to adjust the payment if the recipient's situation changes during the year, as there is with the WfFTC in New Zealand, and there is no need to reconcile the credit at the end of the year, as there was in calculating the AEITC.

The CCB is calculated on prior-year earnings. It is recalculated every July. Taxpayers are required to report any change in marital status during the year to the CRA, because that would affect the benefit amount going forward. Recall, however, that work is not a condition of receiving the CCB. Therefore, unlike the EITC, it is not a programmatic goal to instill a sense of a bonus or reward for having worked.

Certain US social benefits are determined based on past earnings, while others are based on an estimate of current or future earnings. We can look to these designs by way of analogy as we consider an EITC delivery redesign.

Pros and Cons of a Past Earnings Model

Social security is an example of a benefit based on past rather than current or future earnings: retirement and disability benefits are calculated according to lifetime average earnings. Insofar as social security benefits represent a retirement incentive or a reward for work, this is a good analogy to the EITC. Like the EITC, social security also functions as a safety net.

Of course, these benefits generally are paid after retirement, rather than as an annual supplement while working. By the time the benefit begins, the agency can easily calculate the earnings on which the benefits are based. Apart from inflation adjustments, there is no annual fluctuation in a recipient's social security benefits; there is only a possibility that the benefits may be taxed as income if the recipient has sufficient levels of income from a spouse or other sources.

Medicare premiums are also determined in part based on prior-year income; recipients above a certain income level are required to pay higher premiums for Medicare Part B and prescription drug coverage. Unlike social security benefits, which do not fluctuate, the premium associated with this Medicare benefit may fluctuate annually according to income level. The Social Security Administration (SSA) makes this determination using the income reported on the most recently available tax return. For those who have to pay the higher premiums, there is also a form to report a change in circumstance should income be diminished; the agency can use this information to reduce premiums accordingly.

There are other analogies to draw on in the Internal Revenue Code. For example, individuals holding certain tax-favored retirement accounts must take required minimum distributions from the account annually once they reach age seventy years and six months. The minimum amount is calculated by reference to the balance of the account at the end of the prior calendar year. This reference to a temporarily arbitrary, yet fixed, balance is a bright-line rule that provides clarity and ease to the taxpayer when calculating the required minimum.

If EITC periodic payments were based on the prior tax year's earnings, that would retain the current EITC approach and allow for more accurate third-party information reporting before the benefit is paid. It would be relatively straightforward to move to a model of periodic payments based on last year's income. In fact, it would allow the IRS greater certainty in making accurate payments, because it would allow more time for income verification with third parties.

However, from a taxpayer perspective, moving to this model might feel both unfair and paternalistic; it would be a delayed distribution of what the taxpayer is currently entitled to as one lump sum. When first implemented, this would seem like something taken away, not something given, as if it were a deferral rather than an advance. It also presents a temporal disconnect between the work and the bonus; for example, if the United States moved to four quarterly payments, the fourth payment would be paid more than a year after the work had been performed. There would surely be transitional backlash to such a proposal.

A deferred periodic delivery of the EITC coupled with special incentives for savings, such as has been proposed by some scholars and policy makers,[35] could make this past earnings approach more palatable to recipients, especially during a design transition. Short of that, moving to periodic payments based on past earnings might feel like a move backwards for the EITC.

Pros and Cons of a Current/Future Earnings Model

Calculating the EITC according to current or predicted future earnings leaves the taxpayer vulnerable to owing an overpayment at the end of the year. This risk is one reason that many observers believe the AEITC had such a low take-up rate: Taxpayers would rather defer the benefit than risk owing money to the government at the end of the year.

[35] *See, e.g.*, HALPERN-MEEKIN *ET AL.*, *supra* note 1, at 210–13; Greene, *supra* note 3; *see also* David M. Herszenhorn, *Senators Propose Holding Part of Refunds for Taxpayers' 'Rainy Day' Funds*, N.Y. TIMES (Apr. 14, 2016, 6:00 AM), https://www.nytimes.com/politics/first-draft/2016/04/14/senators-propose-holding-portion-of-tax-refunds-for-rainy-day.

Yet many other "safety net" program benefits, such as such as TANF (Temporary Assistance for Needy Families), SNAP, CHIP (Children's Health Insurance Program), and SSI (Supplemental Security Income) are based on information provided about current and expected income. Recipients are expected to report any change in circumstance, including an increase in income, to the appropriate agency. An intentional failure to report such changes can result in a sanction such as suspension of benefits.

When an overpayment occurs in these various social benefit programs, the overpayment generally must be repaid by the recipient. However, one stark difference between the EITC and other programs is that other programs categorize *why* the overpayment occurred and respond accordingly. For example, SNAP has different recoupment options depending on whether an overpayment resulted from an "intentional program violation," "inadvertent household error," or "agency error." Recipients who made an intentional violation are subject to a higher recoupment rate than those who made an inadvertent error or were subject to agency error.[36]

In contrast, the IRS generally has no idea why an EITC overpayment occurred, because it lacks the information or the resources to ascertain whether the ineligible taxpayer made an honest mistake or an intentional one. In general, the IRS responds in the same manner to a taxpayer who knowingly claims an unrelated child who does not live in their household as it responds to a taxpayer who mistakenly claims their own child in a shared-custody situation who lived with them for only 182 days.

For the IRS to distinguish between an "intentional program violation" and an "inadvertent household error," the agency would need to gather more information from the recipient when the benefit is first claimed. Making this determination after the fact is nearly impossible; currently, a significant percentage of taxpayers who are audited on the EITC do not respond to the audit.[37] Presumably, filers don't respond for a variety of reasons. But the IRS cannot make a fair determination in the face of silence.

The flexibility for an agency to change the benefit as circumstances change, and the ability to respond to individual recipients on a regular basis, costs money. As noted, EITC administration is stunningly inexpensive compared to the overhead costs of other social benefit programs, and this is one major

[36] *See, e.g.*, Virginia Department of Social Services, www.dss.virginia.gov/files/division/bp/fs/manual/P17.pdf p. 8.

[37] *See* Taxpayer Advocate Service, 2015 Annual Report to Congress (Vol. 1) 249 (citing a no-response rate of 45 percent in FY 2014, and noting that this rate raises "questions about the accuracy of some default assessments and of the audit's effectiveness as an educational tool for future compliance").

reason why. The drawback, however, is that the agency is underprepared to respond to overpayments and is very slow in its audit determinations. According to IRS performance statistics, the average time for the examination division to resolve an EITC audit is approximately 200 days.[38]

If the EITC were delivered periodically and its amount calculated according to current or predicted earnings, the IRS would continue to struggle with income verification and year-end reconciliation. There are at least two ways to address this struggle, which are not interdependent, but could be designed to work in tandem. The first is by moving to real-time income reporting and using the most recent quarter's earnings; this would facilitate income verification, improving accuracy and thereby reducing the need for year-end reconciliation. I see this as the ideal option, but technology limitations currently make this unrealistic. At the same time, this option presents many worthwhile ideas for envisioning social benefits in the future.

The other solution would calculate benefits using current estimated income but would allow leeway in the event of overpayment and not seek repayment when too much is paid out. As I will discuss, this would mitigate or eliminate recipient concerns about owing money to the government at the end of the year.

Real-Time Income Eligibility: A Worthwhile but Currently Unviable Possibility

My ideal proposal is for the United States to move to a model of quarterly social benefits based on the recipient's most recent three months of work. Messaged properly, this structure would reward work on a regular basis while providing families significant income support several times a year. Because it would be measured by work already performed, this design avoids the difficulties of estimating future income and the risks associated with end-of-year reconciliation.

To move to such a model, it would be necessary to require real-time payroll income reporting from employers, a system not currently in place in the United States. Currently, employers are required to use Form W-2 to report wage information to the SSA by January 31. The SSA then shares this information with the IRS, which uses it to match income reported by taxpayers on their returns.

[38] US Gov't Accountability Off., GAO-14-479, *IRS Correspondence Audits: Better Management Could Improve Tax Compliance and Reduce Taxpayer Burden* 44 (2014), https://www.gao.gov/assets/670/663840.pdf.

Before the enactment of the PATH Act in December 2015, employers had more time to submit Form W-2: If they submitted the forms on paper, they had until the end of February, and if they submitted them electronically, they had until the end of March. A timing mismatch existed under this system: The IRS was processing returns and issuing EITC refunds before it had any verifiable information on file from employers. Concerned about the high EITC overpayment rate, Congress moved the information reporting deadline to January 31 and also required the IRS to hold any refunds that included the EITC or the refundable portion of the CTC until February 15. This allows the IRS a short window to compare information on returns to EITC claims. This law was aimed at reducing large-scale tax return–related identity theft and refundable credit fraud, though it allows an opportunity for verification of all EITC claims. This is appropriate tax administration policy; though low-income taxpayers were accustomed to filing as early as possible to receive their much-needed benefit, by moving the W-2 deadline to January 31, the timing of refunds changed by only a few weeks.

That being said, EITC income verification does not depend on the full Form W-2. Form W-2 contains a lot of information that is not relevant to determining a taxpayer's EITC eligibility: For example, it includes information on deferred compensation, disability pay, employer-sponsored health care coverage, contributions to medical savings accounts and health savings accounts, and contributions to dependent care accounts. Employers must gather this information from multiple third-party sources, and the comprehensive nature of this form makes it difficult for employers to submit it earlier than the January 31 deadline.[39]

To determine income eligibility for the EITC, the IRS needs to determine two things: one, the amount of earned income, which includes wages, salaries, and tips that are includible in gross income, plus the taxpayer's net earnings from self-employment; and two, the amount of "disqualified income," which refers to the limit on investment income. Thus the IRS does not need Form W-2 to determine EITC eligibility. It only needs information about wages, salaries, and tips paid. The IRS already receives this aggregate information quarterly from most employers: Employers whose annual liability for social security, Medicare, and withheld federal income taxes is more than $1,000 are required to file Form 941 quarterly. Form 941 requires information about total wages paid by the employer. While it does not include a breakdown per employee (which is what would be necessary to verify EITC income

[39] *See, e.g.*, Statement of Lori Brown on behalf of the American Payroll Association (Jan. 25, 2012), https://www.irs.gov/pub/irs-utl/lori_brown_american_payroll_association.pdf.

eligibility), certainly employers have that underlying information at hand in their payroll department. Of course, asking employers to break down that information for the IRS in addition to what is already required would impose a new (and some might argue, undue) burden on the employer side.

In 2011, then-IRS Commissioner Doug Shulman outlined a vision for the IRS to move to real-time reporting. His vision of "real time" is different from mine: When he spoke of "real time," Shulman was hoping the IRS could have access to wage information *during*, as opposed to *after*, filing season.[40] My vision of real time is for the IRS to have access to wage information as it is earned and paid throughout the year (which means having it *before* the start of the filing season). The IRS held public forums to gather feedback on Shulman's idea of real-time reporting. Despite pushback from various industries about the burdens and disadvantages of making income information available sooner, Shulman's vision took a big step forward with the PATH Act, which was enacted several years after he introduced the Real Time initiative.

But it is not unrealistic to envision a more ambitious system akin to my vision of real time, one in which the IRS has access to wage information almost instantaneously, with every payment period. In this regard, the United States lags far behind many other countries in its income reporting and wage withholding methods. While the United States does not even have real-time income reporting, many other countries have adopted a pay-as-you-earn (PAYE) structure. Though a move to PAYE is not a prerequisite for real-time income reporting or for my proposal, this system merits a brief discussion because it illustrates how technology can advance and simplify tax administration.

Pay-as-You-Earn

Australia, Ireland, the United Kingdom, New Zealand, and many other countries have moved to PAYE, which in turn has simplified tax filing and reduced burdens on the public. Sometimes referred to as "precision withholding," PAYE involves real-time employer wage reporting to the revenue agency; because the agency has real-time information about cumulative income earned throughout the year, the employer can adjust withholding accordingly on an ongoing basis. The result is that many taxpayers pay exactly the right amount in withholding. They neither owe nor are due a refund, and because

[40] I.R.S. News Release IR-2011-114 (Nov. 30, 2011).

the tax agency already knows this, taxpayers need not even file a tax return.[41] PAYE is intended to simplify tax obligations for wage earners; it does not apply to self-employed taxpayers.[42]

Policy makers and scholars have articulated several advantages to moving to a PAYE system of precision withholding. A major advantage is simplification. Journalist T.R. Reid's recent book, *A Fine Mess: A Global Quest for a Simpler, Fairer, and More Efficient Tax System*, advocates for simplification and a move toward pre-populated returns, which are used in other countries.[43] Reid argues that the act of filing taxes should be made simpler for the public, as it is in many other developed democracies. Pre-populated returns – forms that are individualized for taxpayers based on income information available to the government, such as that reported in the United States on Forms W-2 and 1099 – would lift the burden of information gathering and calculation off taxpayers, and might largely eliminate the need for return preparers in the individual return context.

Michael Hatfield advocates for a move to PAYE on cybersecurity grounds: "[t]o the extent refunds became the exception rather than the rule, the refund payment process could be more tightly controlled, reducing the ease with which fraudulently filed returns succeed at stealing refund payments."[44] As I have noted previously, tax-related identity theft remains a major challenge for the IRS today, with billions of dollars in refunds at stake.

The PAYE model is a stark contrast to the current US model for wage earners, in which employers withhold taxes from each paycheck but do not report wage information to the IRS until the tax year ends. Before the United States could move to a PAYE system, social benefits would have to be decoupled from the tax refund. As Hatfield points out, running social benefits through the tax refund prevents the United States from moving to a cumulative PAYE system, because there can be no precision withholding if employers have to factor in EITC and Child Tax Credit (CTC) eligibility.[45] Having social benefits based upon income but delivered separate from a tax refund

41 William J. Turnier, *PAYE as an Alternative to an Alternative Tax System*, 23 VA. TAX REV. 205 (2003). In his study of the UK system, Turnier found "the coordination between the PAYE system and the income tax law works so well that all but about nine million out of the approximately twenty-six million British taxpayers do not need to file an annual self-assessment." *Id.* at 235.

42 *Id.* at 224.

43 T.R. REID, A FINE MESS: A GLOBAL QUEST FOR A SIMPLER, FAIRER, AND MORE EFFICIENT TAX SYSTEM (Penguin Books 2017).

44 Hatfield, *supra* note 26, at 1196.

45 *Id.* (describing the ways in which the United States would need to simplify its tax system before it could move to PAYE).

would still present a cybersecurity risk (in that significant sums of money are still being transferred from the government to individual recipients), but it splits the information such that there is less aggregate sensitive data in one place.[46]

Moving to a PAYE system would greatly simplify tax filing, which might also improve compliance. Kathleen DeLaney Thomas argues that the procedural complexity of tax filing deters voluntary compliance: Taxpayers may want to be honest, but the filing obligations are mentally draining, causing filers to behave passively and making them more likely to be dishonest.[47] Thomas proposes moving to a system of taxpayer-specific online accounts with third-party data retrieval, which could then be automatically transferred to a tax return for the taxpayer to review.[48]

There are several other features in the Internal Revenue Code that complicate a move to PAYE: different rate structures depending on marital status; the absence of at-source withholding for interest and dividends; the nature of the progressive rate structure; and the treatment of capital gains.[49] To adopt PAYE, the United States would have to consider several simplifications to the current system. Removing family-based refundable credits from the tax return filing process would certainly facilitate a move to PAYE.

As to the question of whether to base family-support benefits on past or future income: Moving to real-time income reporting, even if it were something short of a PAYE system, would facilitate periodic distribution of social benefits because earnings could be periodically calculated and reported to the IRS as they are earned. Real-time information might even allow the government to adjust the size of the credit up or down based on the most recent earnings.

An Ideal Structure: Quarterly Distribution with Real-Time Reporting

There are many ways to envision income measuring. If the United States moved to real-time income reporting coupled with a quarterly distribution of the EITC, each quarter's payment could be calculated on the prior three-month earnings testing period, without regard to what the taxpayer's total annual income might be. For example, a taxpayer whose employment status fluctuates, or whose earnings might vary seasonally, might receive the EITC

46 I am grateful to Michael Hatfield for this conversational insight.

47 Kathleen DeLaney Thomas, *User-Friendly Taxpaying*, 92 Ind. L. J. 1509, 1526–30 (2017).

48 *Id.* at 1542–44.

49 Turnier, *supra* note 41, at 249.

for quarters 1 and 2, but not at all for quarters 3 and 4. This might be because the individual did not work during quarters 3 and 4, or it might be because the individual earned too much in those quarters to receive the benefit. We could design a system in which the recipient would not have to repay any benefit received in quarters 1 and 2 regardless. To the extent that the individual's annual earnings might exceed what we have historically viewed as an appropriate EITC earnings threshold, this quarterly benefit will have helped the worker at a time when the individual had less income to rely on (quarters 1 and 2) and then was absent when the individual was in a better cash-flow position. To the extent that the individual received nothing in quarters 3 and 4 because no work was performed, he or she would have at least received a supplement for quarters 1 and 2 that would help bridge the period of unemployment, as opposed to waiting half a year longer for a lump-sum refund. Either way, the individual can draw a fairly clear connection between the work performed and the benefit received for that quarter. It is critical that recipients not be penalized for being income eligible in one quarter but not the next. The population that receives the EITC is transient, in part because of income fluctuation from year to year. Currently, there is turnover by about one-third as to which individuals are eligible from one year to the next.[50]

Of course, this design would only work if employers moved to real-time income reporting for wages, and it would only work for individuals who are employees rather than independent contractors or self-employed. Perhaps a self-reporting system could allow non-wage earners to receive a quarterly family-support benefit. Some independent contractor income information is available instantly, such as for Uber and Lyft drivers. One concern with self-reporting is that it would leave the benefit open to (even greater) manipulation by cash-based self-employed taxpayers, who might choose to report earnings or expenses in the wrong quarter to maximize their benefit. Another concern is that the EITC measures *net* self-employment income; quarterly self-reporting would have to include calculation of both income and allowable expenses. Perhaps this design would work very well in a cashless world, where every transaction was electronic. But that is not the world we live in now.

One possible design solution would be to treat self-employment income differently than wage income, both for tax purposes and for EITC purposes. For example, in his bill proposing something similar to a PAYE system for the United States, Senator Byron Dorgan suggested a tax exemption for up to $2,500 of non-wage income ($5,000 if married filing jointly). The EITC

50 I.R.S. News Release IR-2016-11 (Jan. 29, 2016).

design could exclude an amount (say $2,500) of non-wage income both from tax and from inclusion in determining the EITC benefit. Thus, at a low income level, non-wage income would not increase the EITC benefit, but it also would not be subject to tax. At an income level above which the EITC starts to phase out, it would not decrease the EITC, and it would still not be subject to tax. For better or for worse, such a design might encourage the working poor to seek out wage earner positions as their primary source of income. But it would not disincentivize nonemployee side work to supplement regular wage income.

A similar but slightly different design solution, which Jonathan Barry Forman proposed many years ago to simplify the EITC, would be to exclude self-employment income from the definition of "earned income" for EITC calculation purposes. Forman argued that doing so would curb the incentive for low-income individuals to report fictitious earnings to maximize their EITC.[51] The state of California experimented with something very similar, also for compliance concerns: When it initially enacted its state-level EITC, it excluded self-employment income from the calculation of earned income.[52] Given the prevalence of alternative work arrangements such as independent contractors, as well as the rise of the gig economy, excluding self-employment earnings might shut out a significant segment of workers who currently are eligible to receive the EITC.

A separate but similar complication with quarterly real-time reporting arises for EITC recipients who hold income-producing assets. Individuals who receive investment income above a certain threshold ($3,750 in 2017) are ineligible to receive the EITC. This rule is intended to disqualify people with amassed wealth from receiving the benefit. For most people, the presence of significant investment income is relatively steady from one year to the next; either one possesses amassed wealth or one does not. Given that, the IRS could easily look to the prior year's income tax return and use any reported investment income to determine eligibility instead of trying to make a real-time determination about quarterly investment income, which would be difficult if not impossible to do accurately.

[51] Jonathan Barry Forman, *Simplification for Low-Income Taxpayers: Some Options* 57 OHIO ST. L. J. 145, 183 (1996).

[52] Leslie Book, *U.S. Refundable Credits: The Taxing Realities of Being Poor*, 4:2 J. OF TAX ADMIN. 71 (2018) (describing California's experiment as "a cautionary tale showing how the EITC compliance problem can contribute to unfairly punishing taxpayers in an economy that they do not have much power over, instead of thinking through the difficult task of compliance and establishing compliance norms"). *Id.* at 84. In 2017, California relaxed this approach and included self-employment income in its calculation. *Id.* at 83.

Another complication with a real-time quarterly benefit is the qualifying child determination. A qualifying child must live with an EITC recipient for more than half the year – but how would this be measured in real time? In many cases, it would be relatively simple: If a child lives with a parent continuously, there could be a presumption of eligibility until a change is reported. But in shared custody situations, the parents may not know until the end of the year where the qualifying child spent more time. My reimagination of the EITC proposes that the EITC be available in part to both parents in a shared-custody situation; this would eliminate the need to make a real-time custody determination.

Quarterly Benefits Based on Current Estimated Income: An Alternate, More Viable Proposal

While I view real-time income reporting and quarterly distribution as the ideal design for distributing the EITC, the United States has far to go in establishing the necessary technology. Short of that, there is a less precise but adequate alternative: quarterly benefits based on current estimated income. Eligible working families would receive a quarterly distribution based on current income estimates, with a cap limiting how much advance they could receive in a given year based on their prior-year EITC. If this proposal were adopted, there must be no clawbacks for overpayment: The recipient should not bear the risk of overpayment. Politically, this might be more viable if the cap on total advance payments was a percentage (50, 65, or perhaps 75 percent) of the recipient's prior-year EITC. In other words, total advance distributions would never be more than what one received the year before.

To illustrate: A taxpayer would be required to file an income tax return by April 15, as always. The payment schedule cycle for the EITC benefit might be, say, April 30, July 31, October 31, and January 31. As proposed in my reimagination, the form for claiming benefits would be decoupled from the tax return. The family would file a tax return for the prior year, but benefits received beginning on April 30 of the current year would be based on the current year's estimated income.

An obvious drawback of this approach is that the process for claiming the benefit based on estimated earnings is more complicated. If the benefit were based on last year's earnings, the taxpayer would not need to provide any estimated income information. Instead, the agency could simply calculate the appropriate benefit and distribute it to the family beginning April 30 of the current year, based on the filing for the prior year.

In contrast, this estimated earnings approach would require recipients to estimate earnings based on their current position. Each year, after filing a tax return for the prior year, taxpayers would have to provide a good-faith estimate of earnings for the current year, and the agency would use that figure to determine the periodic benefit. This is not an insurmountable task; it is what families do in New Zealand. Alternatively, instead of trying to provide an estimate of expected income for the year, taxpayers who have received the benefit for a qualifying child in past years could simply submit their most recent paystub to prove that they are working. We could design the system so that workers would receive the same benefit in Year 2 that they received in Year 1. If, when they filed a Year 2 tax return in Year 3, it turned out they were entitled to a higher benefit, it could be credited towards Year 2's tax liability (or could be refundable in a lump sum if the entitlement exceeded that liability). If it turned out that they had been paid too much in Year 2, there would be no amount due; however, their Year 3 periodic payments would be capped at the total that they *should have* received in Year 2.

As discussed earlier, SNAP and TANF are costly programs in part because of the human resources required; social workers must spend time verifying claims and processing updates. The EITC, on the other hand, is inexpensive to administer because taxpayers self-declare eligibility and the claim is run through computer filters. This proposed good-faith estimate, or "no claw-back," approach would be less expensive to administer than a program in which taxpayers are required to report changes in circumstance. There is an added cost, in that the government bears the risk of overpayment to any taxpayer whose eligibility changes during the year, but the risk is capped: It is limited to the amount paid to that individual in the prior year, and would be recalculated accordingly in the following year.

This proposal requires us to reconceptualize how we view the EITC. It requires us, as a society, to accept some level of individuated overpayment from year to year as an acceptable cost of the program. Is that politically feasible? Perhaps not. This is why messaging matters: The overpayment would be going to working parents at low-income levels; no one would receive it unless without being income eligible the prior year.

This proposal is politically complicated. Many observers will not like the idea of not having clawbacks. Though the EITC is not welfare, strictly speaking, there has long been criticism associated with the idea that some recipients get more than they "deserve" or have "earned." I suggest allowing a cap of up to the full amount the taxpayer received the year prior, but there are more modest design options.

For example, Steve Holt has proposed an accelerated quarterly disbursement of up to 50 percent of the prior year's EITC, to provide a cushion for a year-end adjustment, with a "safe harbor" provision, meaning there is no repayment obligation if the overpayment was based on valid expectations of eligibility.[53] Holt suggests a standard of "presumption of reasonableness for estimates made under penalties of perjury ... coupled with a requirement of timely notification of changes."[54] He illustrates this with an example of those who start a higher-paying job: They would be required to communicate this increase in expected total annual earnings within 30 days; any overpayments after this 30-day deadline that result from the failure to communicate the change would not be covered by the safe harbor. Holt contrasts this example with that of a taxpayer who only learns after the end of the year that someone else would be claiming the child she had previously been qualified to claim for the EITC; that if that change in circumstance was unforeseen, this taxpayer should be protected by the safe harbor.[55] Holt argues that "the design challenge is to keep the inefficiency within reasonable bounds."[56] In other words, some degree of inaccuracy is inevitable and can be tolerated, but it should be minimized so that the program mostly reaches its target population.

The disbursement cap could be something other than 50 percent; it could be 75 percent, for example. A capped percentage approach would be more cost-effective to the government (resulting in fewer dollars overpaid), but the amount of each quarterly payment would be less meaningful to recipients. Still, it would be an improvement over the current system.

Looking to other social benefit programs, there is some precedent for the idea of ignoring overpayments. Other social benefits, such as unemployment insurance and state TANF programs, include an earnings disregard provision. Generally, this works similarly to the current EITC phase out; as earnings increase, the benefit decreases. But in certain contexts, earnings may be tolerated and entirely ignored up to certain limits. For example, Social Security Disability Income (SSDI) recipients can earn any amount above a specific threshold for up to nine months (over a five-year period) without any

[53] *See* Stephen D. Holt, *Periodic Payment of the Earned Income Tax Credit*, The Brookings Inst. (June 5, 2008), https://www.brookings.edu/research/periodic-payment-of-the-earned-income-tax-credit; Steve Holt, *Periodic Payment of the Earned Income Tax Credit Revisited*, The Brookings Inst. (Dec. 17, 2015), https://www.brookings.edu/research/periodic-payment-of-the-earned-income-tax-credit-revisited.

[54] Holt, *Periodic Payment of the Earned Income Tax Credit Revisited*, *supra* note 53, at 20.

[55] *Id.* at 20–21.

[56] Holt, *Periodic Payment of the Earned Income Tax Credit*, *supra* note 53, at 16.

reduction in their benefits, so long as they report their work.[57] The intent is to ease the recipient back into the work force through a "trial work period," but with a safety net in place in case the disability makes work intolerable in the long run. Just as we tolerate a transition period of SSDI benefits when a person with a disability attempts to return to the work force, is there not room to imagine a social policy in which we tolerate economic mobility without a clawback?

As noted, these shifts require us to reconceptualize the EITC and its recipients. What if we viewed EITC recipients similarly to those who receive SSDI benefits? The EITC is an important antipoverty supplement, yet recipients are in part a transient population; as noted, recipient turnover is as high as one-third each year.[58] Some recipients receive the credit inconsistently or only once in a period of years; at the same time, a sizable percentage receives it year after year.[59] If recipients reach the tipping point at which they are no longer income eligible because their family is financially better off, is that not a milestone to be celebrated? To the extent that a family receives an overpayment in the last year of eligibility, or receives a payment for which they are no longer eligible, this represents economic progress for that family. The family should not then receive the benefit in the subsequent year, but the last (over) payment can serve as an extra savings cushion for emergencies if that family experiences a change in circumstances later.

If estimating earnings and providing a no-clawback rule is too complicated or not a politically viable design for EITC reform, there are other ways to design a periodic system. Another design proposal would be to give all parents a small, fixed, quarterly EITC (e.g., $500 per quarter) in the first year they become working parents. They would apply for the benefit using the two-page form and submit a paystub to prove earnings. Congress could choose a minimum amount of earnings – for example, $3,000 – required to establish eligibility; workers would have to submit a paystub or other proof that they met the year-to-date minimum. In effect, this would be a one-time support bonus for all parents in the work force. There would be no clawback or end-of-year adjustment for overpayment in the recipient's first year, though recipients would get a credit if their EITC should have been higher than the sums received. After the first year, quarterly distribution would be based on the *prior year's* income.

57 SSA, *Pub. No.* 64-030 28 (2018), https://www.ssa.gov/redbook/eng/ssdi-only-employment-supports.htm.

58 I.R.S., *supra* note 50.

59 Holt, *Periodic Payment of the Earned Income Tax Credit*, *supra* note 53, at 16 (citing W&I Research, "EITC Trends Analysis" (IRS 2006)).

This option is less administratively complicated (and likely less expensive) than using an estimated approach year after year, though it does not match taxpayers' current cash needs as accurately as an estimated approach would, and taxpayers may view it as a deferral of payment for a benefit already earned. Once again, to reduce the burden on taxpayers to report changes, the administrative time involved for the agency to make those changes, and the risk to taxpayers of owing money, we would need to accept the possibility of first-year overpayments (with no expectation of repayment) as "rough justice" of sorts.

Periodic for All, or Opt In?

Lastly, another critical design question is whether periodic payments should be the only default, or a design opt-in. In New Zealand, recipients choose between weekly, fortnightly, or annual lump-sum payments. In Canada, the default delivery for the WITB is an annual lump sum, but recipients can elect to receive advance payments quarterly. The CCB is delivered monthly, with no option to receive it differently.

I favor either a mandatory periodic payment distribution or a periodic payment default, with the ability for taxpayers to opt instead for a deferred lump sum at the end of the year. Being able to choose a deferred lump sum would give recipients control. Preserving this option would offset the criticism that moving to periodic payment is a paternalistic design choice that strips recipients of autonomy or implies an inability to make rational financial choices.

Scholars who have interviewed lump-sum EITC recipients have proposed ideas to encourage taxpayers to save, rather than spend, their EITC. These ideas include a proposal for a deferred EITC election and an emergency savings account funded by one's EITC.[60] These ideas, which inspired a Senate bill, are intended to address the fact that one in three Americans have no financial savings at all and are ill-prepared to deal with the day-to-day financial emergencies that arise in life, such as a broken-down car or a hiccup in employment.[61] These proposals introduce the idea of a "savings bonus," meaning recipients receive a higher amount if they defer the benefit until the end of the year. I like this concept, but for many taxpayers this undercuts the

[60] *See* HALPERN-MEEKIN *ET AL.*, *supra* note 1, at 210–13; Greene, *supra* note 3.
[61] Press Release, Sen. Cory Booker; Booker, Moran Introduce Bill Empowering Taxpayers to Defer Refund for Rainy Day Savings (Apr. 13, 2016), https://www.booker.senate.gov/?p=press_release&id=403.

usefulness of periodic payments. If recipients cannot access the money when they need it, they may turn to unfavorable financial products or credit cards.

That said, not all EITC recipients are in dire financial straits year after year. Some EITC recipients may already have an emergency savings fund or may be able to routinely rely on a family member or partner when a financial shock hits. These individuals may prefer to elect deferred lump-sum delivery with the option of a savings bonus. In a similar vein, not all EITC recipients are eligible on a regular basis; those who earn too much to be routinely income eligible for the EITC may have a greater need following a year in which their income dropped enough to make them eligible.

The ability to opt out of periodic distribution would give taxpayers greater autonomy and control over their family-support benefit. As a design question, policy makers need to consider which delivery is the default, and which is the "opt out." Behavioral studies suggest that the selection of a default is a significant design question, with inertia potentially playing a role after the default selection. This has been studied in the context of retirement savings contributions, with some scholars suggesting that automatic enrollment of new hires in the company 401(k) plan should be the design default.[62]

One such experiment nudged low-income taxpayers to consider a default at tax return preparation whereby part of their tax refund could be directed into savings bonds. In that experiment, the vast majority of taxpayers opted out of that option, preferring to receive the full lump sum at filing time as they had done in the past.[63]

I would choose a different type of nudge – establishing deferred periodic payments as the default, with the ability to opt out and receive a *deferred* lump sum that would include a savings bonus. The choice would be between receiving smaller benefits sooner and then periodically and waiting an entire year to receive the benefit. If a taxpayer routinely opted out and chose to receive a deferred lump sum with a savings bonus, this would become an annually recurring event that would look much like the current system. However, it would require the taxpayer to opt out initially and then conclude that the delayed lump sum refund worked well for their household. A taxpayer who did not like the delayed lump sum could decide not to opt out in the next cycle – and vice-versa.

[62] *See e.g.*, Brigitte C. Madrian & Dennis F. Shea, *The Power of Suggestion: Inertia in 401(k) Participation and Savings Behavior*, 116 Q. J. OF ECON. 1149 (2001).

[63] Erin T. Bronchetti, Thomas S. Dee, David B. Huffman, & Ellen Magenheim, *When a Nudge Isn't Enough: Defaults and Saving among Low-Income Tax Filers*, 66 NAT'L TAX J. 609 (2013).

SHOWING ELIGIBILITY TO CLAIM THE FAMILY-SUPPORT BENEFIT

Moving to periodic payments would present an opportunity for the IRS to rethink other aspects of EITC delivery, especially if the process for claiming the family-support benefit were decoupled from tax return filing. Reimagining how one would claim the EITC, and redesigning the form and procedure, presents an opportunity to incorporate lessons learned over multiple decades about EITC noncompliance and overpayments. As discussed previously, income misreporting errors are the most common cause of EITC overclaims, but qualifying child and filing status errors also contribute to the high improper payment rate. If the family-support benefit is claimed separately from a tax return, there are several ways that the IRS might improve the benefit eligibility determination.

One improvement would be to require the claimant to provide affirmative information about eligibility on the initial claim form, while keeping the form simple. For example, in the first year in which they claim a child, taxpayers might be asked to provide a brief written explanation about the circumstances of how that child came to live in their house. As discussed previously, claiming dependents as well as the CTC and EITC on a tax return requires a complicated determination of overlapping but different questions, including income, age, and residence – and taxpayers do not always apply the rules correctly.

The Tax Cuts and Jobs Act of 2017 suspended the deduction for personal and dependent exemptions while simultaneously increasing the standard deduction for all filing statuses. These provisions went into effect for tax year 2018 and are temporary; they expire after 2025. If Congress were to make them permanent, in some sense it would simplify tax return filing and reduce complexity. The definition of a dependent is broader than the definition of a qualifying child. When the deduction for personal and dependent exemptions was in effect, a taxpayer generally could claim any person residing in their household as a dependent if the income and support test were met, regardless of whether that person was related to them in any fashion. Thus, it was not uncommon that a taxpayer could claim his or her unmarried partner's children as dependents, even though they were not the taxpayer's children or stepchildren. For many taxpayers, this created a level of confusion; if they supported these children and could claim them as dependents, why were they not allowed to claim them for purposes of the CTC and the EITC?

Among the clients I have represented in EITC audits over a period of more than ten years, this is the most common error I see. It is often hard to ascertain a client's intent in these cases. Some taxpayers seem genuinely confused about why they were not eligible to claim their partner's children for the EITC, given the support they provide. Others likely knew they were ineligible under the letter of the law, but felt entitled to it and assumed the IRS was unlikely to question the return, so they claimed the EITC anyway. In my role as their attorney, I help these clients amend their return and explain why the children meet the test for dependents (assuming they meet the test for "qualifying relatives") but not for the CTC or EITC (because one cannot be a "qualifying child" without a parental or legal relationship).

Imagine if EITC benefits were claimed through an entirely separate process. The family-support form instructions could make it very clear that the application requires a qualifying relative (child, stepchild, nephew, niece, grandchild, etc.). There would be no room for a "good-faith" error, because applicants would no longer be thinking of a broader universe of who can be claimed as a dependent on a tax return.

In Canada, parents claim the CCB on a two-page application form; once the primary caregiver registers the child, there is no need to reapply, and the CRA uses the information for all child benefit programs it administers. The form asks the applicant to provide the child's (or children's) name, gender, place and date of birth, the date the applicant "became primarily responsible for the care and upbringing of this child," and whether the applicant is in a shared-custody situation with respect to the child. The application also asks if this reflects a change in recipient for benefits; if so, the applicant must provide the name, address, and telephone number of the person or agency with whom the child resided previously. If no one has previously claimed the child for benefits, the applicant must enclose proof of birth if either of two situations applies: the child was born outside Canada, or the child is one year of age or older. (Parents can register newborn babies through an automated process.) A female parent generally does not need to enclose supporting documents showing she is the primary caregiver, though the form notes that the agency may need to request other documents later. Because the law presumes that the primary caregiver is female, if a male and female parent live in the same home, the application states that a male applicant must enclose a signed note from the female parent asserting that he is primarily responsible for all the children in the household.

The Canadian approach – a simple one-time registration and an explanation when there is a change in recipient of benefits for a child – makes practical sense. In the United States, if an EITC claimant has not claimed a child in the past, there are only three possible reasons: the claimant has not been income eligible for the benefit; the child was recently born, adopted, or became a stepchild by marriage; and/or the child was living somewhere else. In each case, it would not be unreasonable to ask the claimant for a short explanation of why this is a first-time EITC claim with that child.

The form could simply ask: What changed in your household in relation to last year? Did a qualifying child move in with you, and if so, under what circumstances? Did your income change, making you eligible? If the EITC form were designed to elicit an affirmative response from claimants, it would provide the IRS with additional information for the compliance and enforcement side. Having applicants provide this information affirmatively in written words – instead having them check a box or select from a drop-down box – may also deter claimants from making a misrepresentation, because an applicant would have to lie affirmatively and in writing. On the compliance side, this would make it easier for the agency to determine whether there was an intentional disregard of the rules, in which case the 20 percent accuracy-related penalty should apply to any overpayment. This would align better with SNAP and other social programs that have sanctions for "intentional program violations" and distinguish them from honest mistakes.

As in Canada, once eligibility is established, the United States could presume that the children continue to reside with the recipient until notified otherwise. Income eligibility for the family-support credit would be confirmed by the tax return (or real-time information reporting), whereas qualifying child eligibility would be established by this separate two-page form. Those households in which a child resides with the same parents or guardian year after year would not have to submit a new form.

In Chapter 5, I proposed allowing parents who share custody to split the EITC. Applicants could indicate on the form that they share custody. This would simplify the determination of eligibility, because both parents would receive a family-support benefit every year, with the amount adjusted to reflect the shared custody situation. Currently, many divorced parents switch back and forth from year to year as to who claims the child. In some cases, they do so as an understood agreement, even though it is a fiction insofar as the child may not spend the required residency period with the parent claiming the child in a given year.

The CCB form is very simple. There is no need to pay a preparer or third party to fill out such a form; there are no computations and the questions are very straightforward. Switching to such a form would eliminate the paid preparer industry from the process of claiming social benefits and would eliminate the opportunity for return-related RALs and financial products.

TRANSITIONAL CHALLENGES

It is important to identify transitional challenges as part of this reimagination. I outline here a few that come to mind, but surely there are many more, and these should be part of any conversation about reform.

First, decoupling the family-support element from the tax return would have a significant ripple effect at the state level for many states. Currently, twenty-nine states and the District of Columbia have enacted a state-level EITC. In the most common design, the state piggybacks off federal eligibility and sets its credit as a fixed percentage of what the taxpayer received for a federal EITC. This design keeps administrative costs very low, and allows even states without an income tax to adopt a state-level EITC.[64] States would have to rethink this design, as well as amend their current laws to conform to any new EITC delivery design. This is not insurmountable: Many states had to rethink their income tax laws in the wake of the 2017 federal income tax reform for state provisions that were designed to be complementary to the federal tax law. But should any state simply give up on its EITC rather than amend its provision, this would create a loss for the working poor throughout that state.

Another transitional concern involves the benefit take-up rate. The EITC has been delivered through the Code for decades, and the program enjoys an 80 percent take-up rate, which is relatively high compared to other social benefit programs. If the EITC were decoupled from tax return filing as I recommend, it would be imperative to publicize this change widely and regularly. The most obvious and direct starting point would be to send a letter explaining the change to every taxpayer who received the EITC in their most recent tax refund. More would be required: the IRS could undertake a full-scale marketing campaign, partnering with social agencies, community organizations, and the media. This is not an insurmountable challenge, or a reason not to make these changes, but it is certainly a crucial consideration for any transition.

A second and separate take-up concern is that taxpayers may decide not to claim the benefit if it is based on estimated earnings and the taxpayer risks owing money at year's end. I address this earlier in the chapter, but wish to

[64] Erica Williams & Samantha Waxman, *States Can Adopt or Expand Earned Income Tax Credits to Build a Stronger Future Economy*, CTR. ON BUDGET AND POLICY PRIORITIES (2018), https://www.cbpp.org/research/state-budget-and-tax/states-can-adopt-or-expand-earned-income-tax-credits-to-build-a.

underscore it here again as a reason not to use estimated earnings unless a no-clawback provision or cap is in place.

Jacob Goldin argues that complexity is a barrier to EITC take-up, and that assisted preparation methods (including paid preparers and tax software) reduce this barrier. He argues that efforts to increase take-up should focus on encouraging or inducing taxpayers to file using assisted preparation methods, rather than on increasing awareness of the credit.[65] Splitting EITC claims into a two-step process, in which a taxpayer must both file a return and complete a separate form (even a simple one) may have a negative impact on the take-up rate because claimants would have to complete two steps instead of just one. In all, take-up is a crucial concern and must be given serious consideration; this is one of the greatest hurdles for any change from the status quo. Here, too, we might look to Canada and New Zealand for ideas about how to maximize take-up when the application for benefits is separate from the tax return filing.

The conversation about reforming EITC delivery also implicates a different conversation, one about the challenges that self-employed low-income workers face with their tax compliance. There is no withholding on income paid to independent contractors and self-employed workers. This problem is distinct from benefit delivery, and has been addressed in other literature.[66] The lack of withholding, coupled with the self-employment tax that is calculated on this income, can create a significant liability for even low-income workers. Currently, when those workers receive the EITC and CTC, these credits reduce or eliminate these liabilities. This prevents the financial hardship that would result from a tax liability, though it effectively means their "family-support" supplement is used (in whole or in part) to pay taxes. In theory, if the family-support benefit were delivered quarterly, recipients could set aside some or all of the benefit to make estimated tax payments. That would require significant financial discipline and is not necessarily realistic, especially if the recipient has competing bills to be paid. For budgetary purposes, as well as tax compliance purposes, it would be smoother if self-employed workers were subject to mandatory withholding. This is a topic that also merits serious policy discussion.

65 Jacob Goldin, *Tax Benefit Complexity and Take-Up: Lessons from the Earned Income Tax Credit* (Stan. L. & Econ. Olin Working Paper No. 514, rev. Oct. 25, 2018), https://papers.ssrn.com/sol3/papers.cfm?abstract_id=3101160.

66 *See* Forman, *supra* note 51, at 178 (proposing expanding mandatory withholding to include payments to independent contractors and self-employed individuals).

The reimagination I have outlined in this and the previous chapter includes many proposals. Some have been suggested before by others, some are radical departures from the way the EITC has been delivered for decades, and some are borrowed from other countries. Just as those countries were inspired by the United States to deliver social benefits through their tax system, so the United States can learn from what these countries are doing differently with their analogous benefits.

To reiterate: I do not suggest that these proposals are the only ways forward, nor that these ideas are interdependent. My hope is that my reimagination will spur the continuation of a much-needed conversation about social policy. The United States can do better in delivering this crucial benefit to a vulnerable population: low-income families. To that end, the next chapter turns to an argument for protecting this antipoverty element, in whole or in part, from offset so that low-income families do not have their benefit interrupted.

7

Protecting the Antipoverty Element

Would there be any way to see if they would only take half of it considering that I use most of that money for my son's school stuff, sports, and Christmas?[1]

Taxpayers are often surprised when they do not receive the tax refund they are expecting and instead receive a notice stating that the refund was applied to an outstanding debt. In 2015, more than 1.3 million (4.8 percent) refunds associated with returns claiming the Earned Income Tax Credit (EITC) were offset against other tax debts.[2] For some taxpayers, this notice is the first time they become aware that they have an outstanding tax liability. For other taxpayers, perhaps they were aware of an outstanding tax liability from a prior year or other outstanding debt, such as a federal student loan, but did not expect to lose the tax refund they were anticipating.

Because it is delivered as a tax refund, the taxpayer's EITC and other refundable credits are subject to full offset.[3] Yet the possibility of such offset betrays the EITC's function as an antipoverty supplement. For recipients for whom the EITC is a safety net that helps provide for their family, this is especially frustrating. Though otherwise eligible to receive the working family antipoverty supplement, they do not enjoy the expected lump sum that would

[1] Email from a former client to author (writing sent upon learning that she would not receive her EITC because of other outstanding federal debts) (on file with author).

[2] Taxpayer Advocate Service, 2016 Annual Report to Congress (Vol. 1) 353, n. 141 (2016). This figure does not include offsets against nontax debts. Thus, the number of EITC-related refunds affected by offsets is even higher than stated here.

[3] As this chapter describes, this matter was the subject of litigation, with several courts distinguishing the EITC from a tax refund; ultimately, the Supreme Court held that the EITC is payable as if it were a refund. Sorenson v. Sec'y of Treasury, 475 US 851, 863 (1986) ("[J]ust as eligibility for an earned-income credit does not depend upon an individual's actually having paid any tax, the Code's classification of the credit as an overpayment to be refunded is similarly independent of the individual's actually having made any payment").

otherwise allow them to pay down debt or past-due bills, buy consumer durable goods, or provide small extras for their children. Many working families look forward to the EITC all year long; imagine their disappointment – and the financial repercussions they face – when the anticipated lump sum is unexpectedly diverted to a debt that is less pressing to them than their immediate needs for rent, food, or clothing.

Whether it is appropriate for individuals to receive the EITC if they owe an outstanding tax debt or certain types of other liabilities is a policy question. Despite the EITC's expansions over the years, this question has been neglected, with significant implications for EITC recipients. A reimagination of the EITC offers an opportunity to address this question – but this is a question that deserves attention regardless of any other restructuring of the credit. The EITC is a social benefit for working families, and as such it deserves protection from offset (whether in whole or in part) to better serve its purposes. As I explore in this chapter, this notion is in alignment with protections for other social benefits.

There are several offset mechanisms that the Department of the Treasury uses to recoup debts owed to the United States. One is Internal Revenue Code section 6402, which governs only tax refund offsets. Another is the Debt Collection Improvement Act, codified in Title 31, which governs administrative offsets of federal payments to collect nontax debts. In addition, federal agencies that administer various benefits take different approaches to recoupment of overpayments.

This chapter explores offsets in relation to the EITC, describing how these offsets currently operate and providing some historical background. It then draws analogies from various protections that are available to individuals experiencing financial hardship, both for tax levies and for recoupment or offset of other social benefits. These analogies are useful for considering how offset protections could best serve a social benefit that is an effective antipoverty supplement for low-income families in the United States.

TAX REFUND OFFSETS GENERALLY

Internal Revenue Code section 6402 authorizes the Department of Treasury to offset an "overpayment,"[4] in this context meaning the amount of tax refund

[4] Throughout the book I have used the term *overpayment* to refer to EITC amounts erroneously paid to a taxpayer; the same term is also used to describe the amount due to the taxpayer after the liability is satisfied. Code section 6401(b)(1) provides: "If the amount allowable as credits ... [cross reference to provisions including withholding, EITC, and the CTC] exceeds the tax

due to a taxpayer, against certain other debts owed by the taxpayer. Section 6402(a) provides that a tax refund offset may be applied first against any outstanding federal tax, addition to tax, or interest owed by the taxpayer.[5] If any amount of the refund remains after outstanding federal tax debt is satisfied, the refund is subject to the Treasury Offset Program and is applied against the following in this order of priority: (1) past-due child support payments; (2) outstanding debts to other federal agencies, such as a federal student loan debt; (3) outstanding state income tax debt; and (4) outstanding unemployment compensation debt owed to a state.[6] The Treasury Offset Program is administered by the Treasury Department's Bureau of the Fiscal Service, not by the Internal Revenue Service (IRS).[7]

There are two important scenarios in which a taxpayer with an outstanding liability might seek to prevent a refund offset, in whole or in part.[8] Neither scenario is a statutory entitlement in the Code. Rather, these scenarios are governed by administrative procedures and both scenarios apply only in narrow circumstances. The first scenario is an injured spouse allocation, which arises under operation of property law and is available for any category of outstanding debt. The second scenario, known as an offset bypass refund, involves agency discretion by the IRS, is available only for tax debt, and applies only in cases of serious financial hardship.

Injured Spouse Allocation

An injured spouse allocation applies only when a joint refund is due and one spouse has an outstanding debt for which the other spouse is not liable. Common examples include student loan debt and past-due child support from a prior relationship. It is well established that each spouse has a separate

imposed ... the amount of such excess shall be considered an overpayment." In a sense, one might view this overpayment as going in the other direction: the government owes an excess back to the taxpayer.

5 Satisfaction of a federal tax debt is administered by the IRS, is discretionary, and does not fall within the purview of the Treasury Offset Program.

6 I.R.C. §§ 6402(c)–(f); 42 U.S.C. § 664; IRM 21.4.6.4(4) (Apr. 27, 2017).

7 31 U.S.C. § 3720A.

8 These are not the only exceptions to the refund offset rules. For example, if the taxpayer is in bankruptcy, special rules apply; generally the offset is not permitted because of the automatic stay, but this is not always the case. *See* IRM 5.9.1.5 (Aug. 11, 2014). Another exception that applies only to outstanding tax debt is that the IRS has made a policy decision not to apply a refund toward an outstanding tax debt when that taxpayer has an innocent spouse request pending with respect to that tax year. IRM 25.15.8.7.1.2 (Nov. 13, 2014).

interest in jointly reported income and in any refund due.[9] By default, the IRS will offset the entire joint refund to satisfy the outstanding debt of only one spouse. However, the nonliable spouse (referred to in this context as an "injured spouse") can request an allocation of the refund according to each spouse's interest.[10]

This is not a statutory right granted by the Code; rather, it is an administrative procedure that was created because of the recognized principles of property law. The nonliable (injured) spouse requests relief on IRS Form 8379, either simultaneous with return filing or after the filing. The IRS will determine the portion of the refund to which the nonliable spouse is entitled under applicable state law property rights. The allocation process is different in community property states than in non-community property states.[11]

Because the allocation arises as a matter of property law, the spouse does not have to prove a financial hardship, and the allocation will be made regardless of the type of debt for which the other spouse is liable. For example, if a husband and wife are due a joint refund but the husband owes past-due child support to a former spouse, the wife can request relief and will receive her "share" of what would have been the joint refund; the husband's share will be offset and applied to the past-due child support. Generally speaking, the IRS will determine each spouse's liability by allocating income, deductions, and credits as if they had filed separate returns.[12] It is possible that by such an allocation it will be determined that the nonliable spouse is not entitled to any portion of the refund, and it is also possible that the nonliable spouse would be entitled to the entire refund. This is not a question of financial need or social policy, it is the application of state property law. Generally, the determinative factor is the amount each spouse contributed to the overpaid tax.[13] Imagine a scenario in which only one spouse had income but a joint return was filed: All the earned income and withholding credits would be attributable to the working spouse, with the result that the entire refund is attributable to that spouse. If the working spouse is the liable spouse, the refund will be entirely

9 Rev. Rul. 74-611, 1974-2 C.B. 399 (citing Maragon v. United States, 153 F. Supp. 365 (Ct. Cl. 1957)).

10 Taxpayers are sometimes confused by the terms "innocent spouse" and "injured spouse." The former is a spouse who filed a joint return and subsequently seeks relief from joint and several liability. The latter is a spouse who filed a joint return and has or will have the refund offset to satisfy a debt attributable to the other spouse, for which he or she is not responsible.

11 *See* Rev. Rul. 85-70, 1985-1 C.B. 361; IRM 25.18.5.3 (Mar. 4, 2011); IRM 25.18.5.4 (Feb. 15, 2005).

12 *See* Rev. Rul. 80-7, 1980-1 C.B. 296; *see also* IRM 21.4.6.5.10.1 (Jan. 1, 2001).

13 I.R.S. Chief Couns. Mem. 201012033 (Jan. 8, 2010) (citing Rosen v. United States, 397 F. Supp. 342, 343 (E.D. Pa. 1975); Gens v. United States, 230 Ct. Cl. 42 (1982)).

offset because the nonworking spouse has no property interest in the refund. On the other hand, if the nonworking spouse is the liable spouse, the working spouse may receive the refund in full by requesting such an allocation.[14]

For the EITC specifically, the Internal Revenue Manual directs employees to "determine a new, separate EITC that would be available for each spouse if that spouse had filed a separate return and if EITC were available on a [married filing separate] return. This is a theoretical situation used for computation only."[15] It is theoretical (or perhaps more accurately, hypothetical) because Code section 32(d) provides that a married taxpayer who files using the married filing separate status is not eligible for the EITC. What it means in practice is that the IRS determines what amount of the total EITC shown on the joint return would be allocable to each spouse based on their respective income; if the nonworking spouse is the nonliable spouse, there is no EITC attributable to that spouse, and in such a case the entire EITC will be applied toward the working spouse's past debt. In other words, the work requirement for the EITC comes into play when determining each spouse's interest in the refund.[16]

Offset Bypass Refund

The Code does not *require* the IRS to offset a refund against past-due federal tax liabilities. Section 6402(a) states that the Secretary of the Treasury *may* credit the overpayment (refund due) against a federal tax liability. For all other types of past-due debt, the various subsections of section 6402 state that the Secretary *shall* reduce the overpayment (refund due) and remit it to the appropriate agency.[17]

[14] *See* Rev. Rul. 80-7, *supra* note 12; Keith Fogg, *When One Spouse Files Bankruptcy How Should the Court Split the Refund Resulting from a Joint Return between the Estate of the Debtor Spouse and the non-Debtor Spouse*, Procedurally Taxing (May 2, 2014), http://proceduallytaxing.com/when-one-spouse-files-bankruptcy-how-should-the-court-split-the-refund-resulting-from-a-joint-return-between-the-estate-of-the-debtor-spouse-and-the-non-debtor-spouse.

[15] IRM 21.4.6.5.10.2 para. 3 (Apr. 24, 2012).

[16] Revenue Ruling 87-52 provides the formula the IRS will use in allocating the EITC after the hypothetical amount that would have been available to each spouse on a separate return is computed. Rev. Rul. 87-52, 1987-1 C.B. 347.

[17] Nontax debt is subject to the Treasury Offset Program, which is not administered by the IRS, and the IRS has no discretion over hardship requests for nontax debt. The Internal Revenue Manual instructs IRS employees to refer hardship inquiries involving nontax debt to the Bureau of Fiscal Services. IRM 21.4.6.5.5(5) (Sept. 22, 2017).

Thus, the IRS has the administrative discretion to bypass – allow the refund in spite of – an outstanding federal tax debt, but the agency is obligated to notify the Bureau of Fiscal Services of a refund because the Treasury Offset Program rules apply to any outstanding nontax debt (child support, federal nontax debt, state tax debt, or unemployment compensation debt). The IRS has adopted a policy of not exercising its bypass discretion if the taxpayer has both outstanding federal tax debt and a type of Treasury Offset Program debt.[18]

When the IRS does exercise this discretion, this type of refund is referred to as an "offset bypass refund" (OBR). Unlike an injured spouse allocation request, which can be requested either simultaneously with return filing or after the refund has been offset, an OBR must be requested before the offset has occurred; once a refund has been offset, the IRS cannot initiate an OBR unless a clerical error is associated with the offset.[19]

The procedures for the OBR determination are set forth in the Internal Revenue Manual.[20] The Internal Revenue Manual specifies that "under certain hardship circumstances" the IRS can issue a manual refund without first satisfying an outstanding tax balance liability. It further states:

> Hardship for purposes of an OBR is economic hardship with [sic] the meaning of IRC § 6343, and the corresponding Treasure [sic] regulations (i.e., unable to pay basic living expenses). Handle each OBR on a case by-case basis. There is no exclusive list of expenses which would qualify a taxpayer for an OBR.[21]

The Internal Revenue Manual states that a taxpayer must provide a dollar amount and documents demonstrating specific and immediate financial hardship; the bypass is only granted to the extent of the documented hardship. The Manual provides an example:

> The taxpayer has an overpayment on their return showing $1,000. They have requested a hardship refund of $600 to avoid eviction. A review of their account shows a prior year tax liability of $500. If you decide to honor the

[18] Tax Notes Today, *IRS Clarifies Procedures for Issuing Offset Bypass Refunds*, 2013 TNT 207-12 *Koskinen Kicks off Filing Season with Spotlight on EITC* (Oct. 25 2013).

[19] *See id.*; *see also* IRM 21.4.6.5.11.1 paras. 6, 20 (Sept. 22, 2017).

[20] *See* IRM 21.4.6.5.11.1 (Sept. 22, 2017); IRM 3.17.79.3.17 (July 20, 2016); *see also* Keith Fogg, *Requesting an Offset Bypass Refund and Tracing Offsets to Non-IRS Sources*, Procedurally Taxing (Dec. 9, 2015), http://procedurallytaxing.com/requesting-an-offset-bypass-refund-and-tracing-offsets-to-non-irs-sources.

[21] IRM 21.4.6.5.11.1 para. 1 (Sept. 22, 2017).

hardship request for $600, you must treat $100 of the refund as an OBR. The remaining $400 overpayment offsets to the Federal tax debt.[22]

Generally, the IRS will not grant the OBR request unless the taxpayer demonstrates a serious financial hardship, such as the immediate threat of an eviction, foreclosure, or utility shut-off.[23] As I discuss later in this chapter, the standard for granting an OBR is higher than those required to release a levy (the seizure of assets to cover outstanding debt) in the event of financial hardship. Currently, any refund subject to section 6402 can be spared from offset only by injured spouse allocation or the very narrow circumstance of an OBR.

EITC AS AN OVERPAYMENT SUBJECT TO SECTION 6402

As one of the first refundable tax credits established by Congress, the EITC eventually faced the question of whether it is part of an "overpayment" for purposes of section 6402 – in other words, whether it is part of the tax refund – and whether the credit could be offset and applied to other debts. This question was considered by the Supreme Court in 1986. In *Sorenson v. Secretary of Treasury*,[24] a married couple's tax refund, including both withholding credits and the EITC, was offset and applied to the husband's past-due child support. As required by the terms of the Aid to Families with Dependent Children program, Mr. Sorenson's former wife assigned the past-due child support to the state when she applied for welfare benefits. As a result, the IRS took the position that section 6402(c) required it to intercept any tax refund due to Mr. Sorenson and remit it to the state of Washington to satisfy his unpaid obligation.

Mrs. Sorenson protested the refund offset. Following her protest, the IRS determined that Mrs. Sorenson was entitled to one-half the joint refund under applicable state property law, as their home state, Washington, is a community property state. However, it upheld its determination that Mr. Sorenson's

22 IRM 21.4.6.5.11.1 para. 14 (Sept. 22, 2017).

23 This standard is not explicitly stated in the Internal Revenue Manual, but seems to be the practice. *See* Fogg, *supra* note 20; *see also* IRM 3.17.79.6.4.2 (Oct. 4, 2017) (listing as examples of proof of hardship the following: "Eviction Notice (Court Papers signed by presiding Judge), Official Notice (from water, electric or gas company), Medical Emergency (Physician's statement)").

24 Sorenson, 475 U.S. at 855–56.

one-half interest in the refund was subject to offset, even though it included the EITC.[25]

Mrs. Sorenson, the petitioner, disagreed. She argued that the Code authorized the IRS to offset refunds of federal taxes paid, but did not authorize the interception of EITC benefits. At its heart, *Sorenson* was a statutory interpretation case, with the issue framed as whether the EITC constitutes an "overpayment" within the meaning of section 6402. At the time the Court heard the case, there was a circuit split on this question. Mrs. Sorenson relied on two circuit court cases which had held that refunds attributable to the EITC were *not* overpayments for the purposes of section 6402(c), with those courts concluding that the EITC portion of a refund could not be offset.[26] One of those circuit courts reasoned that the EITC is not a tax refund "because eligibility for the credit is not contingent upon payment of any federal income tax."[27] Both of the circuit courts emphasized that the opposite interpretation would frustrate the Congressional goals of the EITC.[28]

The Supreme Court resolved the circuit split by rejecting the petitioner's interpretation and affirming the Ninth Circuit decision in *Sorenson*, which interpreted the section 6402 definition of overpayment to include the EITC. The Ninth Circuit commented, "the statute provides that the Secretary can intercept not only tax refunds, but any amounts payable as tax refunds."[29]

As an alternative argument, Mrs. Sorenson pointed to the legislative intent of both the EITC and the offset program and reasoned that treating the EITC as an overpayment subject to offset conflicted with Congress' intention to provide benefits to the poor:

> A child in a working-poor family eligible for an earned income credit benefit may be just as needy as, or more needy than, a child in a family receiving AFDC [Aid to Families with Dependent Children]. Interception of an earned income credit benefit destined for the family of such a child means that the relief intended by Congress simply will not arrive. The children in such families will be innocent victims of the intercept law if the Secretary's

[25] *Id.* at 857.

[26] Nelson v. Regan, 731 F.2d 105 (2d Cir. 1984), *cert. denied*, 105 S. Ct. 175 (1984) (noting that the interpretation was a "close one" because the EITC is included in the definition of "overpayment" for purposes of Code section 6401(b)); Rucker v. Sec'y of Treasury, 751 F.2d 351 (10th Cir. 1984).

[27] Rucker, 751 F.2d, at 356.

[28] *Id.* at 357; Nelson, 731 F.2d, at 111–12.

[29] Sorenson v. Sec'y of Treasury, 752 F.2d 1433, 1444 (9th Cir. 1985) ("We believe that the *Nelson* and *Rucker* opinions have misinterpreted the statute by overlooking the fact that the statute provides that the Secretary can intercept not only tax refunds, but any amounts payable as tax refunds").

> interpretation is adopted by this Court. Similarly the earned income credit benefit program's incentive for choosing work over AFDC would be frustrated by the interception of benefits. AFDC benefits are not subject to interception or garnishment by the state seeking reimbursement for assistance previously furnished.[30]

The Supreme Court rejected that argument as well. It noted that the legislative history of the EITC "did not suggest that the earned-income credit was intended primarily as a type of welfare grant; rather, it was meant to negate the disincentive to work caused by Social Security taxes."[31] In addressing the petitioner's policy argument, the Court wrote:

> What petitioner and the Second and Tenth Circuits are really claiming is that the intercept law should be read narrowly to avoid frustrating the goals of the earned-income credit program. The earned-income credit was enacted to reduce the disincentive to work caused by the imposition of Social Security taxes on earned income (welfare payments are not similarly taxed), to stimulate the economy by funneling funds to persons likely to spend the money immediately, and to provide relief for low-income families hurt by rising food and energy prices … It is impossible, however, for us to say that these goals outweigh the goals served by the subsequently enacted tax-intercept program – securing child support from absent parents whenever possible and reducing the number of families on welfare.[32]

While acknowledging the "undeniably important objective[s]" of the EITC, the Court added that "[t]he ordering of competing social policies is a quintessentially legislative function."[33]

In the more than three decades that have passed since *Sorenson*, Congress has not amended Code section 6402 or enacted any legislation to protect the EITC from offset, though it has amended provisions related to the EITC several times since the decision.[34] The expressed goals of the original EITC, cited in *Sorenson*, are narrower than the goals of today's EITC, which since

[30] Sorenson v. Sec'y of Treasury, Br. of the Pet'r, No. 84-1686, 1985 WL 669132 (1985) at *21–22 (9th Cir. Aug. 5, 1985).

[31] Sorenson, 475 U.S. at 858 (1986).

[32] *Id.* at 864–65.

[33] *Id.* at 865.

[34] There has been at least one Senate bill that proposed amending section 32 to protect the EITC from offset against nonfederal debts, and National Taxpayer Advocate Nina Olson has recommended amending section 6402 to protect a percentage of the EITC from offset. *See infra* note 91.

the early 1990s has transformed more expressly into an antipoverty supplement.

I do not believe Congress has ever seriously considered the ordering of these competing social policies; over time the EITC has been expanded more as a political compromise than as a thoughtfully designed social benefit program.[35] If Congress were to adopt the proposals I advance in Chapters 5 and 6 of this book, the EITC would no longer be delivered as part of a tax refund, or as a lump sum annually. If, as I argue it should be, delivery of the EITC is decoupled from tax return filing, the benefit would no longer constitute an overpayment of tax and thus would not be within the purview of section 6402.

In that case, Congress would need to revisit the question of whether having certain outstanding federal or state debts should impact receipt of an EITC-like family-support benefit that was delivered periodically and outside the tax refund context. Given recipients' level of need, when and how is it appropriate to carve out relief – to exempt part of the EITC from offset? Interestingly, in its affirmation of the District Court holding in *Sorenson*, the Ninth Circuit included the following dicta in the opinion's only footnote, which speaks both to the more limited purpose of EITC when the case was decided and to its delivery as an annual lump sum:

> Actually, it appears from the legislative history that although the earned income credit provides some assistance to needy families, it was not designed as a type of welfare grant, but as a work incentive program, by negating the disincentive of Social Security taxes. Social Security taxes apply to earnings received through wages or salaries, whereas they do not apply to funds received through other sources, such as social welfare programs. The purpose of the legislation was to remove the disincentive to work provided by the Social Security taxes that would have to be paid on wages or salaries. See S. Rep. No. 36, 94th Cong., 1st Sess. 12, reprinted in 1975 U.S. Code Cong. & Ad. News, 54, 63–64, 83–84. It is also obvious from the manner in which the earned income credit operates that it was not a type of welfare grant. The wage earner is entitled to receive an income credit of ten percent of his or her earnings up to $5,000. Thus, a person who earns $5,000 would receive a $500 credit, whereas a person who earns $1,000, and would probably be in greater need, would receive only a $100 credit. The funds that the Secretary would

[35] *See* Lawrence Zelenak, *Redesigning the Earned Income Tax Credit as a Family-Size Adjustment to the Minimum Wage*, 57 Tax L. Rev. 301, 346 (2004) (arguing that the "somewhat incoherent nature of current law might be the result of a compromise between conflicting visions of the credit's purpose, rather than the lack of any clear vision, but it is difficult or impossible to find attractive accounts of the purpose of the [EITC] even in the academic literature").

be reaching are in reality more akin to a refund of Social Security taxes than to a type of welfare grant.

The policy considerations are quite different in intercepting such accumulated year-end funds from the policy considerations in the garnishing of weekly wages that the employee is expecting to receive for current living expenses. In this latter instance, Congress has specifically provided for exemptions of certain amounts of wages and salaries from the assessment and collection process. *See* 26 U.S.C. §§ 6305(a) and 6334(d).[36]

Perhaps, extrapolating from the Ninth Circuit's dicta, Congress might view the EITC differently if it were delivered periodically and used for current living expenses, as opposed to viewing it as an annual accumulated windfall. If the EITC were decoupled from the tax return, as I suggest in my reimagination, it would look more like other social benefit programs.

ANALOGIES FROM OTHER CONTEXTS INVOLVING FINANCIAL HARDSHIP

There are several ways that a taxpayer's income and assets, including social benefits, are exempted from offsets and debt collection. These provide useful analogies to consider when and how it is appropriate to protect the EITC from offset. Serious consideration of this issue requires much more than the question of whether the EITC would remain part of a tax refund, or whether it would be decoupled from the tax refund and paid periodically.

Even if the EITC were decoupled from the tax refund, and therefore no longer subject to the section 6402 offset rules, it will remain a federal payment. As such, the EITC would still be subject to the Treasury Offset Program, which applies not just to tax refunds but to many other types of federal payments. The Debt Collection Improvement Act of 1996 (DCIA)[37] requires federal dispersing agencies to offset certain federal payments in order to collect outstanding debts owed to the United States.

Certain federal payments are statutorily exempt from the DCIA,[38] and for other federal payments, the amount that can be offset is limited by the statute.

[36] Sorenson, 752 F.2d at n.1 (emphasis added).

[37] Pub. L. 104-134, 110 Stat. 1321, 1321–58 (Apr. 26, 1996) (codified at 31 U.S.C. § 3716(c)).

[38] The statute specifies that payments under a program administered by the Secretary of Education under Title IV of the Higher Education Act of 1965 cannot be offset. 31 U.S.C. §3716(c)(1)(C). Certain other payments are exempted under other statutory provisions. *See, e.g.*, 38 U.S.C. § 5301(a) (exempting payments administered by the Department of Veterans Affairs).

For example, the DCIA provides that up to $9,000 of certain payments (most notably social security retirement and disability benefits) shall be exempt from offset. This is an annual figure that is prorated monthly, meaning the first $750 of a social security recipient's monthly benefit is exempt from offset.[39] The DCIA leaves open the possibility for exemptions other than those specified by statute: It provides that the Secretary of the Treasury *shall* exempt from administrative offset payments under means tested programs when requested by the head of the respective agency.[40] For this purpose, the Department of Treasury defines a means-tested program as "those programs for which eligibility is based on a determination that income and/or assets of the beneficiary are inadequate to provide the beneficiary with an adequate standard of living without program assistance."[41] The Department of Treasury notes that examples of such programs include, but are not limited to, food stamp programs, SSI programs, and TANF programs.[42]

What about the EITC? While the EITC is generally described as a "means-tested" benefit,[43] it does not satisfy the DCIA standard of means tested for every recipient. Certainly it does for a single minimum wage earner with two children, who in 2017 would have earned approximately $15,000 in annual wages and received an EITC of $5,616: that family would not have an adequate standard of living without the EITC.[44] The EITC provided a significant antipoverty supplement; the benefit was more than one-third of the household's annual wage income. But this is less clear at the higher end of the EITC income phase-out threshold. When a recipient has a higher income and receives a lower EITC benefit, it is harder to say that person's income is inadequate without program assistance. For example, a single worker with two children earning $43,000 would have only received $417 in EITC in 2017; in

[39] 31 U.S.C. § 3716(c)(3)(A)(ii). I.R.C. § 6331(h) provides that the IRS can offset up to 15 percent of monthly social security retirement benefits to satisfy a delinquent tax debt. Though the IRS is not subject to the $9,000 limit provided by the DCIA, a taxpayer whose social security benefits are $750 or less per month would be eligible for hardship exemption from the levy.

[40] 31 U.S.C. § 3716(c)(3)(B).

[41] Dept. of Treasury, Bureau of the Fiscal Serv., Debt Mgmt. Servs., Exemption of Classes of Fed. Payments from the Treasury Offset Program: Standards and Procedures (Jan. 4, 2001, as updated Sept. 3, 2013).

[42] *Id.*

[43] *See, e.g.*, Cong. Budget Office, Growth in Means-Tested Programs and Tax Credits for Low-Income Households (2013).

[44] In 2017, the Department of Health and Human Services provided that the federal poverty guideline for a family of three was $20,420; this hypothetical family would be well below the guideline without the EITC, and barely above it with it.

that case the EITC is likely a welcome addition, but represents less than 1 percent of the family's annual household income.

Even if the EITC is not considered means tested within the standards of the DCIA, the DCIA provides that the Secretary *may* exempt from offset payments under programs that are not means tested upon the written request of the head of the payment certifying agency, so long as the request shows that "administrative offset would tend to interfere substantially with or defeat the purposes of the payment certifying agency's program."[45]

This standard is problematic for the EITC, as the purpose of the EITC described in the 1975 legislative history is not its purpose today. Regardless, if the EITC is meant to lift families above the poverty line, and when it constitutes a significant percentage of a family's living wage, it follows that the EITC should not be offset in full to pay other debts, or even to recoup an EITC overpayment.

Analogies can be drawn from multiple domestic contexts. In particular, I identify two broad categories of analogies. Given its home in the Code, I first consider IRS collection procedures. When a taxpayer has an outstanding federal tax obligation, the IRS has the broad power of levy. Internal Revenue Code section 6331 empowers the IRS to levy, meaning to seize a taxpayer's property to satisfy an outstanding tax debt, generally without first obtaining a court's permission. Section 6334 limits the agency's reach by exempting certain property, and section 6343 provides that the IRS shall release a levy if it creates a financial hardship for the taxpayer. I will describe these limits and suggest that similar limitations should apply to the EITC offset.

Second, I look beyond tax administration and consider how social benefit programs administered by other federal and state agencies approach recoupment of overpayments. Specifically, I examine how overpayments of Supplemental Nutrition Assistance Program (SNAP) and social security benefits are addressed. This analogy is particularly relevant in deciding how Congress might redesign EITC overpayment recoupment.

Federal Tax Liabilities and Levy Exemption

The Code's levy provision grants the IRS the administrative power to seize salary, wages, bank accounts, and other property of a taxpayer who has outstanding federal tax liabilities. However, Congress recognizes that the most

[45] 31 U.S.C. § 3716(c)(3)(B).

vulnerable taxpayers need protection, and it has enacted various provisions to provide taxpayers relief from collections.

For example, section 6334 exempts certain property from levy, including (among other things) specifically limited categories of annuity and pension payments; the wages or salary necessary to comply with a prior court-ordered judgment for child support; a specified amount of wages; disability benefits payable based on military service; and the taxpayer's residence if the tax liability is less than $5,000.[46] Section 6331(h) authorizes the Federal Payment Levy Program (FPLP), which is an automated procedure by which the IRS can levy up to 15 percent of any federal payment, including social security benefits, public assistance payments other than those for which eligibility is based on income or assets, unemployment benefits, and workmen's compensation.[47] The IRS cannot levy Supplemental Security Income (SSI) because it is based on income and assets, and the agency has made a policy decision not to levy Social Security Disability payments even though it is authorized by statute to do so.[48]

The wage levy exemption is calculated based upon the payee's filing status and number of dependents.[49] The exemption is calculated per pay period. Guidance from the IRS provides an example illustrating that in tax year 2018, a married taxpayer with two dependents who is paid bi-weekly will have $1,242.32 exempt from levy; any amount earned above that will be subject to levy.[50] In essence, this rule would protect $32,300 of this hypothetical taxpayer's annual income (though it operates as a per-pay period cap rather than an overall annual threshold).

In addition to these exemptions, section 6343 provides an additional and critical protection: The IRS must release the levy if the taxpayer demonstrates

[46] I.R.C. § 6334(a), (d). Note that I.R.C. § 6334(e) places additional limitations on the service's ability to seize a taxpayer's primary residence; for example, the IRS cannot levy a principal residency without judicial approval. For a comprehensive history and discussion of levies, *see* Mark Howard and Matthew Hutchens, *Obtaining Relief from Federal Tax Levies*, Effectively Representing Your Client Before the IRS (ABA Sec. of Taxation, 7th ed. 2018).

[47] I.R.C. § 6331(h). As a policy matter, the IRS chooses not to apply the automated federal payment to unemployment benefits, workmen's compensation, and certain public assistance payments. IRM 5.11.7.2.1 para. 5 (Sept. 23, 2016).

[48] *See* I.R.S., *Federal Payment Levy Program: Exclude SSA Disability Insurance Payments*, SBSE-05-1015-0067 (Oct. 7, 2015).

[49] Prior to the 2017 tax reform, it was calculated based upon the standard deduction and the total personal exemptions, including dependency exemptions. The text describes the law as in effect for tax years 2018 through 2025. Because the standard deduction was increased for those years, more of the taxpayer's wages are protected.

[50] I.R.S. Pub. No. 1494 (rev. May 2018).

that the levy is creating an economic hardship. Economic hardship is defined to mean that the taxpayer is "unable to pay his or her reasonable living expenses" due to the levy.[51] Taxpayers demonstrate hardship by providing financial information to the IRS; in making these decisions, the IRS relies upon published collection financial standards.

These standards include a national standard based on family size for food, clothing, other household items, and out-of-pocket health care, without questioning the amount actually spent.[52] There are maximum allowances for housing and utilities, which vary by county locality and are based on government standards related to cost of living and transportation, which varies by region of the United States. For those expenses, taxpayers are allowed the amount actually spent, or the maximum allowance – whichever is less.

To illustrate: In 2018, the monthly national standard for household expenses for a family of three is $1,384; the monthly national out-of-pocket health care expense is $156 ($52 per individual under age sixty-five; a higher standard is allowed for individuals sixty-five and older). The maximum housing and utility standard for a family of three in Virginia is as high as $3,440 (in Falls Church, a relatively affluent suburb of Washington, DC) and as low as $1,110 (in Covington, a small town in the rural part of the state near West Virginia). The allowable transportation standard for one car in this region of the country (the "South") is $196 in operating expenses (maintenance, insurance, fuel, repairs, registration, etc.) and up to $497 for ownership expenses (monthly payment on a lease or car loan).

To demonstrate economic hardship for the purposes of having a levy released, it is generally enough to show that one's income does not exceed allowable expenses; unlike in the OBR context, one does not need to show that a levy will result in eviction, foreclosure, or utility shut-off. If individuals can demonstrate economic hardship within these thresholds, the IRS must grant their request to release a levy. The regional variations signal the government's acknowledgment that hardship is a relative term dependent on cost of living. To illustrate: in Covington, Virginia, a single parent with two children with no car payment is in economic hardship if he or she earns $34,152 or less per year. If he or she has a car payment, the allowable amount is increased to $40,116. In Falls Church, Virginia, a single parent with two children and no

[51] *See* I.R.C. § 6343(a)(1)(d); Treas. Reg. § 301.6343-1(b)(4)(i). *See also* Vinatieri v. Comm'r, 133 T.C. 392 (2010) (holding that the regulations require release of a levy that creates an economic hardship regardless of whether the taxpayer is in tax return filing compliance).

[52] I.R.S., Collection Financial Standards (Mar. 26, 2018), https://www.irs.gov/businesses/small-businesses-self-employed/collection-financial-standards.

car payment is experiencing economic hardship if his or her income is less than $62,112.

Although the Code provides all these protections in the *levy* context, a taxpayer's entire *tax refund*, including the EITC, is still subject to offset. However, many taxpayers who are income eligible for the EITC live from day to day in economic hardship. In some cases, it is a condition they never escape. This is why the EITC is so critical to these families. These taxpayers can demonstrate economic hardship in order to have a levy blocked or released, but at tax time they may not receive the antipoverty supplement they so desperately need.

If the EITC is meant to support families in making ends meet, it should be afforded similar protections to wages. In 2017, the maximum EITC available to a single filer with two children begins to slowly phase out at an income of $18,300, and it completely phases out by $45,000. As illustrated above, a family of three within that income range may meet the agency's definition of economic hardship, depending on locality. So why is wage levy impermissible at that income level, but full EITC offset automatic?

Recoupment of Other Social Benefit Overpayments

Every social benefit program is susceptible to overpayment, and agencies have different ways of classifying and recouping overpayments. These provide useful analogies in two regards. First, and most relevant, they can provide ideas for how a tax debt specifically attributable to an EITC overpayment should be recouped. Second, they can provide inspiration for how and in what circumstances part or all of an EITC benefit might be protected from offset toward another tax or nontax debt. These are two separate issues. Where the EITC has been overpaid, the most logical way to recoup the prior overpayment is through offset of a future EITC payment. In other words, even if Congress were to decide that the EITC should not be subject to offset against non-EITC tax debt or other outstanding federal debts, it would likely still insist on recoupment if the outstanding tax debt is due to an EITC overpayment. Thus, one approach toward offset would be that the EITC should not be seized to pay back a debt such as a federal student loan, but that it is appropriate to seize a future EITC upon a finding that the recipient received too high of an EITC in a past year. Even in the latter case, it is not necessarily appropriate to seize the entire EITC in a given year.

This section examines how agencies recoup overpayments of two other benefits: SNAP benefits and social security benefits (including retirement and disability benefits as well as SSI). Like the EITC, SNAP and Social Security are critical parts of the social safety net in the United States. Though neither benefit is contingent on work, both include an income-based eligibility determination, and both programs are intended to help individuals make ends meet.

SNAP

The Supplemental Nutrition Assistance Program is a food benefit program overseen by the federal government and administered primarily by the states. Federal regulations classify benefits overpayments as one of three types: agency error, inadvertent household error, or intentional error.[53] Agency error, as the name implies, means that the recipient was not to blame, but an overpayment was made. The other two types of errors result from the recipient's inactions or actions, and the agency determines whether the error was intentional or not.[54] The recipient has notice and due process rights, including the right to an appeal hearing. Program statistics compiled nationally show that most SNAP overpayments are inadvertent household error or agency error; intentional program violations are less common than either.[55]

Note that this represents a stark contrast to the way that the IRS categorizes EITC overpayments; except in rare circumstances, the IRS has no way of ascertaining the recipient's intentions for an EITC overclaim. Though it has been studying EITC noncompliance for decades, it has not been able to meaningfully categorize overclaims by underlying intent (or lack thereof).

The SNAP benefit recoupment expectation and strategy in turn depends upon the underlying classification. In all three cases, the agency will pursue collection of the overpayment.[56] There is a time limitation: In the case of agency error, the agency generally will collect an overpayment only for the

[53] 7 C.F.R. § 273.18(b). Note that benefit trafficking is a distinct intentional violation, and it is outside the scope of what I am addressing here.

[54] For SNAP benefits, federal regulations define an intentional program violation as "having intentionally made a false or misleading statement, or misrepresented, concealed or withheld facts." 7 C.F.R. § 273.16(c). Intentionality must be established by clear and convincing evidence. 7 C.F.R. § 273.16(e)(6).

[55] Daniel R. Cline and Randy Alison Aussenberg, Cong. Research Serv., R45147, Errors and Fraud in the Supplemental Nutrition Assistance Program 10–12 (2018). (According to the USDA-FNS FY 2016 State Activity Report, of states' established claims for overpayment, approximately 62 percent of total overpayment claim dollars were for recipient errors, about 28 percent were for agency errors, and about 11 percent were due to recipient fraud).

[56] 7 C.F.R. § 273.18(a)(3) (directing each state to "develop a plan for establishing and collecting claims that provides orderly claims processing and results in claims collections similar to recent national rates of collection").

twelve months prior to when the overpayment was discovered; for inadvertent and intentional errors, the agency can collect up to six years back from when the overpayment was discovered.[57]

Recipients have the option to repay the overpayment all at once or enter into a repayment plan.[58] States have the discretion to compromise an overpayment (that is, forgive the overpayment or accept repayment of less than the total owed) if it can be determined that the household will not be able to repay the overpayment within three years.[59] If the recipient does not enter into some form of a repayment plan or receive a compromise, the agency can pursue more aggressive collection options, such as wage garnishment, intercepts of other state payments including unemployment compensation, and participation in the Treasury Offset Program.[60]

However, if the recipient is currently receiving benefits, the state can collect through recoupment of benefits (referred to as "allotment reduction"). The recoupment rate will vary depending on the type of error. For example, if it is determined that the overpayment resulted from an inadvertent household error, the recoupment amount is limited to the greater of $10 or 10 percent of the monthly benefit.[61] For an intentional program violation, the recoupment limit is higher: the greater of $20 per month or 20 percent or the household's monthly allotment or entitlement.[62] If a household is subject to allotment reduction, even for an intentional error, the agency cannot use additional involuntary collection methods against individuals in the house.[63] As long as the household is in a payment plan – be it allotment reduction or a negotiated repayment schedule – and not delinquent, it will not be subject to additional collection action.[64]

Supplemental Nutrition Assistance Program benefits provide a useful analog, but because they are an in-kind benefit rather than cash, they are

57 7 C.F.R. § 273.18(c)(1)(i).

58 7 C.F.R. § 273.18(e)(4).

59 7 C.F.R. § 273.18(e)(7). States can add additional requirements; for example, Maine will only consider a compromise if the overpayment is caused by agency error.

60 7 C.F.R. § 273.18(f).

61 7 C.F.R. § 273.18(g)(1)(iii); the household can agree to have a higher reduction apply.

62 7 C.F.R. § 273.18(g)(1)(ii); the household can agree to have a higher reduction apply. Note that the agency may disqualify recipients from the program upon a finding of an intentional program violation, and the length of the disqualification will depend on the number of violations. *See* 7 C.F.R. § 273.16.

63 7 C.F.R. § 273.18(g)(1)(v); an exception to this is if the source of the payment is "irregular and unexpected such as a State tax refund or lottery winnings offset."

64 7 C.F.R. § 273.18(e)(4), (5).

distinguishable from the EITC. Social security benefits provide a second analog and, like the EITC, are cash payments with no spending restrictions.

Social Security

The Social Security Administration (SSA) pays monthly benefits to claimants who are above a minimum age or are disabled, and to the surviving spouse or children of certain workers. The SSA oversees two distinct benefit programs: Old-Age, Survivors, and Disability Insurance (OASDI) and SSI.[65]

Old-Age, Survivors, and Disability Insurance, commonly referred to as "social security," is a social insurance program and is not means tested. All individuals with the minimum length work history (based on quarters or years of earnings) are eligible for OASDI benefits upon a certain age or a showing of disability. This is true regardless of income level and regardless of whether they continue to work past the age of retirement. Old-Age, Survivors, and Disability Insurance is funded by payroll taxes (Federal Insurance Contributions Act and Self-Employment Contributions Act [FICA/SECA]) and employer contributions, and benefits are calculated based on lifetime earnings, which is why many social security recipients perceive themselves as getting back what they "paid in." Approximately sixty-two million people received social security in 2017.[66]

Supplemental Security Income, described by the agency as "assistance of last resort," is designed for low-income and low-resource elderly, blind, and disabled individuals. It is not based on income, but on need. There is both an income threshold and an asset test to determine eligibility. Supplemental Security Income is not funded by payroll taxes; rather, it is allocated from general revenue. Far fewer people receive SSI than receive social security – between eight and nine million per year.[67] Some people receive both benefits, because they are eligible for social security but their income is low enough to qualify for SSI.[68]

Overpayments occur in both programs. Like SNAP, the overpayment can be the fault of the agency or the recipient (inadvertently or intentionally). Regardless of which party is at fault, the SSA will recoup the erroneous benefit payments.

65 *See* 42 U.S.C. § 401 *et seq.*; 42 U.S.C. § 1381 *et seq.* These programs are sometimes referred to as Title II (OASDI) and Title XVI (SSI), in reference to the Social Security Act.

66 S.S.A., Pub. No. 05-10024, Understanding the Benefits (2018).

67 Ctr. on Budget & Policy Priorities, Intro. to the Supplemental Security Income (SSI) Program (2014), https://www.cbpp.org/sites/default/files/atoms/files/1-10-11socsec.pdf.

68 *Id.* at 1.

Recoupment of SSI overpayments is limited due to the nature of the benefit as means tested assistance. For that reason, the SSA will offset only 10 percent of the recipient's total income (including the SSI payments) until the overpayment is satisfied.[69] The SSI recipient can contact the agency to negotiate a smaller or higher recoupment, based on ability to pay.

There is no such limit on recoupment of OASDI social security; generally the full monthly benefit will be withheld to recoup the overpayment. However, if the recipient no longer has the overpayment funds in his or her possession, he or she can contact the agency to negotiate a smaller withholding based on available income and resources.[70] Specifically, the federal regulations provide than an adjustment to the recoupment is appropriate "[w]here it is determined that withholding the full amount each month would defeat the purpose of title II, i.e., deprive the person of income required for ordinary and necessary living expenses."[71] Such adjustment is not permitted if the overpayment resulted from an intentional act of the recipient.

To request such an adjustment, or a waiver of repayment, the recipient must complete a detailed request form indicating how much they can afford to pay back monthly.[72] The request form requires several written explanations, including an explanation of why the recipient does not believe he or she was at fault for causing the overpayment and accepting the money. The form asks whether the recipient reported the change that resulted in the overpayment and, if the answer is no, provides space to explain why not. The recipient must also provide answers to several pages of questions about assets, household income and expenses, and expected financial changes. The request form also asks whether the recipient loaned, gave away, or sold property after notification of the overpayment. After the recipient submits the request form, the agency reviews it and makes a determination; if the waiver is denied, the recipient can schedule a conference to discuss the request in person.

The SSA request form asks for financial information similar to the information that the IRS uses to determine economic hardship for levy release requests. The federal regulations provide that the determination of whether withholding the full social security benefit would defeat the purpose of the title "depends upon whether the person has an income or financial resources sufficient for more than ordinary and necessary needs, or is dependent upon

[69] 20 C.F.R. § 416.571.

[70] 42 U.S.C. § 404; 20 C.F.R. pt. 404.

[71] 20 C.F.R. § 404.502(c).

[72] *See* SSA, Form SSA-632-BK, Request for Waiver of Overpayment Recovery or Change in Repayment Rate (2018), https://www.ssa.gov/forms/ssa-632.pdf.

all of his current benefits for such needs."[73] Needs are defined to include food, clothing, rent, mortgage payments, utilities, maintenance, life and health insurance, taxes, installment payments, medical expenses, expenses for dependents, and "other miscellaneous expenses which may reasonably be considered as part of the individual's standard of living."[74]

EITC Recoupment and Offsets

Recoupment of EITC overpayments could be modeled on elements of the SNAP and Social Security repayment policies. As noted earlier, as a default rule, recipients who received too much EITC should be expected to repay it in full, regardless of the reason for receiving too much. If it is clearly established that the overpayment resulted from an *intentional* misstatement by the recipient, repayment in full should be required, and as a policy matter it seems appropriate that a penalty should be imposed. Currently, the IRS can impose a 20 percent accuracy-related penalty in these cases (where negligence can be shown or the misstatements resulted in a substantial understatement of tax).[75] The Code also authorizes the IRS to impose a two-year EITC ban for reckless or intentional disregard of eligibility rules, and a ten-year ban for fraudulent claims.

On the other hand, recipients who received an overpayment due to unintentional noncompliance should be treated differently. As a policy matter, they should not be subject to a full EITC offset if they are in fact low-income recipients and currently entitled to it in some amount. Just as SNAP and SSI benefits are reduced, rather than cut off, in the event of an overpayment, the EITC design could include a gradual recoupment set at a default percentage, rather than a total offset. A default percentage recoupment would be simpler to administer and require fewer agency resources; the default could even vary according to income level. Alternatively, EITC recoupment rules could follow a procedure similar to what the SSA has in place for OASDI recipients: EITC-eligible individuals could be given the opportunity to show that recoupment by full withholding of the benefit would deprive their family of the resources required to meet ordinary and necessary living expenses; the agency

[73] 20 C.F.R. § 404.508(a).
[74] 20 C.F.R. § 404.508(a)(4).
[75] I.R.C. § 6662.

could determine what percentage of recoupment is fair on a case-by-case basis.[76]

As I proposed in earlier chapters, the IRS can make changes that would help it better determine whether an EITC overpayment is inadvertent or intentional. Currently, intent is very difficult to ascertain because of a lack of meaningful information. For example, a first-time claimant is not required to explain why he or she has never claimed the qualifying child before. This information could be required, and would only require one or two sentences from most taxpayers. It does not seem unreasonable or unduly burdensome to request this information. As I have argued in prior writing, having to affirmatively provide this information would impress upon claimants the significance of claiming this benefit, and receiving an affirmative written statement would give the IRS a starting point should the return be selected for examination.[77] Any EITC claimants making an inadvertent error should not be treated the same way as those making an intentional one. Those claimants who are actually eligible for the benefit and depend on it to make ends meet deserve a process to negotiate repayment without being immediately deprived of a social benefit they rely upon.

As for offsets, hardship procedures and other workarounds exist for certain of the other debts that are subject to the Treasury Offset Program. For example, an individual who is in default status on a federal student loan can contact the Department of Education to set up a loan rehabilitation agreement; once the borrower makes a specified number of agreed upon voluntary payments and remains in compliance, the loan is removed from default status.[78] Once the loan is removed from default status, it is no longer subject to the Treasury

[76] Drawing on analogies from bankruptcy law, Keith Fogg proposes that the IRS should not require offset of an EITC refund as a term of an offer in compromise where the claimant shows allowable expenses in excess of income. Keith Fogg, *Proper Treatment of Earned Income Tax Credit in Calculating Disposable Income*, PROCEDURALLY TAXING (Oct. 12, 2018), http://proceduraIlytaxing.com/proper-treatment-of-earned-income-tax-credit-in-calculating-disposable-income (citing Marshall v. Blake, 885 F.3d 1065 (7th Cir. 2018) as the analogy in bankruptcy).

[77] *See* Michelle Lyon Drumbl, *Beyond Polemics: Poverty, Taxes, and Noncompliance*, 14 EJOURNAL OF TAX RESEARCH 253 (2016).

[78] The rules for certifying debts to the TOP program are complex; *see* Michelle Lyon Drumbl, *'Defense to Repayment' Protects Taxpayers with Defaulted Student Loans from Treasury Offset Program*, PROCEDURALLY TAXING (Nov. 13, 2018), http://procedurallytaxing.com/defense-to-repayment-protects-taxpayers-with-defaulted-student-loans-from-treasury-offset-program (describing a case in which a federal district judge vacated the Education Secretary's certification of a debt to TOP because the Secretary had not properly considered a defense to repayment raised on behalf of individual student loan borrowers).

Offset Program. These arrangements must be made with the creditor agency rather than by contacting the Treasury Department's Bureau of Fiscal Service.

Under existing law, these sort of procedures remain among the most viable options for protecting the underlying EITC benefit. It requires the debtor to be proactive, and likely will require the debtor to make payments (and stay in compliance with those payments). This is a good option for some individuals, but in some cases it is an unrealistic one, especially for the most financially vulnerable and the least sophisticated EITC recipients.

IMPLICATIONS AND CONSEQUENCES OF PROTECTING THE EITC

It is certainly the case that competing social policies are at stake in ordering debt and making hardship exceptions. A case with facts like *Sorenson* is on the less sympathetic end of the continuum: A father has failed to support his child from a prior marriage, and his current wife does not want her husband's one-half interest in the tax refund going to meet that obligation even though she did receive her one-half interest. Though the one-half refund was technically a repayment to the state of Washington, this repayment was due because the mother of Mr. Sorenson's child had earlier received state welfare benefits at a time when he was not paying the child support he owed her. At the heart of the controversy is the fact that a parent was not meeting his obligation to his child.

Past-due child support presents the most difficult moral argument against EITC offsets, because in principle it necessitates arguing that a working parent should get to keep the EITC to support the child who resides with the parent, instead of having it diverted to support the child from a prior relationship who does not reside with him or her. It follows that as a design choice it may be appropriate to maintain a policy to offset the EITC to satisfy overdue child support, regardless of whether the EITC is separated from the tax refund, delivered periodically, or some combination thereof. This would be consistent with the special rules afforded to child support enforcement more generally, as a matter of public policy, because it involves the support of minor children.[79]

[79] *See* Allen C. Myers, *Untangling the Safety Net: Protecting Federal Benefits from Freezes, Fees, and Garnishment*, 66 WASH. & LEE L. REV. 371 (2009). In discussing exceptions to garnishments of federal benefits, Myers points to 42 U.S.C. § 659(a) (2000) (allowing garnishment of funds otherwise exempted under 42 U.S.C. § 407 to collect child support and alimony payments) and writes of child support and alimony exceptions generally: "Public policy does not view family support as an interest hostile to the beneficiary, nor does it view the need for familial support payments as any less important than the beneficiary's need." *Id.* at 382.

However, even if we agree that past-due child support should always be prioritized over the EITC, a bigger question remains as between the EITC and other types of outstanding debts. Isn't the EITC also designed to help support minor children? This is why the EITC is so much larger for families with children, and why it increases depending on whether a worker has one, two, or three children. As the petitioner in *Sorenson* argued in her brief, children in a working-poor family may very much need the relief the EITC provides.[80]

It is easy, therefore, to imagine several scenarios in which protecting the EITC from offset is morally justified in the interest of prioritizing support for minor children over other types of offsets. For example, many EITC recipients have their refund offset and diverted to past-due student loans.[81] The National Consumer Law Center (NCLC) has studied this particular issue and proposed that Congress should exempt student borrowers' EITC from offset.[82] In its proposal, the NCLC commented that the "main victims of these EITC [offsets] are children, since by far the largest EITC payments go to families with children, and these [offsets] can have a dramatic impact on children's well-being."[83]

Student loan default is a widespread economic issue and a growing problem in the United States. Data on student loan defaulters show "the most vulnerable students at the greatest risk of default":

> Nearly 90 percent of defaulters also received a Pell Grant at one point; 70 percent came from families where neither parent earned a college degree; 40 percent came from the bottom quarter of the income distribution; and 30 percent were African American. These groups are overrepresented among defaulters by double-digit margins.[84]

80 Sorenson v. Sec'y of Treasury, Br. of the Pet'r, No. 84-1686, 1985 WL 669132 at *22 (9th Cir. Aug. 5, 1985). ("Interception of an earned income credit benefit destined for the family of such a child means that the relief intended by Congress simply will not arrive.").

81 In fiscal year 2017, approximately 1.3 million individuals in student loan default status were subject to tax refund offset, and the program collected $2.6 billion owed. While not all of those subject to refund offset are EITC recipients, overlap between low-income working families and student loan defaulters is certainly significant. Kevin McCoy, *Tax Refund Got You Excited? Don't Count on It if Your Student Loans are in Default*, USA TODAY (Apr. 18, 2018), https://www.usatoday.com/story/money/2018/04/18/tax-refunds-seized-pay-defaulted-student-loans/502200002.

82 Yael Shavit & Persis Yu, *Stop Taking the Earned Income Tax Credit from Struggling Student Loan Borrowers*, NAT'L CONSUMER L. CTR. (2016).

83 *Id.* at 1. The report further notes: "It is ironic that the government policy of exempting benefit programs for the poor from government seizure does not protect perhaps the most effective anti-poverty program the government offers." *Id.* at 3.

84 Ben Miller, *Who Are Student Loan Defaulters?*, CTR. FOR AM. PROGRESS, Dec. 14, 2017 at 5.

Thirty-eight percent of student loan defaulters started at a for-profit private institution, even though students at these for-profit schools constitute only 19 percent of all student loan borrowers.[85] Dropouts are at greater risk of default than are college graduates.[86]

This vulnerable population of students that default on loans in turn becomes economically vulnerable. This is a population that desperately needs the EITC to make ends meet, and to support their children, but does not receive it. The NCLC asked student loan borrowers to share stories of EITC offset and compiled a report with the stories of what those borrowers had planned to do with the EITC that they were expecting but did not receive.[87] As the NCLC report points out, some of these borrowers "were denied the promised benefits of education: they were lured in to attend a fraudulent school or a school that closed in mid-course, or life circumstances forced them to leave the school before completing the course of study."[88] The stories recounted in the NCLC report are from parents behind on their rent payments, low-wage workers with cars that barely function, and parents counting on the EITC to get out of debt or to provide for their children.

Other sympathetic scenarios are easy to imagine. For example, how should we treat a working family that was in fact eligible for the EITC, but was paid too much of it? There is a relatively easier moral argument that these individuals should be protected from a full EITC offset, as are SNAP and Social Security recipients in analogous situations.

National Taxpayer Advocate Nina Olson has made prior legislative recommendations to Congress to amend section 6402 to limit offsets of refunds attributable to the EITC to a percentage of the taxpayer's refundable portion of the credit.[89] Olson called the EITC a "trap for the unwary" because of its complexity. She cited an example of a taxpayer who incorrectly claims the EITC in Tax Year 1 because her qualifying child did not live with her for at least half the year, resulting in an audit and assessment of a liability. The same

85 *Id.* at 4.

86 *Id.* at 6.

87 Persis Yu, *Voices of Despair: Student Borrowers Trapped in Poverty When the Government Seizes Their Earned Income Tax Credit*, Nat'l Consumer L. Ctr. (2018).

88 *Id.* at 1–2.

89 Taxpayer Advocate Service, 2009 Annual Report to Congress (Vol. 1) 367 (proposing to limit the offset to 15 percent of the portion attributable to the EITC); Taxpayer Advocate Service, 2016 Annual Report to Congress (Vol. 1) 329. In the same set of recommendations, Olson proposed restructuring the EITC and family status provisions, including a proposal for the creation of a refundable family credit in addition to the EITC. Her proposal relating to offsets is to protect 25 percent of the refundable portion of both the EITC and her proposed Family Credit.

taxpayer would lose the benefit to refund offset in Tax Years 2 and 3 even though she is entitled to it if the child continues to live with her in those years.[90] Olson noted in one of her recommendations that a 2005 Senate bill included a proposed amendment to Internal Revenue Code section 32 that would have protected the EITC from offset against outstanding nonfederal debts, though this would be a smaller universe than the concerns I describe.[91]

The idea of protecting the EITC from offset, in whole or even in part, may be controversial to the public. When I have floated the question to the students enrolled in my low-income taxpayer clinic, many were not sympathetic to the idea. The students raised some very valid counterpoints about why the EITC should not be protected from offset.[92] Generally, they raised concerns that such protection might incentivize irresponsible financial behavior. Students distinguished the EITC from SNAP benefits, arguing that food is a basic necessity, and by extension suggesting that some safety nets are more economically vital than others.[93] For outstanding tax debt, one student raised the point that taxpayers can use the "offer in compromise" option if they are unable to pay the debt in full. The IRS program allows individuals who can establish "doubt as to collectibility" to settle their tax debt for less than the full amount owed.[94] These offers are evaluated based not on the amount owed, but on the individual's reasonable collection potential; accordingly, some individuals settle their tax debt for a fraction of the total owed. As a general term of the Offer in Compromise program, the IRS will additionally seize any refund (including the full EITC) that is due before or including the tax year in which the offer is accepted.[95] After the year in which the offer is accepted, the

90 *Id.* at 365. Olson also notes that due to section 6402, "either the IRS or FMS can grab the social benefit meant to pull taxpayers out of poverty even though the taxpayer remains low income, is otherwise eligible for the EITC, and is relying on the EITC to pay necessities." *Id.* at 367.

91 *Id.* at 367–68 (citing the Taxpayer Abuse Prevention Act, S. 324, 109th Cong. § 2 (Feb. 9, 2005)).

92 I am grateful to my spring 2018 Tax Clinic students for this insightful conversation, in particular Ross LaFour, who made the points included about the Offer in Compromise program and installment agreements.

93 This argument is reminiscent of points made by Viviana Zelizer, which I discussed in Chapter 5. Viviana Zelizer, The Social Meaning of Money (Basic Books 1994). Chapter 4 of Zelizer's book describes the history of public cash relief as opposed to public relief in kind, and the distinctions of public perception.

94 I.R.C. § 7122; Treas. Reg. § 301.7122-1(b)(2) provides that "doubt as to collectibility exists in any case where the taxpayer's assets and income are less than the full amount of the liability."

95 This is the general practice, but the recoupment does not apply to offers accepted under certain conditions, such as under the provisions of an offer accepted for Effective Tax Administration or in special circumstances based on public policy or equity conditions. *See* I.R.S. Form 656 at § 7(e) (rev. Mar. 2018); IRM 5.8.8.8 (Aug. 31, 2018). Note that the IRS cannot collect more than the full amount owed; it can keep only the amount of refund that,

tax debt is considered forgiven so long as the offer's payment and compliance terms are met, and the IRS does not offset future tax refunds.

Other of my students suggested creating collection incentives that would allow individuals to receive their tax refunds (in whole or in part) if certain conditions were met; for example, one student proposed that individuals who are meeting their obligations under an installment agreement should receive the portion of the refund attributable to the EITC. This suggestion is consistent with tax collection policies generally. Returning to the analogies drawn from IRS collection procedures, taxpayers can be exempt from levy even without a showing of economic hardship. Internal Revenue Code section 6331(k) provides that levy cannot be initiated while an offer in compromise is pending or while an installment agreement is in effect.[96] Why not extend the same rule to EITC offset, in whole or in part? In other words, amend the Code to provide that if a taxpayer is making timely payments on an installment agreement, his or her EITC would be protected from offset (at least in part).

As part of a broader reimagination of the EITC and its role as a social benefit program, Congress ought to give serious thought and consideration to the program's legislative intent, the empirical work showing how valuable it is to its recipients, and the analogs from other social benefit programs.

There is no one obvious path forward, but this question of offset protection merits more careful consideration than it has been given. Regardless of whether the EITC is decoupled from the tax return, transitioned to periodic payments, or not reformed at all, the question of whether and how to protect it from offsets is a critical and understudied policy question. This conversation is important, especially if the program were to be reformed, but these concerns could and should be addressed even if the EITC is left exactly as is.

when combined with other payments made, would satisfy the original debt in full (including penalties and interest). IRM 5.19.7.2.21 (Aug. 25, 2017). It may be possible to negotiate the recoupment provision out of the offer contract when entering into the offer; requesting an offset bypass refund would require a reformation to the offer contract. *See* Fogg, *supra* note 20, addressing this possibility in a comment posted subsequent to the original blog post (Mar. 22, 2017, 6:33 AM).

96 *But see* I.R.C. § 6331(k)(3)(A) (providing that continuous levies do not have to be released upon the submission of an offer in compromise. However, the taxpayer can request a release under the economic hardship rules).

8

Beyond EITC Delivery and Administration

How the United States Addresses Poverty

The officials lacked any relationship with the people ... Because they were stuck in their law day and night, they hadn't a true sense of human relationships, and that was a serious deficiency in such cases.[1]

This book is critical of delivery and administration of the Earned Income Tax Credit (EITC). It is skeptical that the status quo is the best way to help the working poor. These are my perceptions after working with low-income taxpayers for more than a decade. Because I am a lawyer, and run a low-income Taxpayer Clinic, I often see the EITC at its worst. I see it when it fails to deliver. I see parents desperately trying to make ends meet and being held at the mercy of the Internal Revenue Service (IRS) while waiting for a monetary benefit that I can see they meet the requirements to receive. I help these clients persevere, sometimes for more than a year, until they receive the sum they are due. I see other individuals making claims to which they are not entitled because they were certain in their own mind that supporting any child means they deserve the EITC, but the statute excludes them because that child is not related to them. I help these clients correct their return, dispute any proposed accuracy-related penalty by showing good faith, and make arrangements to repay the overpayment. Their experiences, too, inform my view of the system.

The EITC design is not perfect. But I cannot underscore enough the importance of the benefit to the families it reaches, many of whom are in

[1] Franz Kafka, The Trial, 84 (Ritchie Robertson ed., Mike Mitchell trans., Oxford University Press 2009), copyright in the translation Mike Mitchell 2009, copyright in the editorial matter Ritchie Robertson 2009, reproduced with permission of the Licensor through PLSclear.

poverty. I hear the importance in my clients' stories, and these stories are corroborated by empirical studies.[2]

It remains unclear what Congress hopes to achieve through refundable tax credits, or whether it has even thought about what it hopes to achieve.[3] Is the goal to move taxpayers off welfare and into the labor force? Is it to address the regressive nature of the social security payroll tax for low earners? Is it to alleviate the low minimum wage? Is it to lift all working taxpayers out of poverty, or is it meant to lift only families with children at home out of poverty? Is it to increase second earner participation in the labor force? To decrease it?

This lack of clarity about what Congress intends can be traced all the way back to the EITC's predecessor, the work bonus plan. "One can look at this as he wants to," said Senator Russell Long of the work bonus plan. "He can look at it as a work subsidy for those making low wages. He can look at it as a tax refund. We decided to call it a work bonus, because, whatever one calls it, it results from tax money collected as a result of the man's working."[4]

As is often common with legislation, today's EITC is a political patchwork. This patchwork is at best the aggregate result of four decades of compromise,[5] and at worse reflects the lack of a serious, thoughtful agenda for addressing poverty. Congress can rethink it carefully and adjust, or even overhaul, the refundable credit structure accordingly. This book draws upon other systems and proposes many ideas for a reimagination. The previous chapters are meant to start a conversation, as well as to provide specific ideas and proposals.

This final chapter asks some broader questions about the way the United States addresses poverty. I review the most recent tax reform, the Tax Cuts and Jobs Act (TCJA) of 2017, the most significant tax legislation in three decades. Not only did the Act neglect an opportunity to improve the EITC, but it has certain troubling implications for low-income filers. And while the EITC helps many people, many others fall beyond its coverage as well as that of other parts of the social safety net. Specifically, I raise the appropriateness of

[2] These are referenced in Chapter 1. The Tax Credits for Workers and Their Families (TCWF), which describes itself as a non-partisan communications initiative, is one resource to find a collection of news and research studies relating to federal and state EITC, as well as other refundable credits. *See* www.taxcreditsforworkersandfamilies.org/resources.

[3] Scholars have been making this observation for decades. *See infra* text accompanying notes 54 and 55; *see especially* Anne L. Alstott, *The Earned Income Tax Credit and the Limitations of Tax-Based Welfare Reform*, 108 Harv. L. Rev. 533, 557 (1995).

[4] 118 Cong. Rec. S33011 (Sept. 30, 1972) (statement of Sen. Long).

[5] *See* Michael B. Adamson, note, *Earned Income Tax Credit: Path Dependence and the Blessing of Undertheorization*, 65 Duke L.J. 1439 (2016).

continuing to condition the largest antipoverty program in the United States on a work requirement without also bolstering other social programs.

Finally, I end with thoughts about asking so much of the Internal Revenue Code, and the IRS, as a vehicle for social programs. There are compelling reasons to keep the EITC in the Code and with the IRS, but I call for a more thoughtful design of both the credit and the way in which the agency implements it.

THE UNITED STATES AND THE PERSISTENT PROBLEM OF POVERTY

The EITC is often framed as a dignified way to deliver social benefits.[6] Dignity, however, is a relative term. *True* dignity would be a living minimum wage, coupled with social policies aimed at eradicating poverty, not least child poverty. The United States is subject to criticism both for its income inequality and for its lack of a comprehensive social safety net, like those found in many other developed nations.

In 2018, the United Nations Special Rapporteur on extreme poverty and human rights, Philip Alston, issued a report after his visit around the United States some months earlier. The report describes the United States as "a land of stark contrasts": "its immense wealth and expertise stand in shocking contrast with the conditions in which vast numbers of its citizens live."[7] Alston cites census data: forty million individuals in the United States live in poverty; 18.5 million in extreme poverty, and 5.3 million in Third World conditions of absolute poverty.[8] Alston describes the United States as having the highest rate of income inequality among Western countries, and raises a concern that the tax reform enacted in 2017 "overwhelmingly benefited the wealthy and worsened inequality" through tax breaks for the rich at a time when other domestic policies resulted in elimination of protections for the middle classes

6 Chapter 2 discusses the work of a number of scholars who distinguish it from welfare on these grounds. *See* Jennifer Sykes, Katrin Križ, Kathryn Edin, & Sarah Halpern-Meekin, *Dignity and Dreams: What the Earned Income Tax Credit (EITC) Means to Low-Income Families*, 80 AM. SOC. REV. (2015) No. 2, 243–67; SARAH HALPERN-MEEKIN, KATHRYN EDIN, LAURA TACH, & JENNIFER SYKES , IT'S NOT LIKE I'M POOR (University of California Press 2015); Sara Sternberg Greene, *The Broken Safety Net: A Study of Earned Income Tax Credit Recipients and a Proposal for Repair*, 88 N.Y.U. L. REV. 515–88 (2013).

7 Philip Alston (Special Rapporteur on Extreme Poverty and Human Rights), *Rep. on His Mission to the United States*, U.N. Doc. A/HRC/38/33/Add.1 (May 4, 2018), https://digitallibrary.un.org/record/1629536/files/A_HRC_38_33_Add-1-EN.pdf.

8 *Id.* at 3.

and poor.[9] Alston argues that there are global consequences to these most recent tax cuts, which he fears will fuel a global race to the bottom, "further reducing the revenues needed by Governments to ensure basic social protection and meet their human rights obligations."[10]

The EITC aids a segment of those whom Alston writes about, and it reaches more than twenty-five million filers annually. Within a discussion of the "shockingly high number of children living in poverty in the United States," Alston credits the EITC and the Child Tax Credit (CTC) as lifting 4.7 million children out of poverty in 2016.[11] Despite its positive impact on a segment of the population, however, the EITC does nothing to help the unemployed or the disabled, and it does very little to help workers who cannot claim a qualifying child.

Alston's report is critical of the recent tax reform, both for neglecting poverty and promoting inequality. The TCJA,[12] signed into law in December 2017, was the most sweeping tax reform enacted in three decades. It reduced individual and corporate rates, made extensive changes to the U.S taxation of international transactions, and introduced a new pass-through deduction regime.[13] Certainly it included provisions that benefited the wealthiest Americans, and it comes at a cost: The Act is expected to reduce federal revenue by more than $1 trillion over the following decade when measured on a static basis. Various economic models predict that it will spur economic growth, creating jobs and higher wages.[14] But even under the more optimistic economic scoring models, the tax cuts are not self-financing, leaving open the possibility that in the future, fiscal conservatives might address the deficit by

[9] *Id.* at 4. The American public shares this perception, at least as of September 2, 2018, when an opinion poll showed that 61 percent of respondents believed the law benefits "large corporations and rich Americans" over "middle class families." Sahil Kapur & Joshua Green, *Internal GOP Poll: 'We've Lost the Messaging Battle' on Tax Cuts*, Bloomberg News (Sept. 20, 2018, 4:55 PM), https://www.bloomberg.com/news/articles/2018-09-20/internal-gop-poll-we-ve-lost-the-messaging-battle-on-tax-cuts.

[10] Alston, *supra* note 7, at 5.

[11] *Id.* at 11.

[12] An Act to provide for reconciliation pursuant to titles II and V of the concurrent resolution on the budget for fiscal year 2018, Pub. L. No. 115-97, § 11022, 131 Stat. 2054 (2017) (known unofficially as "The Tax Cuts and Jobs Act").

[13] As noted in the foreword to a reference book on the legislation, "[e]very U.S. taxpayer, foreign or domestic, individual or business, high-income or low-income, is impacted by the provisions of the act." Tax Cuts and Jobs Act: Law, Explanation, and Analysis (CCH Wolters Kluwer 2018).

[14] *See, e.g.*, Tax Found. *Preliminary Details and Analysis of the Tax Cuts and Jobs Act* (Dec. 2017), https://files.taxfoundation.org/20171220113959/TaxFoundation-SR241-TCJA-3.pdf; William G. Gale, Hilary Gelfond, Aaron Krupkin, Mark J. Mazur, & Eric Toder, *Effects of the Tax Cuts and Jobs Act: A Preliminary Analysis*, Tax Policy Ctr. (June 13, 2018).

overhauling other social programs, namely Medicare, Medicaid, and Social Security.[15]

Alston is correct that the TCJA disproportionately benefits the wealthy and misses an opportunity to address poverty.[16] Despite its sweeping changes, the Act did not include any changes to the EITC. It did not expand the EITC for childless workers, as some had proposed in the years leading up to the reform. The TCJA did, however, include a change that will indirectly and negatively impact EITC recipients over time: Calculation of annual inflation adjustments will be made using the Chained Consumer Price Index for All Urban Consumers (C-CPI-U); previously, the adjustments were made using the Consumer Price Index (CPI).[17] The difference in the two methods of calculating inflation is "not insignificant," with the effect being that adjustments for inflation will be smaller under the new method.[18] Chuck Marr from the Center on Budget and Policy Priorities points out that this means the maximum EITC will rise more slowly over time than under prior law, "eroding the credit's value for millions of working-class people."[19] Marr projects that by 2027 a married couple with two children earning $20,000 will see their EITC reduced by $168, while a married couple with two children earning $40,000 will receive $319 less. Ironically, this is one of the only provisions impacting individual filers that is permanent rather than temporary.[20]

While the TCJA did not amend the EITC, it did increase the CTC. However, it did so in a way that favors the wealthy as much as or more than it does the poor. Before the 2017 tax reform, the CTC was characterized as a lower- and middle-income credit. In tax year 2017, the CTC was a maximum

[15] Heather Long, *The Republican Tax Bill Was the Easy Part: The Next Debate Could Be Much Uglier*, WASH. POST (Dec. 19, 2017), https://www.washingtonpost.com/business/economy/the-republican-tax-bill-was-the-easy-part-the-next-debate-could-be-much-uglier/2017/12/19/a9c94e2c-e4df-11e7-a65d-1ac0fd7f097e_story.html?utm_term=.75a648840ac2.

[16] The Tax Policy Center estimated that in 2018, "taxpayers in the bottom quintile (those with income less than $25,000) would see an average tax cut of $60, or 0.4 percent of after-tax income" while "taxpayers in the top 1 percent of the income distribution (those with income more than $733,000) would receive an average cut of $51,000, or 3.4 percent of after-tax income." Tax Policy Ctr., *Distributional Analysis of the Conference Agreement for the Tax Cut and Jobs Act* (Dec. 8, 2017), https://www.taxpolicycenter.org/sites/default/files/publication/150816/2001641_distributional_analysis_of_the_conference_agreement_for_the_tax_cuts_and_jobs_act_0.pdf.

[17] IRC §1(f)(3) and (6), as amended by the Tax Cuts and Jobs Act (P.L. 115-97).

[18] CCH Wolters Kluwer, *supra* note 13, at 60.

[19] Chuck Marr, *Instead of Boosting Working-Family Tax Credit, GOP Tax Bill Erodes It over Time*, CTR. ON BUDGET AND POLICY PRIORITIES BLOG (Dec. 21, 2017, 10:15 AM), https://www.cbpp.org/blog/instead-of-boosting-working-family-tax-credit-gop-tax-bill-erodes-it-over-time.

[20] Marr points out that the bill makes the chained CPI permanent "in order to help cover the long-term cost of its corporate tax cuts, which the bill also makes permanent." *Id.*

of $1,000 per child. The income phase out for calculating the credit began at $75,000 for a taxpayer filing as single or head of household; it was $110,000 for a married couple filing a joint return. The credit was refundable to the extent it exceeded the tax due. The refundable portion was limited to the lesser of 15 percent of the filer's earned income in excess of $3,000 or the unused portion of the credit. In other words, workers had to meet a minimum income threshold of $3,000 for it to be refundable at all, and whether it was fully refundable depended on how much the worker earned above that.

The TCJA doubled the maximum CTC to $2,000 per child. Like most of the individual tax provisions in the legislation, this provision is temporary; it is effective for years 2018–25. At first blush, doubling the credit sounds like it should provide a tremendous boost to low-income families. In fact, the Act also lowered the minimum income threshold to $2,500 so that the credit would phase in more quickly. However, the increased CTC is not fully refundable even once the threshold is met (at an income level of approximately $12,000 for filers with one child); the Act limits the maximum refundable portion of the CTC to $1,400 per qualifying child.[21] To be sure, filers who benefit from refundability will find themselves slightly better off – but not by much. Compared to the previous law, an estimated eleven million children in low-income families will see an increase of $75 or less, while another fifteen million children in low-income families will receive more than $75 but less than the full $1,000-per-child increase that higher income families will get.[22]

Congress made an interesting – and revealing – policy choice in not making the full $2,000 refundable. Certainly, to do so would have been quite costly from a revenue outlay perspective. However, the Act also dramatically increased the income phase out for the CTC. For the years the increase is effective, the CTC only begins to phase out at $200,000 ($400,000 for married taxpayers filing jointly). In choosing to more than double the income phase-out level for single filers, and to more than triple it for married filers, Congress converted this from a low- to moderate-income benefit to a benefit for virtually

[21] In other words, $600 of the credit is nonrefundable: It can reduce the filer's taxable income, but not below zero. The $1,400 refund limit per qualifying child will be indexed annually for inflation after 2018.

[22] Higher-income families benefit from the full credit to the extent that their taxable income exceeds $2,000 per child. Ctr. on Budget and Policy Priorities, *2017 Tax Law's Child Credit: A Token or Less-Than-Full Increase for 26 Million Kids in Working Families* (2018), https://www.cbpp.org/sites/default/files/atoms/files/8-27-18tax.pdf.

all families, even reaching some families with household incomes in the top 5 percent of earners.[23]

All this stands in striking contrast to the original vision for a refundable child tax credit. As first discussed in Chapter 1, in 1987 President Reagan signed a bill passed by a Democratic-controlled Congress establishing the bipartisan National Commission on Children.[24] The commission spent years examining issues and challenges of American families and children. It did not limit its work to experts and data; it reached out to the American people. It sponsored a national opinion research project to survey parents and children in order to better understand public perceptions, and it held hearings, town meetings, site visits, focus groups, and other forums in eleven communities nationwide, in urban, rural, and suburban America.[25] In 1991, as part of a unanimous comprehensive report, the commission recommended the creation of a new $1,000 refundable credit for each child, which would not be contingent on a work requirement.[26] The proposed credit would have been available even to the unemployed. The commission report recommended this credit in addition to (not as a replacement for) the EITC, which it recognized as a successful supplement for low-income families.[27] To partially offset the cost of this proposal, the commission suggested the elimination of the personal exemption for dependent children.[28] Congress did not adopt the committee's

[23] In 2015, the mean income for the top 5 percent of household incomes was $350,870. Tax Policy Ctr, *Household Income Quintiles 1967 to 2015* (May 3, 2017), https://www.taxpolicycenter.org/statistics/household-income-quintiles. An earlier Senate version of the bill had proposed increasing the CTC to $1,650 and increasing the income phase-out level to a somewhat astonishing $1,000,000. Chuck Marr, *Senate Tax Bill Limits Child Tax Credit Expansion for Low-Income Children, Extends Credit to Wealthy Households*, Ctr. on Budget and Policy Priorities (Nov. 10, 2017, 12:30 PM), https://www.cbpp.org/blog/senate-tax-bill-limits-child-tax-credit-expansion-for-low-income-children-extends-credit-to.

[24] The bipartisan commission was created by Public Law 100-203, which was signed into law by President Ronald Reagan on December 22, 1987. The commission's thirty-four members were appointed in equal numbers by President of the United States, the President pro tempore of the US Senate, and the Speaker of the US House of Representatives. Nat'l Commission on Children, Beyond Rhetoric: A New Am. Agenda for Child. & Fams.: Final Rep. of the Nat'l Commission on Child. viii (1991). Most of the members of the Commission were representatives of organizations providing services to children and representatives from parents' organizations, rather than politicians, though then-Governor of Arkansas Bill Clinton was a member. The commission was chaired by Senator John D. Rockefeller IV, a Democrat from West Virginia. For a list of commission members, *see id.* at iii.

[25] *Id.* at ix–x.

[26] *Id.* at x.

[27] *Id.* at 88.

[28] *Id.* at x.

recommendation, though in 1997 it enacted the CTC with its work requirement.

Fast-forward twenty-some years. As part of the TCJA of 2017, Congress did eliminate the exemption for dependent children, at least temporarily (for tax years 2018–25). It also temporarily repealed personal exemptions for the filer and, for joint returns, the filer's spouse. In combination, this temporary repeal of all personal exemptions saved an estimated $1.31 billion in static revenue over ten years, meaning it helped offset significant losses in revenue created by other parts of the bill.[29] For a family of four, this change represents a loss of $16,600 in deductions. While this sounds like it will in effect create a tax hike for low-income families, that is not necessarily so: At the same time, the Act nearly doubled the standard deductions, to $12,000 for single filers, $18,000 for heads of households, and $24,000 for married couples filing jointly (this is an increase from $6,500, $9,550, and $13,000, which would have been the respective standard deduction amounts in 2018 if not for the legislation).

This feels somewhat like a shell game – with one hand, all personal exemptions disappear, but another hand increases the standard deduction; the CTC is doubled, and the phase-in amount lowered, but it is no longer fully refundable. How all these changes, in effect from 2018–25, will impact low-income families depends very much on household composition, including marital status and the number of children (if any) in the house. Many lower-income households will fare slightly better, most will see no material change, and a small percentage will be worse off: The Tax Policy Center estimates that only 27 percent of households in the lowest income quintile (those with income less than $25,000) will receive a tax cut (in some cases, this will mean an increased refund), while 1 percent will have a tax *increase* relative to the existing law.[30] Among those households who will receive a tax cut (or increased refund), the average savings will be $190. Among the small percentage of households that will experience a tax increase, the average tax increase will be $750.[31] When aggregated against all lowest quintile

[29] Tax Found., *supra* note 14, at 9 tbl. 5. By contrast, reducing individual rates across the board created an estimated ten-year static revenue loss of $1.87 billion, and lowering the corporate tax rate to 21 percent will result in an estimated ten-year static revenue loss of $1.42 billion.

[30] Frank Sammartino, Philip Stallworth, & David Weiner, *The Effect of the TCJA Individual Income Tax Provisions Across Income Groups and Across the States*, Tax Policy Ctr. (Mar. 28, 2018), https://www.urban.org/sites/default/files/publication/97556/the_effect_of_the_tcja_individual_income_tax_provisions_across_income_groups_and_across_the_states.pdf.

[31] *Id.* at tbl. 2.

households (those facing a cut, no change, or an increase) the average tax savings resulting from the legislation is only $40.[32]

The Tax Policy Center's analysis of the second income quintile (those with income greater than $25,000 but less than $49,000 – a quintile that includes many EITC recipients) looks a bit different, in part because the CTC expansion benefits those taxpayers a bit more: Nearly 65 percent of households will experience a tax cut, with an average savings of $550, while 5.6 percent of households will experience an average tax increase of $660. The remainder will see no change.[33] The average tax savings across all households in this income quintile is projected to be $320.[34]

Republicans would like to make the changes to these individual provisions permanent, but that will require additional legislation later.[35] Senate procedural rules (related to the revenue loss projections stemming from the bill) made this a political necessity; if a provision will sunset within ten years, that provision is ignored for purposes of calculating the deficit impact.[36] When tax cut provisions have been enacted with a sunset date in past legislation, such as in 2001 and 2003, Congress later had to calculate the political fallout of letting those provisions expire (effectively resulting in a tax increase for all taxpayers) or voting to make them permanent; many of those temporary provisions of 2001 and 2003 were extended in 2010 and then made permanent in 2012.[37]

In sum, the most sweeping tax reform in three decades did little to address poverty in America. Optimistically, the TCJA may not be the only bellwether, but in the country's current political climate, with its polarized and highly partisan state, it is hard to imagine a president working with Congressional leaders from the other party to address any broad social policy issues. Moreover, if the 2017 tax cuts are made permanent, Congress will have to find new sources of revenue or dramatically cut spending. In addition, the current administration has suggested reform of other social entitlement programs. Weeks after signing the TCJA, President Trump proposed a 2019 budget that included substantial cuts to nondefense discretionary programs, including

[32] *Id.* at tbl. 1.

[33] *Id.* at tbl. 2.

[34] *Id.* at tbl. 1.

[35] Jeff Stein, *Republicans Explain Why Their Tax Cuts Are Temporary, But Not Really Temporary*, WASH. POST (Nov. 30, 2017), https://www.washingtonpost.com/news/wonk/wp/2017/11/30/republicans-explain-why-their-tax-cuts-are-temporary-but-not-really-temporary/?utm_term=.8956a1d2218c.

[36] *Id.*

[37] *See* Emily Horton, *The Legacy of the 2001 and 2003 'Bush' Tax Cuts*, CTR. ON BUDGET AND POLICY PRIORITIES (2017).

health care subsidies, the Supplemental Nutrition Assistance Program (SNAP), housing and energy assistance, disability benefits (including both Social Security Disability Insurance [SSDI] and Supplemental Security Income [SSI]), Temporary Assistance for Needy Families (TANF), and education grants and loans.[38] Weeks later, the president signed an executive order directing agencies to strengthen existing work requirements and introduce new ones for recipients of Medicaid, SNAP, public housing benefits, and TANF.[39]

These proposed cuts involve several of the same concerns that Alston, the U.N. Special Rapporteur, outlined in his 2018 report on extreme poverty and human rights in the United States. When asked to respond to the report, U.N. Ambassador Nikki Haley replied that it was "misleading and politically motivated" and that it is "patently ridiculous for the United Nations to examine poverty in America," suggesting that the United Nations would be better off focusing on poverty and human rights abuses in Burundi and the Democratic Republic of Congo.[40] The Trump administration, Haley asserted, takes the issue of poverty very seriously and believes that "the best way to help people get out of poverty is to help them get a job."[41]

This emphasis on working is by no means limited to Republicans: In October 2018, Democratic Senator Kamala Harris unveiled a detailed proposal to establish a new refundable tax credit to supplement the EITC. Her credit would match earnings, including Pell Grants, of up to $3,000 for individuals and $6,000 for married couples. Harris proposed an option of making the credit available monthly. The credit would require work, but in a departure from the EITC model, it would be available regardless of whether one has any children, making it significantly more valuable to workers without children at home.[42]

38 Sharon Parrott, Aviva Aron-Dine, Dottie Rosenbaum, Douglas Rice, Ife Floyd, & Kathleen Romig, *Trump Budget Deeply Cuts Health, Housing, Other Assistance for Low- and Moderate-Income Families*, Ctr. on Budget and Policy Priorities (2018).

39 Tracy Jan, *Trump Executive Order Strengthens Work Requirements for Neediest Americans*, WASH. POST (Apr. 10, 2018), https://www.washingtonpost.com/business/economy/trump-executive-order-strengthens-work-requirements-for-neediest-americans/2018/04/10/21e21382-3d08-11e8-974f-aacd97698cef_story.html?utm_term=.ec5102503O4c.

40 Letter from Nikki Haley, Rep. of the US to the UN, to Senator Bernard Sanders (June 21, 2018), https://www.sanders.senate.gov/download/haley-response-to-sanders?id=EFF61D64-853F-4445-BCC8-2F6374F04537&download=1&inline=file.

41 *Id.*

42 Harris termed her proposal the "LIFT (Livable Incomes for Families Today) the Middle Class Act."

USING THE CODE TO BOOST MORE THAN JUST WORKERS

The central ideas in the reimagination proposed in this book revolve around the premise that refundable credits should be tied to work. I accepted this premise because I start from a place of pessimism – the assumption that it would be a political nonstarter to detach the EITC from a work requirement. I also acknowledge that an expanding economy with more jobs is an important part of reducing poverty, at least with respect to those who are able to work.

Fundamentally, however, I agree with the U.N. Special Rapporteur: There are "shortcomings in basic social protection"[43] in the United States, and our domestic policy has an "illusory emphasis on employment."[44] Sociologists Kathryn Edin and Luke Shaefer illustrate this problem in their 2015 book, *$2.00 a Day: Living on Almost Nothing in America*.[45] Edin and Shaefer describe the deepest level of poverty in America, acknowledging the success of the EITC program but highlighting those left behind (and left outside the coverage of the EITC's safety net) because they cannot find or keep a job. "Extending the nation's safety net [to the working poor] has improved the lives of millions of Americans," they write. "But there are simply not enough jobs, much less good jobs, to go around. And for those without work, there is no longer a guarantee of cash assistance."[46]

Among the working poor, refundable credits have worked as a measure to drive down poverty rates. When measured to include the impact of both government aid and refundable tax credits, the United States has been successful in reducing child poverty: between 1967 and 2016, the rate dropped from 28.4 percent to 15.6 percent.[47] Researchers at the Center on Budget and Policy Priorities show how this drop is primarily attributable to social programs such as the EITC, CTC, and SNAP.[48] By analyzing poverty measurements before taking into account government aid and refundable credits, they did identify specific short periods of years in which a strengthening economy did

[43] Alston, *supra* note 7, at 8–12.

[44] *Id.* at 9.

[45] Kathryn J. Edin & H. Luke Shaefer, $2.00 a Day: Living on Almost Nothing in America (Houghton Mifflin Harcourt 2015).

[46] *Id.* at xxiv.

[47] Isaac Shapiro & Danilo Trisi, *Child Poverty Falls to Record Low, Comprehensive Measure Shows Stronger Government Policies Account for Long-Term Improvement*, Ctr. on Budget & Policy Priorities (2017); Annie Lowrey, *America's Child-Poverty Rate Has Hit a Record Low*, The Atlantic (Oct. 5, 2017).

[48] Shapiro & Trisi, *supra* note 47.

result in a drop in child poverty.[49] However, by that measurement, child poverty has declined only modestly, from 27.4 percent in 1967 to 25.1 percent in 2016.[50] Isaac Shapiro and Danilo Trisi thus conclude from their analysis that in the four decades between 1967 and 2016, "labor market trends and developments in the private economy have not, on balance, led to a large reduction in child poverty."[51] In sum, it is government programs, not the economy, that have most impacted child poverty.

These programs, however, are not accessible to all low-income households, and benefit access is inconsistent, depending on an individual's or household's specific situation. So while I do believe that we should continue to incentivize and reward work, recognizing that the EITC and CTC have played a critical role in reducing poverty, it is also imperative to bolster the safety net for those who are not able to work. The reimagination I set forth in this book is limited to the EITC, but there are also ways Congress can provide dignity to non-working individuals by providing social benefits to them through the Code, as we do for working families.

In recent years, there has been considerable scholarly focus on the merits of a universal basic income, sometimes referred to as a citizen's dividend or a demogrant because it would be paid to all individuals rather than only those who demonstrate need.[52] Some countries (most notably Finland) have experimented with the idea. The idea of universal basic income has its historical roots in Milton Friedman's negative income tax proposal, which I discussed in earlier chapters. The general idea of universal basic income is an unconditional cash payment to all individuals. For example, everyone receives the same payment, regardless of whether they have low incomes, high incomes, or have no income at all. Many proposals are designed such that the cash payment is recaptured through a graduated surtax at higher income levels, meaning the wealthiest receive the benefit in the literal sense but pay for it through their own taxes. At least some versions of such a proposal envision a

[49] *Id.* at 3–4. Specifically, they conclude economic growth reduced child poverty from 2014 to 2016 and in the late 1990s.

[50] *Id.* at 3 and tbl. 1.

[51] *Id.*

[52] *See, e.g.*, Miranda Perry Fleischer & Daniel Hemel, *Atlas Nods: The Libertarian Case for a Basic Income*, 2017 Wisc. L. Rev. 1189; Ari Glogower & Clint Wallace, *Shades of Basic Income*, Sharing the Gains of the Global Economy: Proceedings of the New York University 70th Annual Conference on Labor (forthcoming 2018); Benjamin M. Leff, *EITC for All: A Universal Basic Income Compromise Proposal*, 25 Wash. & Lee J. Civ. Rts. & Soc. Just. (forthcoming).

universal basic income as a replacement for other social benefit programs, similar to Friedman's vision.[53]

One advantage of a universal payment that reaches all individuals is that people who have no earned income would not have an incentive to "give away" their dependent to someone else who can demonstrate work eligibility, because their household would receive the benefit regardless. In addition, this benefit would reach children in the poorest families – the ones Edin and Shaefer describe in *$2.00 a Day* as unable to qualify for the EITC but no longer able to access traditional welfare. Putting aside the question of political feasibility, a universal basic income would be a radical departure from our current social safety net, and would be one way to address poverty and income inequality.

Alternatively, the United States could consider less pure variants of a universal basic income that would be targeted only at households with children. For example, Congress could enact a modest fixed credit for all primary caregivers of minor children (adopting a definition of *caregiver* similar to what Canada and New Zealand have done), which would be paid regardless of income level and regardless of whether the caregiver works outside the home.

For the same reasons that the Internal Revenue Code has been the vehicle for other refundable credits, universal basic income or other nonwork-related credits could be enacted as part of the Code. Canada and New Zealand include such credits in their revenue law. One primary advantage is that doing so lends dignity to recipients – a key advantage of the EITC. But if we are to continue asking so much of the IRS, and indeed of the Internal Revenue Code, Congress needs to properly fund the IRS and redesign the agency to better fit its mission.

WHAT ARE WE ASKING OF TAX?

In Franz Kafka's dystopian novel *The Trial*, Josef K. is arrested but is never told the nature of the crime. Though he is represented by counsel, his case seems to never progress; he endures an opaque criminal prosecution at the hands of a faceless bureaucracy. When I think of this story, I am reminded of the many oddities of EITC administration. Where Kafka speaks of the nameless officials who lack any relationship with the people, I think of the anonymous IRS

[53] *See, e.g.*, Charles Murray, In Our Hands: A Plan to Replace the Welfare State (AEI Press 2016); Michael Tanner, *The Pros and Cons of a Guaranteed National Income*, CATO Inst. Policy Analysis No. 773 (May 12, 2015).

auditors who examine my clients' lives through documents and not through conversation. They ask for school records as a bright-line determination of the child's residence, without engaging the parent who claimed the EITC in conversation about when and why the child moved in with them, who else lives in the house, or, if applicable, what their shared-custody arrangement looks like.

So many elements of our EITC administration present a paradox. Individuals receive large amounts of money designated as a tax refund, but it does not represent taxes paid. What is intended as a social benefit to help overcome poverty is often diverted to pay off credit card debt or a payday loan, or to pay a tax return preparer. Sometimes the impoverished individuals do not even receive their social benefit, because they are too poor to have paid off another type of outstanding debt, such as a prior year tax liability or an unpaid student loan.

As discussed in an earlier chapter, tax scholar Lawrence Zelenak has critiqued the EITC as an undertheorized policy, citing the program for "the absence of any definitive statement of legislative purpose, or any coherent purpose discernible from the structure of the credit."[54] Scholar Jennifer Bird-Pollan, referencing Zelenak's critique, comments that "not only was there no expressed purpose in creating the EITC, various reports offer conflicting intentions and purposes."[55]

Building on Zelenak's ideas about undertheorization of the EITC, Michael Adamson describes the modern EITC as the product of legislative path dependence.[56] He refers to the EITC as "an ambiguous jumble of a policy" that has been expanded incrementally and for an assortment of different purposes, some of which are no longer relevant; hence, its lack of "a single coherent purpose."[57] However, Adamson argues that this ambiguity is politically *valuable*, because it has preserved its bipartisan support.[58] His argument underscores the political difficulties and realities of the task at hand, and here I am conflicted, because certainly I do not wish to jeopardize the success of

54 Lawrence Zelenak, *Redesigning the Earned Income Tax Credit as a Family-Size Adjustment to the Minimum Wage*, 57 Tax. L. Rev. 301 (2004).

55 Jennifer Bird-Pollan, *Who's Afraid of Redistribution? An Analysis of the Earned Income Tax Credit*, 74 Missouri L. Rev. 251, 258 (2009). Bird-Pollan also cites the work of Anne Alstott, who framed the different possible goals of the EITC as having "unacknowledged normative tensions." Alstott, *supra* note 3, at 557.

56 Adamson, *supra* note 5.

57 *Id.* at 1474–75. Adamson describes the legislative motivations behind the EITC expansions that occurred under various presidential administrations of both political parties.

58 *Id.* at 1476 ("If policymakers convert ink blots into a more vivid picture, everyone might not like what they see any more.")

the EITC by advocating for coherence. Perhaps it is enough for Congress to acknowledge that the EITC has many goals and these need not be ranked ordinally; perhaps Senator Long was right that it is enough for Congress simply to draw a clear line between such a social benefit and work.

These concessions and complexities give rise to other questions: Are we asking too much of tax? Is it appropriate to look to the Internal Revenue Code to address poverty? After years of personal reflection on this question, I conclude that the EITC should remain within the Internal Revenue Code, and its administration within the IRS. If keeping the EITC administration within the IRS protects the political viability of the credit, then that alone is a compelling reason. But there are other reasons as well. First, the connection to work (and by extension, to income) makes it a logical fit. Second, it is not practical to create a new federal agency to oversee the EITC, and no existing agency is better suited to administer it. As National Taxpayer Advocate Nina Olson points out, the IRS has ready access to income information from taxpayers and third parties.[59] Furthermore, housing social benefits within the IRS reduces stigma for recipients.

At the same time, Olson observes that the IRS is not well equipped to administer social benefits, in part because its culture is that of a revenue collection and enforcement agency.[60] In a subsequent report, Olson called on the IRS to evaluate its organizational structure to better reflect its dual role as tax collector and social benefit administrator, noting that the "current IRS workforce generally lacks the social welfare or caseworker background necessary to interact with taxpayers on social benefit issues."[61] Olson recommended structural changes for the agency, such as the creation of a Deputy Commissioner position to "create policy and develop strategic direction for all social benefit initiatives."[62]

I like these ideas. As part of a structural reimagination, offices within the IRS could be restructured and designed to better administer social programs. Congress should increase funding to the agency. Perhaps it could create a centralized unit within the IRS dedicated to the administration of social benefits, such as the one created for innocent spouse determinations. Given the nature of their work, employees in the innocent spouse unit are given different training than other IRS employees; for example, they are trained on

59 Taxpayer Advocate Service, 2009 Annual Report to Congress (Vol. 2) 83.

60 *Id.* at 86.

61 Taxpayer Advocate Service, 2010 Annual Report to Congress (Vol. 1) 22.

62 *Id.* at 23. Currently there are two Deputy Commissioners, one for services and enforcement, and one for operations support.

issues of domestic violence. Why not use a similar approach with respect to poverty and family support so that the IRS is better equipped to oversee these programs? EITC returns subject to exam could be sent to an examination division within the centralized unit. Specially trained examiners could make an effort to speak to the taxpayers they audit, to engage in a common-sense conversation about the household. These examiners could be empowered, and encouraged, to accept a variety of forms of substantiation, rather than limited to the narrow list of documents specified in the exam notices.

If EITC administration were centralized within a specific part of the IRS, those employees could be trained to approach problems with the mindset of a social worker rather than an enforcement agent. Indeed, the role of such an office need not be limited to enforcement. Olson has also proposed ideas for increasing pre-filing assistance with the EITC, such as creating a dedicated toll-free IRS helpline to assist taxpayers who wish to check their EITC eligibility.[63] Such a centralized unit of the IRS could be encouraged to embrace its role as an administrator of social benefits, as a partner with society in providing a safety net.

In doing so, the agency should work harder to understand the complexity of households, and it should engage with taxpayers more efficiently on an individual basis when necessary. Recall that the Taxpayer Advocate Service studied a sample of docketed EITC Tax Court cases in which the IRS fully conceded (without going to trial) the taxpayer was entitled to the EITC, and found that in 20 percent of those cases the Appeals Officer of Chief Counsel accepted the very documents that the Tax Examiner had rejected.[64] Separate studies by the National Taxpayer Advocate show that "enhanced communication techniques" between IRS employees and EITC claimants result in a higher likelihood of substantiation of the claim.[65] Olson concludes that IRS EITC examiners could be trained on flexible approaches to evaluating substantiation evidence, and recommends that the IRS engage taxpayers in "meaningful conversation" earlier in the process.[66]

63 Taxpayer Advocate Service, Fiscal Year 2017 Objectives Report to Congress (Vol. 2) 139. Olson recommends that this phone line be staffed by employees "with excellent listening and communication skills who have completed training in social work." *Id.*

64 Taxpayer Advocate Service, 2012 Annual Report to Congress (Vol. 2) 72.

65 *Id.* at 75.

66 *Id.* at 92. Olson notes that when taxpayers with meritorious claims must go to Tax Court to resolve their claims, the IRS is required to pay interest on the delayed refund. A system in which taxpayers must go to Tax Court is also costlier in terms of employee resources (more employees are touching the case, including attorneys, who are higher paid than examiners). For the taxpayer, it results in an even longer delay in receiving the refund.

Meanwhile, it is up to the executive and legislative branches to design policy solutions to effectively address poverty in its many forms. Poverty has many causes and many faces; do these branches of government fully appreciate the underlying reasons for poverty, or try to empathize with what it is like to raise a family from paycheck to paycheck? No one elected to the White House or to Congress lives in poverty; to the contrary, most have lived a life of great privilege. To borrow from Kafka, without a "true sense of human relationships," without "any relationship with the people," the law may not be well suited for the reality on the ground.

This need for understanding applies equally to Congress, which designs solutions, and to the IRS, which implements the administration of those solutions. The National Commission on Children created by President Reagan spent time surveying and listening to parents across America, and valued those perspectives in its policy recommendations. Such a comprehensive conversation with the people who are affected by these choices – people like my clients – could better inform Congress about what these families' daily lives are really like. While it remains important to involve economists and policy experts in redesigning social programs, it would be remiss not to hear from the very population those programs are intended to support.

The EITC lifts millions out of poverty. With thoughtful changes to its design and administration, it can do better still, and this book aims to fuel a conversation about how. That may mean introducing social workers into the ranks of the IRS, and it may mean accepting improper payments as the trade-off for cheap administration of social benefits. It may involve decoupling the EITC from the tax filing process while keeping the IRS involved in administering the benefit, and someday it may conceivably include delivering benefits to those who are not working at all, as other countries do via their income tax systems.

There is no simple fix for the difficult work of addressing relatively widespread poverty in a nation that also has the world's largest economy, but the United States can do better than the direction it took in its most recent tax reform. Congress can make the Internal Revenue Code more effective in delivering this family-support benefit, and perhaps someday the Code can serve as a vehicle to boost all Americans, not just those who can find work.

Index